Oral Tradition
and the Internet

Oral Tradition and the Internet

Pathways of the Mind

JOHN MILES FOLEY

UNIVERSITY OF ILLINOIS PRESS

Urbana, Chicago, and Springfield

Library of Congress Cataloging-in-Publication Data
Foley, John Miles.
Oral tradition and the internet: pathways of the mind /
John Miles Foley.
  p.   cm.
Includes bibliographical references and index.
ISBN 978-0-252-03718-4 (cloth) — ISBN 978-0-252-07869-9 (pbk.)
1. Folklore and the Internet.
2. Oral tradition—Computer network resources.
I. Title.
GR44.E43F63   2012
398.2—dc23   2012003385

The Pathways Project is for Joe and Bella Foley
Loyal friends, always elegantly dressed
Κύνας μοι ἔννεπε, Μοῦσα, ξείνοις κέδνους αἰεί
Sing about my dogs, O Muse, ever beloved to guest-strangers

Table of Nodes

Preface

A preface (literally, a "fore-speaking") conventionally serves a number of purposes. It can, for example, provide a point of entry, chart a map for the journey to follow, and describe what the book that it's introducing aims to accomplish, and also not to accomplish. But whether you're reading these words on paper or in pixels, you will quickly realize that such conventions don't really apply here.

In the morphing book (Morphing Book) and wiki-website (Wiki) alike, the *pre*-face doesn't necessarily come first. You can profitably start experiencing the Pathways Project at some other entry point, indeed *any* other entry point, without deferring to this node. As for charting a map, that's largely your responsibility. All the Project can do is present you with options for surfing and advice about how the media work (Getting Started); from that juncture, you're on your own. In the same cocreative vein, what the book and site seek to accomplish is to enlist you in the experience and demonstration of the core premise: namely, that *oral tradition (OT) and Internet technology (IT) operate similarly by navigating through networks.*

So why create a node called "Preface"? Because the Project needs a place where we can address some OT-IT generalities not covered in the Response node (Response) and where we can thank some of the generous fellow travelers who have helped to bring the overall initiative to this stage (notice I didn't say "to completion"). To make this node a more likely destination on your itinerary, I've maintained the designation of "preface" and placed it in a position of prominence—near the linear beginning of the morphing book and as a bold-faced link in the left menu-bar of the website. My hope is that you will run into it sooner or later.

Questions and Answers

First, the generalities, which I present here as economically as possible in a skeletal question-and-answer format. Let me emphasize that these four questions were actually asked, in various forms, by colleagues, students, or friends.

Q1: How did you decide on this particular set of linkages among nodes? Did you have a specific strategy or organization in mind?

A1: The link-system is suggestive, not prescriptive. Both the morphing book and the wiki-website could be configured and linked in infinite ways, and indeed that's just the point: at every level the Pathways Project is contingent (Contingency), allowing reality to remain in play (Reality Remains in Play).

Q2: Why did you choose to order the nodes alphabetically in the Table of Nodes and to feature Preface, Disclaimer, Response, and other Nodes (by placing them early in the book and in the left menu-bar on the website)?

A2: In the Nodes (Table of Nodes), I am suggesting that the most important order is not the one I impose but rather the one you choose. Alphabetizing the list confers an artificial, largely meaningless organization on the content parts; it makes them easy to find, but in no way constitutes any logical sequence of ideas. That logic is your responsibility. As for the featured nodes, I highlight them in order to increase the likelihood that you will encounter the discussion-based observations they contain. Hopefully, the ready availability of prominent links will motivate you to surf toward their content—especially toward the Preface on OT-IT generalities, the Disclaimer on what the Project isn't claiming (Disclaimer), and the Response on my reactions to reviewers' prepublication critiques of the morphing book manuscript (Response).

Q3: This is a big discussion. Are you satisfied that you've covered everything thoroughly?

A3: Yes, it's a big discussion, but "thorough coverage" is an ideologically inspired illusion (Ideology of the Text). The goal of the Pathways Project is to serve as a heuristic, as a way into some of the most important media challenges of our time. It does not pretend—nor should any contribution pretend—to do anything more (or, for that matter, less). No initiative prospers by aiming to be the final word.

Q4: What do you expect in the way of reaction to the Project and its OT-IT thesis?

A4: The Pathways Project is intended as a provocation, not a solution. I expect variety in responses, some of them impassioned. For citizens accustomed to exchanges limited to the textual marketplace (tAgora), the oral (oAgora) and electronic (eAgora) marketplaces can seem undependable and even forbidding. Trying to get behind ideology, which by definition shuts down exploration before it can begin, is a difficult process, parallel in a sense to the culture shock we've all felt at one point or another (Culture Shock). Some will embrace the OT-IT homology, some will resist it, but hopefully the Project will make a reasonable case for why we need to become citizens of all three marketplaces (Citizenship in Multiple Agoras). And as the Project continues to evolve with contributions to the wiki-website,[1] there will be an opportunity for us to learn more by sharing our ideas and reactions.

From here on

Some questions remain. Where does the "the future" of the media-universe lie? What new initiatives will emerge to challenge and enlighten us? What role will stand-alone texts occupy as we start to feel more and more comfortable with electronic media and with the plasticity and interactivity they foster? What mixture of methods and strategies for creation, transmission, and reception of knowledge, art, and ideas will be current ten years from now? Reasonable questions, to be sure, but perhaps the most intriguing part of the game is that we can't in fact predict its outcome. More to the point, "outcome" seems the wrong word here, since reality and experience, as the Pathways Project explains, just won't hold still. To my mind, the best preparation one can make for a (delightfully) unpredictable media-future is to remain imaginative and undefaulted. As Walter Ong was fond of observing, the conversation is never over. My hope is that the Pathways Project will help stir the pot.

Appreciation

One of the most pleasant tasks associated with finishing a book or website is thanking those who helped. Even when, as in the present case, the verb *finish* isn't quite suitable, I want to take the opportunity to express my gratitude to the diverse group of collaborators, advisors, students, colleagues, mentors, institutions, and events that have made the ongoing journey so interesting and rewarding.

The dual nature of the Pathways Project would have been impossible without the remarkable expertise and imagination of Mark Jarvis and Jamie Stephens, IT Managers at the Center for Studies in Oral Tradition and Center for eResearch. In earlier days, George Maiewski and David Woods helped me to understand what computers could do in humanities and social science, or more precisely how we could use them to think; Mark, the creator of the wonderful mind map,[2] and Jamie have continued my education as well as tolerated and implemented any number of ePipedreams. Morgan Grey heroically shouldered the demanding burden of research assistant on the Project for the last two years and has worked intelligently, assiduously, and goodnaturedly, even contributing a node on mash-ups[3] to the network. Through his support of the Centers and his encouragement for our research, Michael O'Brien, Dean of the College of Arts and Science at the University of Missouri, has made a real difference. The Pathways Project origi-nated as the inaugural lecture in the University of Missouri's Twenty-first Century Corps of Discovery series, an annual campus event championed by Chancellor Brady Deaton and Chancellor Emeritus Richard Wallace.

Individuals who have pointed the way, whether through discussion or via their own inquiries and discoveries, include Mark Amodio, Aodong, Justin Arft, Benjamin Bagby, Ćamil Bajgorić, Halil Bajgorić, Margaret Hiebert Beissinger, David Bouvier, Leslie Cahill, Chogjin, Whendi Cook, Adam Davis, Thomas DuBois, Casey Dué, Andoni Egaña, David Elmer, Fazool, William Ferris, Ruth Finnegan, Elizabeth Foley, Lori Peterson Garner, Scott Garner, Joxerra Garzía, Joseph Harris, Lauri Harvilahti, Michael Holland, Kati Kallio, Werner Kelber, Anne Mackay, Heather Maring, Richard Martin, Mariana Masera, John Mc-Dowell, Stephen Mitchell, Robin Moore, Rebecca Mouser, Gregory Nagy, Jožsi Nagy, John D. Niles, Xabier Paya, Thomas Pettitt, Andrew Porter, Peter Ramey, Karl Reichl, Paula Sanders, Jon Sarasua, John Shaw, Lotte Tarkka, Frederick Turner, Lee Edgar Tyler, Yang Enhong, Paulu Zedda, and Zhu Gang.

In addition, I have profited enormously from activities surrounding lectures and conferences at a wide variety of institutions during the past five years: Amherst College, Beijing Normal University, Bertsozale Elkartea in the Basque Country, Brown University, Bryn Mawr College, Cambridge University, the Chinese Acad-emy of Social Sciences, the Dahesh Museum in New York City, the Graduate In-stitute, Harvard University, Massachusetts Institute of Technology, the National University for Nationalities in Lanzhou, Rice University, St. Louis University, Turku University, the Universidad Nacional Autónoma de México, the Università di Cagliari, the University of Bergen, the University of California Los Angeles, the University of Edinburgh, the University of Gothenburg, the University of Helsinki, the University of Southern Denmark in Odense, the University of St. Andrews, and the University of Victoria. Let me also remember my core teachers and mentors: Robert Payson Creed, Joel Halpern, Lauri Honko (*in memoriam*), Barbara Kerewsky-Halpern, Albert Bates Lord (*in memoriam*), and Walter J. Ong (*in memoriam*). I am grateful as well to my editors at the University of Illinois Press, Joan Catapano, who encouraged the project right from the beginning and offered much-needed counsel and support during its evolution; and Willis Regier, whose steady hand and good judgment have guided it ever since.

Finally, the Pathways Project reached this stage during a difficult passage in my life, and I offer my heartfelt thanks to my family for their support through the hardest of times: Anne-Marie the smiling and steadfast, Lizzie the wordsmith and bosom friend of Cyrus, Isaac the faithful and ever so musical, and Joshua the paterfamilias and *cuisinier nonpareil* have in their diverse ways been remarkably strong and unfailingly cheerful. Nor can I forget to celebrate the loving, whimsical wisdom of Bud Stone, who knows more about life than anyone else. The dedication of *Oral Tradition and the Internet: Pathways of the Mind*, and of its wiki-website counterpart, speaks for itself.

Oral Tradition
and the Internet

For Book-readers Only

A Local Disclaimer

This node was created to serve as one possible introduction to (one of several avenues into) *Oral Tradition and the Internet: Pathways of the Mind*, the book associated with the Pathways Project. For that purpose it emphasizes the disorientation necessarily involved in abandoning the default medium of the book in order to grasp the dynamics of alternative media—specifically OT and IT. As such, it explains how tAgora-speak (tAgora) doesn't and can't translate to the eAgora (eAgora).

The Book in Your Hands

You've picked up this book, gently cradling it in your hands as you've done so many times throughout your life in so many different situations. It's a cozy, familiar action, essentially a reflex, as you prepare to set sail through the smooth, silent seas of letters, words, lines, paragraphs, pages, and chapters. Everything lies before you in expectable sequence, reassuringly formatted and configured. Even the artifact itself comes complete with trusty features—a title embedded in an eye-catching design; a back-cover blurb to summarize the argument; the soft, cool feel of the pages as you turn them one by one. In ways that you don't consciously register, the book provides a powerful and uniquely welcome frame of reference (Texts and Intertextuality). You're ensconced on the sofa, the light's adjusted, your cup of tea's in place, peace reigns. You're about to reenter a world apart, a world you've visited before and long to revisit.

Let the Reader Beware

Comfortable, then? Well, *caveat lector*: let the reader beware! This particular book doesn't fit that tried-and-true mold; in fact, it seeks to expose the mold as an ideology we've adopted (Ideology of the Text), a tacit compromise we've forged with a much messier and more complex reality. For that reason it's a book more likely to enervate than entertain, at least until you get used to how it works (Getting Started). Instead of the dependable calm that proceeds from opening the dependably put-together artifact, what awaits you is, frankly, an unsettling experience. You may undergo a kind of culture shock, not so different from the disorientation we feel when we're suddenly immersed in a foreign society with language and customs far from our own (Culture Shock). And no apologies: *Oral Tradition and the Internet: Pathways of the Mind* is actively intended to generate just that kind of disquiet and dissonance.

Why? Because we'll be doing nothing less fundamental than challenging the default medium of the linear book and page and all that they entail. We'll be addressing the very nature of text (Reading Backwards) and asking whether that's all there is to communication. Worse yet, perhaps, we'll be finding that there is indeed much, much more that we've made a cultural habit of ignoring or suppressing. We'll learn that there are large, complex, wholly viable, alternative worlds of media-technology (Agora Correspondences) out there—if only we're willing to explore, to think outside the usual, culturally constructed categories. We'll learn that oral tradition and Internet technology support thinking and creating and communicating in ways that books can't match. And we'll find that OT and IT work in strikingly similar fashion, offering us networks to navigate, webs of potentials that we will be in a position to activate. And that won't be a comfortable experience, at least initially. Not at all.

A Way Out . . . If You Want One

Too much to ask? Well, there's a way out, of course, a strategy to avoid the discomfort (Agoraphobia). We can simply choose not to think outside the book—not to jump off the dock—and thus avoid the reshuffling of our cognitive categories that the Pathways Project demands. The sun will still rise in the east and set in the west, the twin illusions of object (Illusion of Object) and stasis (Illusion of Stasis) will remain (artificially) in force, and our hard-won and desperately held convictions about the certainty, permanence, and primacy of the book and page will rest undisturbed.

And perhaps there's a reasonable argument for doing just that. Having labored since Gutenberg to convert knowledge, art, and ideas to an item-based economy (Accuracy), are we now to throw away centuries of hard-won victories?

Now that we've developed this marvelous textual prosthesis to help us manage the slippage that threatens to undo communication at every turn, are we now to discard it in favor of a broader view we can't yet appreciate and may not be able to control? Maybe, given all that texts have meant and continue to mean to myriad readers, including you and me, that's an irresponsible and indefensible act. Maybe we should remain on the dock. Maybe we should just close this book and return it to the shelf.

Opportunities Ahead

But that would be a mistake, and a missed opportunity. For the process ahead also promises to be exciting and rewarding, as long as we're willing to honestly confront some basic, unexamined assumptions and preconceived notions. That's the catch, of course: in order to make our way through the ideas housed within this book and networked within the Pathways Project in general, we're going to have to jump off the end of that proverbial dock and learn how to swim in a new and different environment. Only by relinquishing the relative safety of the stand-alone book can we start to understand how major media-types—oral tradition, Internet technology, and, yes, the book as well—really function. Only then can we then reorient ourselves and see how human communication actually works from a pluralistic, informed perspective (Citizenship in Multiple Agoras). Only by first letting go can we realistically recalibrate our thinking.

Culture shock can lead to acculturation. Or, to put it proverbially: *no media pain, no media gain.*

If you're ready to proceed, please turn the page to—or click on—Welcome to the Pathways Project[1] (the book's Home Page) or Getting Started (Getting Started) and begin your journey.

Home Page:
Welcome to the Pathways Project

The major purpose of the Pathways Project is to illustrate and explain the fundamental similarities and correspondences between humankind's oldest and newest thought-technologies: oral tradition and the Internet.

Despite superficial differences, both technologies are radically alike in depending not on static products but rather on continuous processes, not on "What?" but on "How do I get there?" In contrast to the fixed spatial organization of the page and book, the technologies of oral tradition and the Internet *mime the way we think* by processing along pathways within a network. In both media it's pathways—not things—that matter.

The Pathways Project consists of a website[1] and a brick-and-mortar book, *Oral Tradition and the Internet: Pathways of the Mind*. The website serves as the focal point for a suite of media that includes a network of linked topics (called nodes), suggested reading-routes through those nodes (called linkmaps), audio and video eCompanions (eCompanions), multimedia eEditions (eEditions), and eventually a moderated forum for user contributions.[2]

To begin your journey, please turn the page or click on Getting Started (Getting Started).

Getting Started:
How to Surf the Pathways Project

The Multimedia Project

What you're scrolling through on your virtual desktop or physically holding in your hands is in some ways a text, but it's also a great deal more than that. The Pathways Project departs from a stand-alone, linear text in two fundamental ways.

First, the online version of the Pathways Project consists of a network of linked nodes that presents the contents of the book but also adds many connections and opportunities that books just can't support.

Second, even the brick-and-mortar book entitled *Oral Tradition and the Internet: Pathways of the Mind* is not simply a conventional text. It's a *morphing book* (Morphing Book), capable of being read in innumerable different ways.

In other words, you can surf the online facility or you can "read" the book, but in either case your experience will differ from the usual text-consuming scenario. More about those two options in a moment, but first a word about the general thesis of the Pathways Project.

The Homology

The goal of the Project is to explain and illustrate a central thesis—namely, that humankind's oldest and newest thought-technologies, oral tradition and the Internet (abbreviated throughout as OT and IT), are fundamentally alike. Hardly identical (Disclaimer), of course, but surprisingly similar in their structure and dynamics.

And how are they alike (Agora Correspondences)? Both media depend not on static products but on continuous processes, not on stationary points but on vectors with direction and magnitude, not on "What?" but on "How do I get there?" In contrast to the fixed, spatial linearity of the conventional page and the book, the twin technologies of OT and IT *mime the way we think*—by navigating along pathways within an interactive network.

In both cases, then, it's linked pathways—and not things—that matter. OT and IT don't operate by spatializing, sequencing, or objectifying. They don't fossilize ideas into freestanding museum exhibits (Museum of Verbal Art), as books typically do. Instead, they invite and require active participation and support a rich diversity of individual, one-time-only experiences. In place of the single, predetermined route typical of texts, they offer myriad different routes for exploration by engaging each user in nothing less than cocreating his or her own contingent reality (Contingency).

This built-in, rule-governed variability marks the crucial difference between the closed arena (Arena of the Text) of a textual script—what we'll be calling the tAgora (tAgora)—and the open, multiform environment of oral tradition and the electronic world of the Internet—the oAgora (oAgora) and eAgora (eAgora), respectively. Because of their inherent dynamics, both OT and IT are always in flux; they remain open, emergent, and forever under construction rather than closed, determined, and complete (Reality Remains in Play).

Key Terminology: o-, e-, and t-

Before we turn to the question of how to surf the online network and read the morphing book, let's add a brief note on terminology. Throughout both modes of presentation, we'll be using an extended version of web-speak to describe words, pathways, and other phenomena across the three agoras (Three Agoras). Thus oral words will be oWords (oWords), electronic pathways will be ePathways (ePathways), textual agoraphobia will be tAgoraphobia, and so forth.

Surfing the Wiki

Instead of wrestling with the built-in barriers of book technology and the tAgora, the online facility allows you to fashion a unique, individualized encounter with its assets by choosing among practically innumerable combinations of pathways. Instead of interpreting a monolithic text, you immerse yourself in a *wiki*, a collaborative electronic space where you can choose your route and contribute in various ways. In practical terms, you are responsible for molding the wiki's networked, interactive contents into your own personal experience. You are an active participant in charge of a process: you set the agenda and prescribe the itinerary. And your experience happens—actually takes living shape—even as you click through the network. Note that the Pathways Project wiki supports contributions—in Contributions[1]—but not direct editing of preexisting contents.

Options

Here are four ways you can proceed:

1. *Via the default method: "straight through."* The Pathways Project wiki can be read straight through, so to speak, by following the alphabetical order given in the Full Table of Nodes continuously available in the left menu-bar. Mirroring the page-turning sequence of *Oral Tradition and the Internet: Pathways of the Mind* (itself only one choice among myriad alternatives), this nominal sequence amounts to merely one of many potential routes through the network.

2. *Via the three principal media environments.* Another way to surf the wiki is to focus on one of the three principal media environments—the oAgora, tAgora, and eAgora—that lie at the heart of the OT-IT thesis and at the foundation of the Pathways Project as a whole. All three agoras are always accessible from the top menu-bar.

   The oAgora is the word-marketplace (Agora As Verbal Marketplace) or the arena for oral tradition (Arena of Oral Tradition), the "place" where OT is performed for audiences. As demonstrated elsewhere (Homo Sapiens' Calendar Year), it serves as the site for humankind's oldest and most pervasive communications technology. The tAgora, next in historical succession, names the communications technology that involves the creation of texts as cognitive prostheses for thinking and exchanging ideas. The eAgora, or electronic marketplace, is of course the virtual world of the Internet and digital media. Today these technologies coexist in a complex array of media channels, a situation that the Pathways Project aims to represent as well as explain.

   If you choose to start with one or more of these three major ideas, you can then proceed from that basic frame of reference to any other part of the wiki. (One radical advantage of this eTool is that you're offered numerous opportunities to explore related links at any and all points in your "reading.")

3. *Via linkmaps.* Linkmaps amount to suggested routes through the wiki network, particular sequences of ePathways that we have clicked through and found illuminating in one way or another. An example is the eWorld (Linkmaps), a series of nodes that leads from Leapfrogging the Text, to Museum of Verbal Art, to Resynchronizing the Event, to Systems versus Things. En route the surfer will have an opportunity to think about a textless world, the new-media landscape for literature and oral tradition, an ancient Greek myth of transformation, the re-creation of performance

events, and communication without "things." What's more, the entire itinerary revolves around the core OT-IT thesis of the Pathways Project.

But that's just one option. Potential surfers may opt to follow this or some other predesignated pattern (any of which they can always exit at any point). Or they may choose to strike out on their own, fashioning their own experiences at every juncture—effectively creating their own linkmaps as they go. The freedom to explore and to construe is nearly absolute (Variation within Limits), and all we ask in return is that surfers consider the option of contributing their newly discovered itineraries to the Pathways Project linkmap digest as possible "guidebooks" for future users.

4. *Via branches*. All topic nodes contain multiple branches, links that allow navigation to other internal or external nodes related in some fashion to the particular idea under discussion. As with other aspects of the online facility, the choice of how to proceed rests with the surfer. You may decide to keep on reading past the branch or to "depart" the present topic node for another destination. Of course, the whole point of the online digital configuration is to erase the tAgora notion of departure and to image the pathways of OT and IT.

Here is a screenshot of the Pathways Project wiki with all of its features described simply:

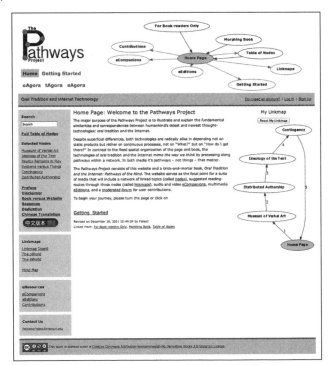

Welcome to the Pathways Project. Webpage by the author and Mark Jarvis.

A Brief Tour of the Pathways Project Home Page

[This section is intended most immediately for those of you who are interacting with the website, but may also serve as an incentive and guide for readers of *Oral Tradition and the Internet: Pathways of the Mind* who wish to explore the website.]

General

The features described below appear on every electronic page and will follow you wherever you travel within the Pathways Project, always available to support your cocreative surfing.

Horizontal orange menu-bar

Here you have the option of creating an account to surf the Pathways Project website. You're welcome to surf the site without an account; it is free and open to anyone with a web connection and a browser. If you choose to establish an account, however, you can contribute linkmaps of your own design to our linkmap digest (for the benefit of others) and, eventually, offer comments, responses, and other reactions to the site.

Above the horizontal menu-bar

The animated Pathways Project logo is meant as a continual reminder of the core theorem of the Project, namely that oral tradition and Internet technology operate via navigation through networks. Just below the logo you see five orange hyperlinks. The *Home* link brings you back to the home page, "Welcome to the Pathways Project," while *Getting Started* will take you to a detailed explanation of how to begin using both the site and the book. The other three links—*oAgora*, *tAgora*, and *eAgora*—lead to the three principal media nodes: substantial discussions of the oral, textual, and electronic marketplaces, respectively. To the right of these five links is a diagram that indicates your position at the present moment (here, Home Page), which is always colored orange, along with all of the other nodes that are linked to the current node. Notice the color differentiation: all linked node-names are circumscribed by white ellipses, but "linked-to" nodes have orange arrows and outlines, while "linked-from" nodes have brown arrows and outlines.

Left menu-bar

The *Search* field is indexed by keyword; it allows you to pursue important concepts through the entire website. Just below, clicking on *Full Table of Nodes* yields a complete alphabetical listing of the more than 100 nodes that constitute the

Pathways Project. From this collection I have chosen six that may be of special interest and provided direct access under the heading *Selected Nodes* (we plan to rotate this selection periodically). Next in vertical order comes the *Preface*, followed by the crucially important *Disclaimer*, a node that emphasizes the nature of the core comparison at the basis of the Pathways Project—that oral tradition and Internet technology are meant to be understood as homologous, and definitely not as simply equivalent. We are looking at similarities, not identities. The next link in the left menu-bar, *Book versus Website*, sketches some of the necessary differences between *Oral Tradition and the Internet* and the wiki-website experience. Just below this link is another entitled *Response*, which presents my reaction to the reports of the two anonymous reviewers commissioned by the University of Illinois Press. After the *Dedication*, the surfer has the opportunity to visit several of the most important nodes in *Chinese Translation*. Under *Linkmaps* you will find suggested itineraries through the Project's web, itineraries consisting of several nodes that collectively illustrate a particular topic. The *Mind Map*, a three-dimensional schematic, images the thousands of linkages that make the Pathways Project web the unique exploratory experience it is. The *eResources* box houses two kinds of electronic strategies for representing OT via IT (*eCompanions* and *eEditions*), as well as the Contributions link,[2] which will soon offer participation typical of a wiki with gatekeeping. Finally, the *Contact Us* e-mail allows users to share impressions, report problems, and make suggestions.

My linkmap feature

As you surf through the Pathways Project, the *My Linkmap* feature will track your progress wherever you go. Arrows and numbers indicate the sequence of your clicking, and the node where you presently are will be marked in orange. For example, in the screenshot shown earlier, the surfer started on Home Page and then moved on to Museum of Verbal Art, followed by the nodes on Distributed Authorship, Ideology of the Text, and Contingency before returning to Home Page. At any point you can erase your linkmap simply by clicking on "Reset My Linkmap," and the tracking process will begin anew from your present location.

Bottom bar

The Pathways Project is licensed for use under a Creative Commons contract that can be viewed by clicking on the link that appears at the bottom of every node.

"Reading" the Morphing Book

Contents

The contents of *Oral Tradition and the Internet: Pathways of the Mind*, the brick-and-mortar aspect of the Pathways Project, consist of items eligible for exchange within the tAgora, plus a few unusual options. That is, the book contains approximately 65 percent of the electronic node-texts composed and posted as of its date of issue, its copyright date. Naturally enough, it cannot house any subsequent additions unless it proceeds to a second edition, which would in turn involve a sequel set of limitations. The truth is that by their very nature books can't remain open-ended or under construction (as OT and IT can and must).

Options

Unlike conventional books, *Oral Tradition and the Internet: Pathways of the Mind* is built and intended to be "read" in multiple, alternate ways. Of course, a book is not a website; no text can ever wholly emulate the virtual arena (Arena of the Web). But to the limited degree that the tAgora allows, you will be able to "sort" your experience according to facsimiles of the four reading strategies available in the online wiki:

1. *Via the default method: "straight through."* You can opt to march straight through from the opening page to the last, like a novel-reader tracking the story as it unfolds according to a singular, fixed blueprint? This alphabetical order is intended to mirror the default logic of the tAgora, but without the customary hierarchy of chapters, sections, and other book-matrices that act as cognitive and rhetorical support for the reading process. As in the wiki, the "straight through" order is merely alphabetical and is probably best likened to reading page after page of definitions in a dictionary, or trolling through a telephone directory in ruthlessly linear sequence, name after name. Each of the nodes is (hopefully) interesting and helpful, but responsibility for assembling them into a coherent whole rests in large part with you, the reader.
2. *Via the three principal media environments.* Or you can read according to any of the three principal media environments—the oAgora, tAgora, or eAgora. Once you reach your chosen agora, more options await you within that section. You'll need to flip back and forth in uncustomary (because nonlinear) ways, but you will be able to manufacture a partial facsimile of what the wiki offers along these lines. It's an awkward repurposing of tAgora technology, but that very awkwardness exposes the fundamental assumptions of the book-and-page medium.

3. *Via linkmaps.* You can decide to use one or more of the linkmaps (Link-maps) that are also available in the volume's opening pages, a set of pre-designated itineraries that are offered as alternate viable routes through Pathways Project contents. Of course, you won't be able to exit and reenter the prescribed sequences as easily as in the wiki, but such is the nature of eAgora strategies deployed nonnatively within the tAgora. There aren't any · "back" buttons or clickable links in the book.

4. *Via branches.* You can exercise any of myriad options to explore the branches that are contained within each node and marked by parenthetical cross-references, but here the book really struggles to morph acceptably. It's inconvenient to interrupt the linear page-to-page logic too often if you can't immediately return to your point of departure with a simple click. More tell-ingly, all those branches that lead to external media-rich sites are effectively dead; audio, video, and the like can't be forced between two covers. You can explore branches with a mouse in one hand and the paperback in the other, of course, but there are built-in constraints as to how far the book itself can morph to imitate eAgora (and oAgora) technology (Online with OT).

Experimental limitations

Naturally, the inter-agora experiment can go only so far before agoraphobia sets in (Agoraphobia). We can't wholly retool book technology and force it to become something it isn't. Pages, paragraphs, chapters, and other dimen-sions of order-by-sequence constitute a cognitive rhetoric seated deep in our text-disposed psyches (Texts and Intertextuality), so deep that it functions as automatically and invisibly as a computer's operating system, well below the level of conscious awareness. Like it or not, our thinking and communication process has been defaulted—tDefaulted, in fact.

But to the extent that the medium of texts can support more than the usual slate of textual activities—and that's precisely the experiment we're conduct-ing with *Oral Tradition and the Internet: Pathways of the Mind*—you can "click through" this morphing book, charting your own idiosyncratic route as you go. No "hard" text can ever entirely simulate OT or IT, of course; it may morph to an extent, but it's still a book. If suggestively constructed, however, it can ac-complish two related goals. It can remind us how those nonlinear, participatory technologies work even as it reveals the inherent conditions of exchange within the tAgora marketplace.

There's a good reason our experiment can be pushed only so far.

One last point before you get started . . .

One small but fundamental caveat before you begin. You'll notice that certain topics will recur over the various nodes of the Pathways Project. You will have an opportunity to weigh their importance in a number of different contexts as well as numerous chances to visit every node in the network. Let me be clear: this recurrence is a wholly intentional aspect of both the morphing book and the online wiki, a crucial feature that has been "written into" both components for two purposes.

1. The dynamic difference between *recurrence* and *repetition* is a key theme of the Pathways Project (Recur Not Repeat). And the contrast aligns with the homology between OT and IT on the one hand, as opposed to textual technology (TT) on the other.

   Repetition demands a linear framework with a predetermined sequence, in other words a tAgora environment. Each instance refers back to the previous instance(s) for its meaning. This cognitive setup can generate emphasis or ennui: repetition can be effective or annoying, depending on how the author handles the transaction.

   Recurrence happens independently each time, with meaning invested idiomatically and equivalently in each occurrence. Phrases such as "Once upon a time" are recurrent, not repetitive, in that they signal an event about to emerge—in this case a Grimm Brothers fairy tale. Recurrence is typical of web-navigation in the oAgora and eAgora.

2. I have built recurrence into the Pathways Project to empower exploration. Just as there should be more than one set of pathways to navigate, so there should also be more than one way to "get there"—wherever "there" may be. No matter how you choose to surf, you should have ready access to core ideas and many different avenues leading to every destination.

   Remember: you won't have the one-way street of the text guiding you and making your decisions for you, determining every move you make by meticulously mapping the exclusive itinerary ahead of your journey. To take up the cognitive slack, I have created multiple opportunities at every juncture that will allow and support many different itineraries, with the starting, ending, and intermediate points left for you to decide as you go. Recurrence keeps the network functional and cocreativity alive (Reality Remains in Play).

   As you work your way through the Project, navigating pathways as you see fit in either the morphing book or the online wiki, please keep this most basic of mantras in mind: *OT and IT recur, TT repeats.*

Disclaimer

Overview

The Pathways Project is devoted to exploring the homology between oral tradition (OT) and Internet technology (IT). But let me be careful to stipulate a basic and very important disclaimer: *homology does not mean absolute equivalence*. On the web,[1] and I would add on the web we call OT (Online with OT), it means "the quality of being similar or corresponding in position or value or structure or function."

Nowhere in either the morphing book or the online wiki (Getting Started) do I make the reductive claim that these two media-technologies are simply identical. Nowhere is it argued—nor should it be—that the oAgora and eAgora are "the same place."

What the Project seeks to explain and represent is the striking reality that, despite the many obvious contrasts between OT and IT, the two media share a fundamental functionality: navigating through linked networks of potentials. They offer comparable vehicles or sets of strategies for the creation and transmission of knowledge, art, and ideas—strategies that are categorically different from those used in the tAgora. The oAgora and eAgora present similar—even cognate—opportunities for virtual surfing rather than for tAgora trekking.

In other words, the Pathways Project explores a comparison/contrast of remarkably similar but nonidentical ways of construing and shaping reality (Reality Remains in Play). How do OT and IT affect and even determine the ways in which we communicate? How do the cognitive prostheses they provide differ from our trusty, ideologically ingrained medium of texts (Ideology of the Text)? In broadest perspective, then, the central thesis of the Project maintains that OT and IT are homologous in *miming the way we think*—notwithstanding the many obvious contrasts in design and usage between the oAgora and the eAgora.

The "Fine Print"

To make certain that the scale stays balanced and to avoid simplistic equation of technologies, here are a few ways in which the OT-IT homology resists reductionism and makes room for the innate complexity of media-worlds:

1. *Texts can exist online.* Static eFiles,[2] which differ from the more usual tAgora fare only in that they are composed of pixels (rather than shredded trees) and available 24/7/365 to a much larger group of readers, are essentially texts (Texts and Intertextuality). Once they begin to link outside themselves and offer user options beyond the one-way street of linear sequence, they start to fulfill the cocreative, participatory mandate of the eAgora.

2. *OT can morph into texts and enter the tAgora.* For most of its history and even today, the field of studies in oral tradition has, quite ironically, pointed toward the tAgora. Not only do we freeze living performances by writing down (some aspects of) them, but we also manufacture static, immutable audio- and video-texts. The truth is that while the kinetic dimensions of voice and visual action are a welcome restoration that helps to fill out the thin slice of reality portrayable via printed pages, audios and videos are likewise and inescapably frozen texts. They are cenotaphs of performance; they have no pathways in them (Impossibility of tPathways). By consulting not one but many such fixations we can begin to glimpse a kinetic, emergent reality—much as flip books[3] or films simulate motion through persistence of vision. But collating instances provides at best a facsimile, a creditable illusion, and not at all the real experience.

3. *Communication can move into and out of multiple agoras.* Music, for example American blues songs, can be learned and transmitted via person-to-person exchange (in the oAgora), but also through published sheet music (in the tAgora) and online resources such as YouTube. Avdo Medjedović, the most accomplished of the South Slavic epic singers recorded by Milman Parry and Albert Lord, acquired his most famous song, *The Wedding of Smailagić Meho*, by having a colleague read a printed text aloud—a text that was of course itself an earlier transferral from the oAgora to the tAgora (A Foot in Each World). Evidence is mounting that scribes and poets can plug into OT language and expressive strategies even when composing pen-in-hand, or finger-on-keyboard. Sometimes it's even possible to leapfrog the tAgora (Leapfrogging the Text) altogether, moving from voice to virtuality directly. If research over the past quarter-century has shown

anything, it's that the so-called Great Divide of orality versus literacy amounts to an illusion that has outlived its usefulness. As marketplaces brimming with all of the verbal complexity humans can muster, agoras are anything but one-dimensional.

4. *Communication in the contemporary world requires multiple citizenship.* Taking these realities into account, the best solution for the contemporary mix of communicative modes is to establish citizenship in all three agoras—a primary goal of the Pathways Project (Citizenship in Multiple Agoras). As a first step we need to stop defaulting to textual ideology as our exclusive way of thinking about knowledge, art, and ideas. More positively, we need to start understanding how navigation works in the oAgora, how performers and audiences negotiate the pathways of an oral tradition that they share and participate in. In pursuing this kind of new awareness, we already have a powerful analogy ready at hand and in daily (if not hourly) use: namely, our navigation of the Internet as an interactive, rule-governed, ever-evolving experience. By getting inside of IT—by recognizing that everything it offers is necessarily contingent (Contingency) upon our and others' activities and contributions (Distributed Authorship)—we can also begin to understand how OT works within all societies as a fundamental communications technology.

5. *The conversation continues.* As part of the presentation in both media, and in the spirit of the Pathways Project, I have included my reactions to the reports by the two anonymous reviewers commissioned by the University of Illinois Press in a node entitled Response (Response).

Coda: Homology and Diversity

Once again, then, homology describes a relationship of *similarity, but not of identity* (Agora Correspondences). Any idea or concept worth entertaining must account for complexity, counterexamples, and general untidiness, and the OT-IT homology at the basis of the Pathways Project is no exception. As the Project seeks to illustrate in many different areas, OT and IT do their media-work not by adhering to verbatim singularity but by navigating pathways through networks of potentials. Variation within limits is the ultimate source of their strength and their staying power (Variation within Limits). Both of these verbal marketplaces thrive, in other words, by remaining forever "under construction."

The oAgora and eAgora are hardly identical or superimposable, but they are importantly alike in fostering activities that—in their own particular, highly diverse ways—mime the way we think.

Book versus Website

As the Pathways Project has matured and *Oral Tradition and the Internet* has moved toward publication, the relationship between the wiki-website and the book has changed in interesting ways. Applying the Golden Rule of multiple media—to leverage each medium to do what it does best—I have abbreviated and focused the tAgora presentation. While the online resource retains all of the nodes and numerous accompanying images, *Oral Tradition and the Internet* features the most prominent and significant nodes with a few selected images. Part of the motivation for this focusing was practical (issues of length, cost, and the like). But the more important reason was strategic: the book is meant to house the core theory in a familiar, default format, while the online resource offers more materials, additional options for exploration, and the built-in possibility of growth.

To read *Oral Tradition and the Internet* is to engage in the tried-and-true commerce of the tAgora. Although as a morphing book it supports and reflects some online-like activities (Morphing Book), its primary value derives from textual dynamics. You have room to navigate to a degree, but you're also provided a single, direct route—at least within each node—through the shorter, guided, brick-and-mortar presentation.

To surf the Pathways Project wiki-website[1] is to take advantage of the emerging technology of the eAgora. Its contents are more copious as well as interactive and non-predetermined, so you can formulate your own experience to a radically greater extent. Navigation means cocreation, as the network licenses (and requires) your ongoing participation.

Both media are economical and productive in their own ways, the one for tThinking and the other for eThinking (which parallels oThinking). The single best way to experience the Pathways Project is to engage both tools.

Response

The University of Illinois Press[1] engaged two anonymous readers to review the manuscript of *Oral Tradition and the Internet: Pathways of the Mind* in the context of its accompanying wiki-website. Their comments and suggestions have led to additions, subtractions, and revisions that have substantially improved the Pathways Project as a whole. In the spirit of interactive exchange that lies at the foundation of the Project, let me enumerate their major points and offer my response and perspective. Hopefully, this sort of conversation can continue in the Contributions node of the site.[2]

Five Critiques

1. *The "further reading" section should be more comprehensive.*

First, the Pathways Project—morphing book and wiki-website alike (Getting Started)—is meant to stand chiefly on its own, at a level suitable for the general reader and surfer. In response to the reviewers' encouragement, however, I have added an appreciable number of references that may prove useful for those who want to pursue various issues raised and discussed in the Pathways Project. These references are provided according to a carefully designed policy: "Further Reading" is intended not as a conventional academic bibliography, but primarily as an optional extension of the Project to serve the needs of nonspecialists. In other words, there is no attempt to include "all" relevant books, articles, and sites on any subject (an illusion in any case), and I have specifically excluded items that demand an expert's preparation. Within this policy, "Further Reading" emphasizes resources on oral tradition, since that is my principal field and since of the three agoras or marketplaces (Three Agoras) it is the oAgora that in my experience usually requires the most explanation. The Project's dependence on Wikipedia entries is intentional, both because of the ready availability of primary information and the second-level opportunities presented by those entries' links out to other eAgora-based information. We have accessed all external sites successfully as of February 25, 2012. As with any aspect of the Pathways Project, this section is open-ended, suggestive, and eligible for ongoing development through the website.

2. *What are the limits on the OT-IT correspondence?*

As emphasized in the Disclaimer node (Disclaimer), the OT-IT correspondence is meant as a homology, not an identity. There are of course myriad differences between oral tradition and Internet technology, from the physical through the conceptual, and these disparities should not be ignored. But it is the Project's purpose to point out fundamental analogies in how the two media-technologies work: they operate by navigating through networks of potentials rather than tracking along a one-way route; they are emergent, cocreative, and forever under construction; they mime the way we think. Does textual technology share some features of OT and IT? Most certainly, both theoretically and practically. All three agoras are, after all, arenas for human verbal exchange. But instead of focusing on the differences between OT and IT, or on their shared function with TT, I choose in this book and wiki-website to foreground the basic homology and its implications for citizens of all three agoras (Citizenship in Multiple Agoras). I concentrate on highlighting the importance of network-driven exchange—of how we imagine, transmit, and preserve knowledge, art, and ideas.

3. *Don't texts support and encourage a variety of interpretation that parallels user-driven activities in the oAgora and eAgora?*

It's true: no one reads the same text exactly the same as any other reader. Immutable artifacts aren't understood in precisely the same way by any two human beings, no matter how congruent their attitudes, life experiences, and personal profiles. As philosophy and literary criticism over the last thirty to forty years have shown beyond any doubt, the idea of a stable, core meaning is an illusion (Illusion of Stasis). We all come to texts—even word-for-word the very same text—with preconceptions and frames of reference developed over a lifetime, and the result is an inescapable diversity of interpretation and reception. Some critics have even observed that a wholly transparent text, a fixed and stable item that could be understood in only one way, would fail to engage its readership, since there would be nothing left for the reader to contribute. So, to that extent, texts in fact do sponsor and encourage alternate receptions, and we should not pretend that they don't.

But here's the distinction: in the tAgora you aren't navigating, you're trekking. In the oAgora and eAgora, every decision you make generates a new constellation of possibilities; when you make that next choice, another network of options presents itself, and so on. Sentences don't appear in fossilized, predictable order, and you can't (without considerable trouble) repeat the same blazed trail tomorrow. Why not? Because the interactivity of OT and IT is contingent (Contingency), real-time (Real-time versus Asynchronous), and ever-morphing. oSurfers and eSurfers aren't readers; they aren't reacting disparately to a fixed item. Instead, they're cocreating a "non-item" by negotiating a linked route-system (Systems versus Things). In the arenas of oral performance and the web, we must remember, it's *pathways* rather than *objects* that constitute the platform for exchange. Reality remains in play, not just in variant reactions to letter-by-letter, page-by-page instructions for reception, but because the network itself just doesn't hold still (Reality Remains in Play).

4. What is the source of authority in each of the three agoras or verbal marketplaces?

One of the reviewers suggested the formulation *a/Authority* to deal with the multi-agora variety of performers, makers, and users. So let's try that out. At the core of tAgora exchange lie an Author, a Work, and Permission to read. Even if there is no author-name or title attached to the item that reaches us, as is the case with many ancient and medieval texts, we feel compelled to assign—and if necessary to invent—such identifiers. Insistence on using the catchall designation "anonymous," or on coining titles where none exist, makes the point. Such is the overwhelming power of textual ideology (Ideology of Text).

But in the oAgora and eAgora, authority (now with lowercase *a*) resides not in owning things but in sharing systems (Owning versus Sharing). Because OT and IT authorship are distributed rather than singular (Distributed Authorship), no one person can claim absolute control over the ongoing process of rule-governed exploration. Likewise, since there isn't just one road to follow, how can "Big-C" *Copyright*—close kin to "Big-A" *Authority*—ever apply to the surfing that goes on in the oAgora and eAgora? (In recent years we've certainly seen how desperately that application has been attempted in the realm of digital media, and how spectacularly it has failed.) In order for Authority to reign, we need a finished and pathwayless product (Impossibility of tPathways), a platform that supports repetition rather than recurrence (Recur Not Repeat). Distinguishing between *Authority* and *authority* is a matter of responsible agora-business (Responsible Agora-business), and of becoming a citizen of not one but multiple marketplaces.

5. Isn't there a problem with universal access to eMedia? Practically speaking, who will be able to actually use the Pathways Project?

It's undeniably true that access to the eAgora, and therefore to the Pathways Project wiki-website and to URLs cited in the morphing book, is endemically limited. In fact, I would go further: outside the Wired West, whatever web access, hardware, and software are available may well be relatively unsophisticated and behind the technological curve.

I have two responses. First, all media are restrictive to some degree, but open Internet media are enormously more accessible than written and printed media. As detailed in the wiki node chronicling its publication history,[3] our journal *Oral Tradition* saw its readership explode from an annual high of about 1200 in the paper format to more than 20,000 unique visitors from 216 countries and territories for the open-access website. Although there are limitations on any facility or transaction in any agora, it's abundantly clear that open eMedia foster a radical and unprecedented democracy of access. Second, and in keeping with the new diversity of audiences involved in eAgora-business, we have a responsibility to construct delivery systems that serve the whole spectrum of potential users. That's why the *Oral Tradition* site was built as a platform for downloadable PDF files with linked eCompanions, for example, opting for simplicity and relatively small download size while still preserving the option to engage heavier media such as video, audio, photo slideshows, and the like via links. It's also why the Pathways Project sits on top of a simple wiki engine that, while password-protected, aims to offer users an uncomplicated experience of surfing through its network.

Provoking Exchange

Finally, let me close this node with a blanket response to all reactions and suggestions, large and small, positive and negative, from these two reviewers or from the audience of the morphing book and wiki-website. The Pathways Project is meant first and foremost as a provocation, and certainly not as a "final answer." In my view any contribution or intervention worth the name has as its most basic responsibility the stimulation of dialogue—more accurately, polylogue (Polytaxis)—that will lead to greater understanding than any single contribution can ever engender. As Walter Ong so often put it, "the conversation is never over."

In that respect the Project follows its own credo: it is a heuristic, a stimulation toward further discovery, and as such it must remain forever under construction. Once the blinders of textual ideology are removed, perhaps we can see that the Pathways Project is hardly an exception to communicative rules. All initiatives, no matter how finely crafted, are essentially provocations in a long, continuous, and unpredictable series—they're never finished things (Illusion of Object) but always experiences in search of "completion." The larger process amounts to navigating through networks, and the purpose of that navigation is to gain fresh (but always contingent) perspectives on the creation, transmission, and reception of knowledge, art, and ideas. You're involved in that process right now and with every book, website, and oral performance you engage.

After all, tAgora reflexes aside, that's the way we think.

Linkmaps

Linkmaps amount to suggested routes through the wiki network, particular sequences of ePathways that have been found to be illuminating in one way or another. An example is eWorld, a linkmap of nodes that leads from *Leapfrogging the Text* to *Museum of Verbal Art* to *Resynchronizing the Event* to *Systems versus Things*. En route the surfer will have an opportunity to think about a textless world, the new-media landscape for literature and oral tradition, an ancient Greek myth of transformation, the re-creation of performance events, and communication without "things." What's more, the entire itinerary revolves around the core OT/IT thesis of the Pathways Project.

But that's just one option. Potential surfers may opt to follow this or another of the predesignated patterns listed below (any of which they can always exit at any point). Or they may choose to strike out on their own, fashioning their experiences at every juncture—effectively creating their own linkmaps as they go. The freedom to explore and to construe is nearly absolute (Variation within Limits), and all we ask in return is that web-surfers consider the option of visiting the site and contributing their newly discovered itineraries to the Pathways Project **Linkmap Digest** as possible "guidebooks" for future users. To share your linkmap, you will need to create an account by clicking on the **Sign Up** link at the right of the horizontal orange bar that appears before the start of every node.

Linkmap Digest

Broadening your Horizons: This linkmap looks at what "literature" and "performance" can mean in different settings.

Citizenship in Multiple Agoras → A Foot in Each World → Misnavigation → Excavating an Epic

The eWorld: This node-sequence explores several aspects of the electronic world, or eAgora, and its trademark activities.

Leapfrogging the Text → Museum of Verbal Art → Resynchronizing the Event → Systems versus Things

The oWorld: This linkmap offers a perspective on the oral world, with emphasis on its similarity to the eWorld and difference from the world of texts.

Excavating an Epic → Homo Sapiens' Calendar Year → Online with OT → Museum of Verbal Art → Why Not Textualize? → oAgora

Textual Limits: These nodes collectively discuss and argue against cultural assumptions regarding textual superiority.

Ideology of the Text → tAgora → Don't Trust Everything You Read in Books → Impossibility of tPathways

Nodes in Alphabetical Order

A Foot in Each World

Counterintuitive behavior

Common sense and agora-savvy would seem to indicate that the individual person who feels completely at home in more than one verbal marketplace must be rare indeed. Of course, the Pathways Project actively encourages citizenship in multiple agoras (Citizenship in Multiple Agoras) as a way to avoid agoraphobia (Agoraphobia) and culture shock (Culture Shock). But full fluency—full media-bilingualism or even-trilingualism—is another matter. Cognitive habits run deep, as we textualists (Ideology of the Text) can come to realize if we're willing to look beyond our buried assumptions and conditioned reflexes about media.

Occasionally, though, we do encounter an exception that proves the rule: an individual who somehow manages to transact verbal business equally well in two different marketplaces. More than simply getting along in another, "nonmother" medium, such individuals fluently understand and fluently manage more than one cognitive technology. Because they live and act and communicate outside the monomedium paradigms that restrict most of us, they truly do qualify for more than just multiple citizenship. Wherever they're located at any given time, they have a foot in each of two worlds.

Nikola Vujnović

The famous expedition to study South Slavic oral epic in its natural setting, conceived and carried out by Milman Parry and Albert Lord, could not have happened without the invaluable and often underappreciated contribution of Nikola Vujnović. For Vujnović was that rare individual: a person with a foot planted securely in each of two worlds. A performing *guslar* himself, he sang a number of epics that were recorded acoustically or via dictation for the American scholars. But he also had enough literacy to be able to write down other poets' performed epics from dictation.

What did this native experience in both the oAgora and tAgora mean? Much more than a mere translator between languages, Vujnović served as a fully credentialed guide and intermediary between cultures and between agoras. On the one hand, he understood the South Slavic oral epic tradition from an insider's point of view. After all, he was himself a member of that epic tradition. As a result, he was able to interview other *guslari* as a colleague whom they could trust and respect.

But there was another, complementary side to Vujnović's crucially important role. To the oral world of the epic bards he could also bring inquiries conceived in the world of writing, reading, and texts (Arena of the Text), translating his employers' questions about South Slavic epic, Homer, and oral tradition into terms the other singers could grasp.

Still another benefit of his serviceable literacy emerged later on, when Lord brought him to the Parry Collection[1] at Harvard University to transcribe the oral epics they had recorded acoustically on large aluminum disks. Indeed, it seemed the perfect situation: a transcriber who was not only steeped in the epic register but also himself a *guslar*. And in many ways it was an ideal arrangement, although not in every respect. But that's another story (Singing on the Page).

If there were ever any question of whether a single individual could acquire native fluency and profitably use it in more than a single agora, Nikola Vujnović certainly provides a "textbook" answer.

Paolu Zedda

The island of Sardinia boasts a vigorous tradition of competitive oral poetry that reaches back for many centuries. Similar in its general outlines to Basque *bertsolaritza* and numerous other contest-song traditions worldwide (including some conducted via the Internet),[2] this genre of verbal dueling, called *mutetu longu* by the community, customarily involves from three to six poets. The duelers take turns "fighting" one another by improvising short poems, back and forth, on an assigned topic over a two- to three-hour period. The audience includes long-time aficionados who sit close to the action (often with recording equipment to preserve these improvised creations), as well as a cross section of the community somewhat more removed, physically and interactively, from the central stage.

The rules for composition are forbiddingly complex, prescribing not only verse-form and vocal melody but also a complicated spatial arrangement in which the word order within individual verses must be shuffled while maintaining rhyme. And all this while simultaneously responding cleverly to one's competitors! Making a Sardinian *mutetu*, referred to as a *cantada* when it is sung, is truly a tour de force of oral poetic composition, usually requiring many years of listening and practicing. It emphatically puts the lie to the common ideologically based conviction that complexity in poetic composition must always involve writing.

The foremost improviser or *cantadori*, as poets call themselves, in the southern Sardinian (Campidano) tradition of contest poetry is forty-two–year-old

(Left panel) Nikola Vujnović playing the *gusle*. Permission from David Elmer, associate curator of the Milman Parry Collection, Harvard University.

(Right panel) Paolu Zedda performing in Sardinia, 2007. Photograph by the author.

Paolu Flavio Zedda. His case is remarkable, and remarkably instructive for inquiries into inter-agora activities. For he is not only a respected and articulate citizen of the oAgora, highly skilled and widely admired for his performances in the oral marketplace, but also—and equally—a fully participating citizen in excellent standing in the tAgora.

And in what way, you might ask, does he keep a foot in each of these two worlds? Well, Zedda is a faculty member teaching ethnomusicology at the Università di Cagliari, with a focus on Sardinian oral traditions. And if that weren't enough, he is also a practicing orthodontist with a substantial clientele in the Cagliari area. In other words, he isn't only a leading oral poet in high demand (which would itself be quite an achievement) or a professor (again, a creditable position) or a dentist who specializes in straightening teeth (which of course requires advanced training). He is all three at once.

With his dual perspective of oral poet and trained academic/health care professional, and with his firsthand experience in both the oAgora and tAgora, Paolu Zedda is uniquely qualified to explain the oral tradition of *mutetu longu*.[3]

Accuracy

A tricky concept, *accuracy*. And very often a code word summoned to praise tAgora activities while denigrating transactions in the oAgora and eAgora. We're told that oral traditions can't preserve history accurately, for example, or that the web is far too subject to change or multiplicity to be a really dependable medium. We're asked to subscribe to (literally, to "underwrite") the credo that text is the only possible vehicle for safely and faithfully conveying the immutable data we need to run our cultures. Beware the oral and the virtual; fidelity lies solely in the brick-and-mortar. Or so goes the widespread and enduring myth of Textual Accuracy.

Five propositions

To refute this heavily biased and crippling belief, and to restore an appreciation of each agora on its own terms, I offer five propositions designed to recall the civic responsibility of achieving and maintaining citizenship in multiple agoras (Citizenship in Multiple Agoras). Each of these propositions emphasizes the importance of understanding diversity among media, technologies, and verbal marketplaces. As a group they are intended to approach the common problem of "tAgora default"—and the agoraphobia (Agoraphobia) it engenders—from different perspectives. They're all getting at the same inconvenient truth, in other words.

1. *Accuracy is as accuracy does.* This proverbial-sounding observation (Proverbs) is a "literal" reaffirmation of communicative democracy. To paraphrase, only if our ideal of fidelity to truth meets the requirements of the particular agora in which we find ourselves can it have any meaning. Otherwise, it remains a foreign and unintelligible term (even if we suppose ourselves fluent, we're simply imposing an irrelevant and distorting frame of reference).

2. *Accuracy is in the eye of the beholder.* This proposition emphasizes the myopia induced by parochial, ideologically driven tAgora prejudice (Ideology of the Text). In conceiving of the very idea of "being accurate," we unconsciously attune the concept solely to transactions that take place within the tAgora (Arena of the Text), subordinating everything to the rule and model of text. But tAgora accuracy doesn't fit the oAgora or eAgora.

3. *Accuracy is usually, and wrongly, understood as [textual] accuracy.* Though we don't pause to consider the distortion, by accuracy we conventionally mean accuracy as applied to texts, as literal truth, as indisputable fact (Just the Facts). As a post-Gutenberg culture, as people of the book, we always and everywhere include the bracketed adjective as an indispensable part of the definition, subscribing ideologically to [textual] accuracy.

4. *Accuracy is "marked" by its covert reference to textuality and the tAgora.* Accuracy already means tAccuracy (Texts and Intertextuality). The proof of this hidden agenda lies in the preordained focus of the term. Consider how parochially we use the word: in order to describe or even imagine other kinds of accuracy, we have to undo the presumption (Reading Backwards), remove the default. We have to add qualifiers to the monolithic concept in order to deflect its inherent thrust. To designate anything else we need an intervention—as in oAgora accuracy, or eAgora accuracy. We might compare the situation to the coining of "oral literature" as a term designed to overcome the inherent tAgora bias of "literature," marked for letters and texts. It's only too easy to see where the cultural conventions lie, and how hard we have to labor to get beyond them.

5. *At root, accuracy simply means "taking care of."* It may come as a surprise, but there is nothing fundamental in the term itself that mandates textual definition. The English word derives from Latin *accuratus*, with the meaning "taken care of, exact."[4] And who's to say that we can't take care of our verbal business with great precision in the oAgora and eAgora as well—as long as we construe accuracy within their own frames of reference? True enough, sentencing either OT (oral tradition) or IT (Internet technology) to unnatural confinement in the tAgora causes nothing but problems, inducing agoraphobia at every turn. Who can aspire to be accurate when speaking in an unintelligible foreign tongue?

But we can do better than that. Let's attempt to understand accuracy within the individual agora, according to the applicable rules.

Rethinking accuracy

One of the primary tenets of the Pathways Project is that experience, perception, and communication are always and everywhere filtered by the media and technologies we use. It's not a question of whether this self-evident proposition is true, but simply how it works out in the case of each medium and technology.

But cognitive habits are hard to break, or even consciously recognize. We are so fluent in tAgora communication that we don't stop to assess its influence on how we interrelate and transfer knowledge, art, and ideas; without further thought, we take textuality and its arena as the common denominator, the standard, the bedrock. Of course, that working assumption is patently wrong: to map living, multidimensional experience onto a printed page raises as many problems as it putatively solves. Most museums only remember reality (Museum of Verbal Art). They can't ever contain it.

Fundamentally, there is no such thing as a one-for-one, mimetic portrayal of reality in any medium, never mind transferal of that experience to another person. Reality can only be sampled, hinted at, and then always in fragmented and reduced form (Reality Remains in Play). The overpowering ideology of text—ultimately a deal with the devil—has bewitched us into accepting the tAgora credo that texts can capture and contain reality, but nothing could be further from the truth. It is never a matter of freezing knowledge, art, and ideas for later consumption. It is always a matter of choosing which medium or technology we wish to use and fully appreciating its built-in liabilities as well as its endemic advantages. And there are always both kinds of features to consider.

In regard to media, then, there are no perfect and complete—no universally accurate—representations. There is only a selection of lenses, each of which offers a particular kind of accuracy, an idiosyncratic take on reality. From this principle it follows that a lack of [textual] accuracy in the oAgora or eAgora should not necessarily be interpreted as an error or shortcoming, but, at least potentially, as its own, agora-specific brand of accuracy.

What is oAccuracy?

If you're looking for absolute stasis—cold, hard fact that refuses to adjust as the environment around it morphs—don't bother searching the oAgora. Such immutable, inflexible items are in short supply. And why? Because they serve no useful purpose in a constantly morphing agora. To put it most plainly, all they can accomplish is to inhibit the natural dynamics of navigating through networks of potentials. Accuracy in this marketplace doesn't have anything to do with the brittleness of verbatim repetition (Recur Not Repeat). oAccuracy means fidelity to the system, not the thing (Systems versus Things).

When a South Slavic *bajalica*, or conjurer, diagnoses her patient's malady and adjusts her healing charm to fit the disease, she is oAccurate. When an African society responds to the advent of a new king by systematically "forgetting" one person in the royal lineage, thus keeping the official cultural history of kingship at the authoritative seven individuals, they are cultivating oAccuracy. When Basque *bertsolaris* fashion never-before-uttered verses that respond competitively to their opponents' verses and will never be uttered again, everyone involved is behaving oAccurately. When a Rajasthani epic bard narrates what we textualists would consider only a "part" of the overall story-cycle, leaving the whole implied (but in the oAgora very much present to the communicative act for both bard and audience), he is practicing oAccuracy.

Three oPrinciples   In short, then, we can affirm three counterintuitive principles that govern accuracy in the oAgora. First, the operative dynamic is not stasis (Illusion of Stasis)—real or imagined—but rather malleability and rule-governed variation (Variation within Limits). Patterned variation (as opposed to willy-nilly change) (Not So Willy-nilly) is the name of the game. Second, to be oAccurate is to navigate through networks of potentials, where each choice generates a host of opportunities and no two itineraries are identical. Dead ends—textual culminations—are death to oAgora transactions. Third, and perhaps hardest to grasp for those pledged to textual ideology, in the oAgora accuracy is the opposite of singularity. *Not* to morph, *not* to adjust to an ever-changing environment, is necessarily to become oInaccurate, oImprecise.

What is eAccuracy?

Reference "books"—static files of pixel-pages[5]—are certainly common enough on the web, and sometimes more conveniently accessed on a website than in their home marketplace, the tAgora. Indeed, an argument could be made that such items are best understood as located in what amounts to a recently constructed electronic wing of the tAgora marketplace.

But true eAgora systems are a breed apart. If you're choosing your route, navigating pathways interactively, and exploring via potentials rather than predetermined sequences, then you will search in vain for singular, text-defined accuracy. Given our unexamined bias in favor of tAgora thinking and communication, you may well be disappointed at the nonstop morphing, the refusal of the system to hold still—never mind your own uncertainty about the "best" or "prescribed" way to proceed. You may well experience a severe case of agoraphobia and find yourself categorically dismissive of the web-based, interactive medium itself, criticizing it for not performing textually. You may conclude that you just can't depend on the web.

But things aren't that simple. Once again it's a matter of what activities are appropriate to and licensed by the particular agora in question. If at some point your Internet expedition leads to the kind of tAgora accuracy we're taught to admire and count on, then you've stalled and your eExploration is at an end. Why? Because the networked medium that serves by presenting alternatives, by fostering connections, by offering the user participation within a rule-governed system, has ceased any useful function. If your next choice is your last choice, in other words, the systemic power of linked possibilities has failed. Living potential has collapsed to a museum exhibit. A vivid, continuous present has yielded to a flattened, frozen past. You might as well go read a book (Don't Trust Everything You Read in Books).

eAccuracy, on the other hand, promises its own kind of fidelity and for that reason must be assessed on its own terms. Suppose you're in search of something more than the conversion factor between liters and quarts. Let's say you're hoping to learn more about how Buddhism flourished or struggled under various political regimes, and further that you want to take into account different opinions and evolving situations. eAccuracy means plotting a course through dozens of interactive web assets, some of them mutually contradictory, and entertaining multiple perspectives. And don't forget: even the sites and links you follow can and will change over time—as they must to reflect evolving realities. Charting your own path through continuously updated medical websites in pursuit of a deeper awareness of species of multiple sclerosis is to surf eAccurately (even if, as is likely, none of the sites can ever properly aspire to singular authority). Listening to multiple versions of an Irish folksong posted by many different fieldworkers over many regions and years—and programmatically denying priority to any single one—will go a long way toward providing a facsimile, eAccurate sense of the song's many-sided, irreducible character. eAccuracy is like a video continuously being shot and (re-)edited rather than a photograph filed in a shoebox.

Three ePrinciples   As in the case of the oAgora, we can affirm three counterintuitive principles that govern accuracy in the eAgora. First, to be eAccurate means to accept and engage malleability and rule-governed variation. Don't expect either stasis or willy-nilly modulation, both of which are signals that you're operating outside the network. Second, concentrate on navigation, with full awareness that you're in charge—and no hesitation or apology is needed. Finally, realize that singularity, epitome, and ultimate authority are foreign values that only compromise eAccuracy.

Accuracy depends on the agora

Data or experience? Item-centric or system-driven? One-way street or route network? No matter how strong our ideological presumptions and cognitive habits may be, the answer is not to choose one alternative or the other. The answer is to choose the alternative that suits the marketplace. No notion of accuracy is universal, and commitment to an impossible universality can engender only flawed perspectives and flawed communication.

To be accurate—to "take care of"—is clearly an agora-dependent activity. And in the oAgora and eAgora, accuracy means fidelity not to things but to systems.

Agora As Verbal Marketplace

The ancient Greek word *agora* originally names a brick-and-mortar marketplace, a physical site for exchange, in general a center for municipal interactions of many sorts. The Athenian agora,[6] for example, situated northwest of the Acropolis, seems to have been a bustling center for political, commercial, and religious activities throughout the fourth and fifth centuries BCE. It served its constituency uniquely as a designated public space and nexus for social transactions.

The Pathways Project uses the term "agora" to denote a *verbal marketplace*, a virtual site for exchange, a public space and nexus where ideas and knowledge are shared via whatever medium the community has adopted as the default technology. As such, it takes three forms: oral (the oAgora), electronic (the eAgora), and textual (the tAgora). Each of these three venues operates according to its own dynamics for creation and transmission, but the root correspondences between the first two—the home environments for OT and IT—are striking and important (Agora Correspondences).

Agora Correspondences

As explained in each of the three involved nodes—the oAgora, the tAgora, and the eAgora—our discussions of these verbal marketplaces and principal media-types follows a mirroring logic. Each section within a node is explicitly matched to corresponding, parallel sections in the other two nodes. The purpose of this structural strategy is to highlight the comparisons and contrasts (Three Agoras) that constitute the major subject of the Pathways Project (Getting Started).

The following table lists the section titles, with (in the wiki) anchored links to the relevant section in each of the three nodes. In the spirit of the Project, of both the wiki-website (Wiki) and the morphing book (Morphing Book), this interactive list offers yet another way to navigate available contents.

Agora Correspondences

oAgora	tAgora	eAgora
Genus and species	Genus and species	Genus and species
Word-markets	Word-markets	Word-markets
Public, not proprietary	Proprietary, not public	Public, not proprietary
The evolutionary fallacy	The evolutionary fallacy	The evolutionary fallacy
Five OT word-markets	Five TT word-markets	Five IT word-markets
No real authors	Real authors	No real authors
Five nonauthors	Five real authors	Five nonauthors
oAgora sharing and reuse	tAgora sharing and reuse	eAgora sharing and reuse
Variation within limits	Verbatim means no variation	Variation within limits
The analogy to language	The contrast to language	The analogy to language
Recurrence, not repetition	Repetition, not recurrence	Recurrence, not repetition
Built-in "copyright"	Imposed copyright	Built-in "copyright"
Survival of the fittest	Survival of the "fixed-est"	Survival of the fittest

Agoraphobia

The online Merriam Webster English dictionary[7] defines *agoraphobia* as an "abnormal fear of being helpless in an embarrassing or unescapable situation that is characterized especially by the avoidance of open or public places." Does this phenomenon apply to our three agoras—the oral, textual, and electronic marketplaces (Agora As Verbal Marketplace)—that lie at the basis of the Pathways Project (Agora Correspondences)? Can a person be phobic about media dynamics?

Before we start . . .

Let's offer a trial answer to these questions before we begin to address the issue of agoraphobia in detail.

In short, for well-indoctrinated citizens of the tAgora, steeped in texts as the primary vehicle for communicative exchange, the oAgora and (to an ever-decreasing extent) the eAgora represent "the other." In broad terms, most of us reading this book or clicking through this wiki don't suffer from tAgoraphobia, simply because the textual medium is so familiar and so comfortable. It's the major marketplace in which we live and work and think. There are certainly text-based activities with which we're uncomfortable: some of us fear the writing of reports or seminar papers, some are anxious about spreadsheets, others enervated over the prospect of poring over long and complex books. Nonetheless, the tAgora remains—at least for the moment—our "home field," the default arena for the kinds of culturally driven knowledge-exchange we practice on a daily basis. Even when we use the web, we're often simply creating more texts.

Not so within the oAgora, where most of us lack fluency. In an unfamiliar environment that requires an ability to navigate networks, page-turners (or screen-scrollers) like us are mostly lost. And, as an easily threatened and technologically parochial species, what we don't understand we characteristically either ignore or devalue, summarily pronouncing it outside (or even beneath) our attention. OT seems opaque, so we denigrate it as an inefficient technology. Dealing with an indecipherable reality by denying its existence or declaring it primitive, inaccurate, or just plain flawed—these amount to "textbook" symptoms of oAgoraphobia.

We do much better—better by the week, in fact—with the new "other" of the eAgora. We're already getting accustomed to the strength and power of the electronic network, already gaining some fluency and know-how in the languages associated with this emerging verbal marketplace. We're still flummoxed by its inherent plasticity and array of options, of course, often being content to copy our static text files straight to a website and consider the job done, or to employ one crude but familiar eTool when a more useful tool or suite of tools would vastly improve our work and experience. For these reasons, many times the "nontechies" among us sometimes find the eAgora forbidding, falling victim to a state of mind that translates only too easily to fear, helplessness, and disempowerment, that is, to eAgoraphobia. And a substantial number of us are to one degree or another eAgoraphobic.

So that's the irony. Because of our predisposition as creators, users, and traders of fixed, spatialized texts, we may struggle to communicate fluently within the eAgora, and most of us fail utterly to gain fluency in the oAgora. The diagnosis? "Thoroughgoing oAgoraphobia complicated by a milder and diminishing but still chronic case of eAgoraphobia." tAgoraphobia doesn't enter the picture as a major disorder for most of us, but we'll come to appreciate how that apparent sign of health actually amounts to a crippling problem in itself.

Curing agoraphobia

The way past our media-based limitations will be to experience all three phobias, understand their sources and resources, and learn to transact the business of communication not monotechnologically but diversely (A Foot in Each World). We will need to understand the tAgora as merely one possible marketplace, one possible arena supported by a set of arbitrary conventions. Then texts will be seen for what they are: one strategy within a pull-down menu of options, one channel within a group of channels. It may be difficult and frustrating to cast ourselves adrift from the ingrained, almost autonomic reflex of thinking through texts, but it's a necessary preliminary. And eventually it will prove an exciting and liberating step, as we take the next step and learn to think through other media. In the end, diversifying our repertoire of media-technologies (Citizenship in Multiple Agoras)—a central goal of the Pathways Project—is the best remedy for agoraphobia.

As an intervention designed to help cure agoraphobia by suggesting a continuous conversation rather than a one-dimensional statement, let me direct the reader and surfer to the Response node (Response). This section amounts to a brief reaction to the reports by the two individuals commissioned by the University of Illinois Press to review the Pathways Project.

Arena of Oral Tradition

What does it mean to enter the oAgora? Why do you go there? Whom will you meet in that marketplace (Agora As Verbal Marketplace)? What kind of verbal exchange can you reasonably expect to happen there? How do you leave and how do you return?

Try conceiving of the experience as entering an arena, a space defined by the activities that transpire there rather than by geography or other physical attributes. It is a space for recurrent rather than repetitive activities (Recur Not Repeat), and you can get there only by following oPathways (oPathways)—which means by cocreating your own route and your own destination. Not surprisingly, it is a space that closely resembles the arena of the web (Arena of the Web) but differs markedly from the arena of the text (Arena of the Text). In other words, the Pathways Project homology (Disclaimer) holds for arenas as well.

Access

Subject to rules imposed by the oAgora group in question, access to the oArena is open to all who wish and are qualified to take part. Some oral traditions do discriminate by ethnicity, age, or gender, but by far the greater number involve open-ended, diverse audiences as participating, present partners. In effect, participating means getting online with OT (Online with OT).

Fluency in the specialized language

Successfully negotiating the oArena, and successfully navigating oPathways, requires reasonable fluency in the special language of the oAgora. Whether performer(s) or audience, you must control both the structure and the idiomatic content of that powerful language, and you must recognize the emergent, right-now nature of the communication. If not, you'll fall prey to agoraphobia (Agoraphobia) and culture shock (Culture Shock), and all attempts at arena-based communication, no matter how earnest or intense, will fail.

Partnership

Open access and fluency are important because OTs are responsible for all kinds of crucial cultural work. Far more than entertainment or vaguely defined instruction, they serve as vehicles for history, trade, social criticism, medicine, philosophy, maintenance of personal and group identity, and a vast array of recurring social activities, to name a few important areas. Different cultures handle partnership differently, but they have one aspect in common: in each and every case there is built-in provision for continuity, for transmission of knowledge, art, and ideas to others. OTs are real-time partnerships (Real-time versus Asynchronous) that prosper by remaining forever under construction (Reality Remains in Play) by the people who make and remake them.

Becoming part of the event

Once you've gained access to the oArena, put your fluency to work, and established an ongoing partnership, you're ready to enjoy the event. For the Basque community of poets and audiences participating in the improvisational competition called *bertsolaritza*,[8] this means living inside the matrix of rules and practices that govern the verbal transaction of contest poetry in that oral tradition. To take delight in the improvisers' clever solutions to the problems posed by topics and competitors, to feel the emotion of nationalistic scenarios playing out as brief narratives, to sing those last few lines of a never-before-composed poem ensemble; these are some of the core experiences awaiting you in this oArena.

Exiting and returning

If you exit the oArena and stop engaging with an oral performance, the experience that you exited won't be waiting for you on your return. Why not? Simply because there is no freestanding "it" to return to, no object or item to reclaim. Those other oSurfers you left behind, who have continued their cocreation of the event along with the performer(s), will have kept the connection alive, but reality will have morphed in the meantime. And they weren't having precisely the same experience anyway. For all of these reasons, "it" won't hold still, despite the ideologically based claims we unthinkingly cling to (Ideology of the Text). Exiting means that your shared, ongoing experience is over.

But all is not lost. The oAgora will offer another performance of the same story, another chance to hear your group's history, another opportunity to learn a medical procedure or assist in a familiar ritual. At that juncture you can reenter the living network of options that you navigate, essentially the "same" oArena and the "same" dedicated language—though we must be careful not to impose a brick-and-mortar definition of what "same" means. Every choice you're offered and every choice you make helps to determine your always-evolving experience. Expressive power in this medium derives from rule-governed flexibility (Variation within Limits).

The oArena is nothing if not a platform for cocreativity.

Arena of the Text

What does it mean to enter the tAgora? Why do you go there? Whom will you meet in that marketplace (Agora As Verbal Marketplace)? What kind of verbal exchange can you reasonably expect to happen there? How do you leave and how do you return?

Try conceiving of the experience as entering an arena, a space defined by the activities that transpire there rather than by geography or other physical attributes. It is a space for repetitive rather than recurrent activities (Recur Not Repeat), and you can't get there by following pathways because the tAgora is pathwayless (Impossibility of tPathways). Although you will interpret the journey individually, you will follow the unique route and reach the unique destination prescribed by the artifact that serves as your guide and predetermined source. Not surprisingly, it is a space that differs markedly from the arena of oral tradition (Arena of Oral Tradition) and the arena of the web (Arena of the Web). In other words, the Pathways Project homology (Disclaimer) holds for arenas as well.

Access

Access to the tArena is limited and selective. Eligibility depends on the availability of textual objects and the affordability of using them. Many prospective users will not qualify simply because they cannot lay hands on the requisite materials or because those materials are out of reach financially or because distribution channels are closed to them. Discrimination can inhibit or prevent access on any number of grounds, and, unfortunately, in many cases there's no way for a certain segment of the population to participate.

Language fixed in amber

Although specialized languages do exist in the tArena (for example, official languages such as those employed for law codes), the structure and idiomatic content of most communication is less densely coded than is typical of communication in the oAgora and eAgora. Moreover, tAgora languages support a nonemergent, asynchronous (Real-time versus Asynchronous) kind of exchange that is accomplished by transferring knowledge, art, and ideas to the cognitive prosthesis of texts. Not recognizing the freestanding, unenmeshed quality of this kind of communication will lead to agoraphobia (Agoraphobia) and culture shock (Culture Shock), and all attempts at outside-the-arena communication, no matter how earnest or intense, will fail.

Proprietorship and consumership

The tArena restricts access according to a proprietor-consumer relationship that governs the legalized use of things rather than provides gateways to systems (Systems versus Things). Although this arena is responsible for hosting verbal traffic of all sorts, disparities in access lead inevitably to imbalances stemming from eligibility requirements. Can you afford a book or a subscription? Can the item be bought with your currency or reach you through presently available distribution channels? Brick-and-mortar texts may seem to insure continuity and permanence, but as disembodied containers they are subject to loss, wear, and other kinds of failure. Textual technology is an asynchronous medium that supports only secondhand partnerships and prospers by resisting change (Reality Remains in Play) and affirming the illusions of object (Illusion of Object) and stasis (Illusion of Stasis).

Standing aloof from the event

Once you've gained access to the tArena, either by buying or by selling under the rules of ownership, the textual object (Texts and Intertextuality) is ready for use. For a reader of physical books, this means opening to page 1 and following the well-blazed trail (the only trail through the text). For the reader of eBooks, which amount to static eFiles,[9] this means turning on your Kindle, Nook, or iPad; downloading a virtual object; and proceeding without detours along the same kind of one-way, never-branching trail. The reading experience happens as the text user reacts to a fixed, invariable item, and for that reason seems both highly economical and highly repeatable. Uniformity and stability in the item—which is created *in advance of* rather than *during* its use—encourages the impression of uniformity and stability in experience. Or at least that's how we conventionally understand the transmission of knowledge, art, and ideas in the tAgora (Ideology of the Text).

Exiting and returning

If you exit the tArena and stop engaging with a text, have no fear: it will be waiting for you on your return. Why? Simply because there is a finite, freestanding "it" to return to, an object or item to reclaim. Maybe you signaled where you left off by placing a physical or virtual bookmark between pages, or paused or stopped the mp3 music file or the DVD film (aren't those "continue from last session" options handy?). Meanwhile, you go to the kitchen for a cup of coffee or resume your reading or listening or watching tomorrow night after work. "It" will in fact hold still, subject of course to technological problems of various sorts. "It" won't have morphed in the meantime. Exiting does not mean that your tArena experience is over. You most certainly *can* go home again.

All this is possible because you are not navigating through a system or network but trekking through a text. And according to the operative ideology you can stop and start the process as you wish, without disturbing or foreshortening or distorting the experience. Expressive power in this medium derives from inflexibility (Variation within Limits).

The tArena is nothing if not a platform for scripted communication on your own terms.

Arena of the Web

What does it mean to enter the eAgora? Why do you go there? Whom will you meet in that marketplace (Agora As Verbal Marketplace)? What kind of verbal exchange can you reasonably expect to happen there? How do you leave and how do you return?

Try conceiving of the experience as entering an arena, a space defined by the activities that transpire there rather than by geography or other physical attributes. It is a space for recurrent rather than repetitive activities (Recur not Repeat), and you can get there only by following ePathways (ePathways)—which means by cocreating your own route and your own destination. Not surprisingly, it is a space that closely resembles the arena of oral tradition (Arena of Oral Tradition) but differs markedly from the arena of the text (Arena of the Text). In other words, the Pathways Project homology (Disclaimer) holds for arenas as well.

Access

Subject to rules imposed by the eAgora group in question, access to the eArena is open to all who wish and are qualified to take part. Some networks discriminate by username, password, or locality, but by far the greater number involve open-ended, diverse audiences as participating, present partners. In effect, participating means getting online with IT (Online with OT).

Fluency in the specialized language

Successfully negotiating the eArena, and successfully navigating ePathways, requires reasonable fluency in the special language of the eAgora. Whether web-designer or -surfer, you must control both the structure and the idiomatic content of that powerful language, and you must recognize the emergent, right-now nature of the communication. If not, you'll fall prey to agoraphobia (Agoraphobia) and culture shock (Culture Shock), and all attempts at arena-based communication, no matter how earnest or intense, will fail.

Partnership

Open access and fluency are important because IT events are responsible for all kinds of crucial cultural work. Far more than entertainment or vaguely defined instruction, they serve as vehicles for history, trade, social criticism, medicine, philosophy, maintenance of personal and group identity, and a vast array of recurring social activities, to name a few important areas. Different networks handle partnership differently, but they have one aspect in common: in each and every case there is built-in provision for continuity, for transmission of knowledge, art, and ideas to others. IT events are real-time partnerships (Real-time versus Asynchronous) that prosper by remaining forever under construction by the people who make and remake them (Reality Remains in Play).

Becoming part of the event

Once you've gained access to the eArena, put your fluency to work, and established your ongoing partnership, you're ready to enjoy the event. And the repertoire of events is both open-ended and always morphing in real time. You can decide to explore the legalities of digital sharing, Tweet about your latest concert, converse with your Facebook friends, surf through the Pathways Project, or navigate various international perspectives and live discussions on war and peace; these are some of the core experiences awaiting you in the eArena.

Exiting and returning

If you exit the eArena and close your browser, the experience that you exited won't be waiting for you on your return. Why not? Simply because there is no freestanding "it" to return to, no object or item to reclaim. Those other eSurfers you left behind, who have continued their cocreation of the event, will have kept the connection alive, but reality will have morphed in the meantime. And they weren't having precisely the same experience anyway. For all of these reasons, "it" won't hold still, despite the ideologically based claims we unthinkingly cling to (Ideology of the Text). Exiting means that your shared, ongoing experience is over.

But all is not lost. The eAgora will offer another opportunity to investigate digital sharing, tweet, friend, or surf. At that juncture you can reenter the living network of options that you navigate, essentially the "same" eArena and the "same" dedicated language—though we must be careful not to impose a brick-and-mortar definition of what "same" means. Every choice you're offered and every choice you make helps to determine your always-evolving experience. Expressive power in this medium derives from rule-governed flexibility (Variation within Limits).

The eArena is nothing if not a platform for cocreativity.

Audience Critique

Most of our elite contemporary forms of performance—drama, classical music concerts, ballet, opera, formal poetry readings, and so on—call for polite, narrowly defined participation by audiences. We're encouraged to applaud and perhaps allowed to quietly express our disapproval, but these reactions are customarily permitted only after the performance has finished. To interrupt an ongoing event with audible comments or visible responses is normally considered rude and inappropriate; in the context of that kind of performance arena, such actions are unidiomatic.

Audience protocol is often radically different in the oAgora. Of course there are some forms of OT that demand rapt silence and careful observance of ritual constraints, but there are also a great many varieties that license or even require real-time contribution and intervention.

Working together

One case in point is slam poetry, which fosters a continuous, usually positive interaction between performing poets and their audiences as part of the ongoing event. Another is Basque *bertsolaritza*,[10] a form of contest poetry in which mass audiences who know the rules for extemporaneous composition actually sing the last few lines of never-before-composed oral poems along with their composers. In a vital sense both OT groups are collectively surfing the pathways of a living network, cocreating the performed poem. Their interactions are positive and mutually reinforcing. Everyone is playing by the accepted rules of the oAgora.

For another instance of working together, please visit the Response node (Response), which briefly presents my reaction to the reader reports on the Pathways Project as commissioned by the University of Illinois Press.

Disapproval

But what about the negative side of things—criticism? What about the equivalent of the harsh morning-after reviews of Broadway plays that mercilessly pan the production? Or critics' scathing indictments of an opera, ballet, or symphony performance? Is there any outlet in the oAgora for audiences to disapprove or at least to query what the performer or group is doing?

One answer comes from Matija Murko,[11] a Slovenian scholar and fieldworker who studied then-thriving South Slavic oral epic traditions in the early decades of the twentieth century and offers us this amusing firsthand report:

> The audience listens to the singer with maximum attention, interest, and sympathy for the heroes, and is sometimes extremely moved by the whole of a poem or by certain episodes. During pauses for rest, the members of the audience make various remarks, question the singer, and critique him, to which criticism he does not fail to respond. One time I reproached a singer for having given a favorite Moslem hero, Hrnjica Mujo, four brothers instead of the two he is credited with elsewhere; he retorted in a bitter tone: "That's how another told it to me; I wasn't there when they were born!" There is one mode of criticism that does not lack originality: when the singer is absent during a pause for rest, someone greases the string and the bow of his instrument with tallow, which makes it impossible for him to continue.

It's one thing to feel the sting of a bad review, quite another to have your string greased!

Bellerophon and His Tablet

It's endemically difficult to comprehend in our present tAgora-dominated environment, but letters and pages and books didn't always have the upper hand (Texts and Intertextuality). They didn't always represent the trump technology, the medium through which all other media had to be interpreted. Nowhere is this more evident than in a tale from Homer's *Iliad*, a perilous episode that at first sight may seem like unexpected evidence for writing within the oAgora.

The story concerns the victimization of the Greek hero Bellerophon, who incurs the wrath of Proitos's wife by denying her advances. His refusal so infuriates her that she spitefully reports him to her husband as the instigator, causing Proitos to attempt a kind of vicarious, long-distance revenge (which eventually fails, by the way). In short, Proitos sends Bellerophon to the Lykian king with a "folding tablet" bearing the encoded message to "kill the bearer." Homer calls the kill-code *sêmata lugra*, literally "baneful signs," and it's hard to argue with that description.

But Homer and his tradition, good citizens of the oAgora, weren't simply defaulting to the tAgora here. The logic runs the other way. By calling the written message a series of signs, Homer was explaining that inscription, a technology he doesn't use, amounts to a species of sign language, an OT technology that he does use. He is characterizing the momentous communication in the only way that he can—as a species of the expressive signals known within his tradition as *sêmata* and used to describe such phenomena and objects as divinely inspired omens, tomb markers for heroes, and Odysseus's and Penelope's olive-tree bed.

And Homer is absolutely consistent in his media dynamics. Wherever these *sêmata* occur in the *Iliad* and *Odyssey*, and for whatever specific purpose, they share one principal function: *they serve as symbols rife with hidden meaning that can be discovered in no other way.* As such, these dedicated signs (Accuracy) remain as mysterious as they are powerful, as superficially opaque as they are effective. In other words, Homer interprets the tablet and its murderous code from within his own oAgora by comparing the written message to a meaning-making strategy that lies at the heart of his OT craft.

Homer does not struggle to escape the ideology of texts. He does not suffer from the modern plague of agoraphobia. He's many centuries too early to worry over the reaccreditation of the Museum of Verbal Art. For once, the tables are turned: oral tradition sets the frame of reference, and we're asked to understand a text in terms of oAgora technology, not vice versa.

Citizenship in Multiple Agoras

You know how it goes. You're planning a trip to another country and find you need a passport, maybe a visa, perhaps even a special travel permit beyond that. Documents in hand, you get off the plane, pass through immigration and customs, change some currency, and—if you're able—switch to the local language. But even if your vocabulary isn't spotty, even if your syntax and grammar prove serviceable, you can't simply assume immediate membership in the new culture. Remembering a few words and stringing correct sentences together is one thing. Achieving cultural fluency (Culture As Network)—which requires a set of habits borne of years of experience and subliminal learning—is quite another, and well beyond your reach.

Unless, of course, you've learned more than one system. Unless you feel entirely at home and at ease configuring more than one reality. Unless, in short, you're a full-fledged member of more than one culture (A Foot in Each World).

The benefits of agora citizenship

To belong to an agora (Agora As Verbal Marketplace) as a citizen in good standing is like belonging to a culture. The marketplace feels native, and you can transact your business fluently—without hesitation and without conscious adjustments and recalculations.

Your tItinerary   Let's begin with our usual default agora, the textual marketplace. You have a report to write? Then your tAgora facility with memos, executive summaries, or whatever form your employer uses, kicks in and you compose within a familiar frame of reference. You have a research paper due in two weeks? Then your text-mastery (Texts and Intertextuality) guides you through the library, through websites loaded with static eFiles,[12] through the format preferred by the course instructor, and so forth. Whatever the challenge, the point is that you don't have to rediscover the most basic aspects of the procedure. You don't have to relearn the routine. Instead, you enter the tAgora (Arena of the Text) and proceed according to its rules for creating and exchanging text-objects.

Your eItinerary   It's becoming easier all the time for many of us to enter and use the eAgora—which explicitly does *not* mean to consult fixed texts on the web but specifically to engage in interactive and cocreative activities online (Disclaimer). We find ourselves increasingly comfortable with instruments such as Wikipedia, we build our own electronic sites and intranets for many purposes, and in general we are getting accustomed to another way of thinking and expressing ourselves. However, it's a relatively small percentage of us, disproportionately located in industrialized, wired environments, who have achieved real eCitizenship. While the balance tips further every day toward the arena of the web (Arena of the Web), it still has a long way to go.

Your oItinerary   Less familiarly yet for most of us, the performers and audiences of oral traditions also work within well-defined arenas (Arena of Oral Tradition) with built-in rules for the creation, transmission, and reception of knowledge, art, and ideas. Performers of contest poetry don't search through handbooks for melodies or verse-forms, lamenters don't reinvent their practice on each occasion or iteration, and epic singers don't parse oWords. They simply know how to proceed, how to surf the oPathways of their particular oral tradition, and their audiences know how to follow along and how to contribute to the process as active, fluent partners and oCitizens.

The drawbacks of agora citizenship

Fluency in the language and customs of one agora is a double-edged sword, however, because it involves restriction as well as license. Perhaps you've had the experience of cognitive dissonance in dealing with another culture (Culture Shock)—something as simple as a gesture that unintentionally offended someone, or your own uneasiness in bartering over a price when bartering is expected, or a political faux pas of some sort. In none of these cases did you set out to cause problems, but your blind adherence to the wrong set of cultural rules got you into trouble in the new, nonnative context.

Why was that adherence blind? Simply because it was ideological—reflexive, autonomic, and thus beyond the reach of considered analysis. No matter which agora you're a citizen of, the other ways of thinking will inherently seem foreign and illogical, and you will be tempted to disparage them because of their radical unfamiliarity and the discomfort involved (Agoraphobia). Once again, this reaction—let's call it intolerance, because that's what it becomes—does not amount to a tempered, well-considered opposition based on calm, careful appraisal of the issues from all possible perspectives. Not at all. It's an ideological short circuit: the dirty underbelly of hard-won, longstanding, and deeply embedded agora-fluency.

The most obvious version of this short circuit is what the Pathways Project calls the ideology of the text (Ideology of the Text). Under the tAgora bias, oral traditions have often been characterized as primitive, inaccurate, and in need of textualization (How to Build a Book). Of course, that approach automatically blocks any kind of faithful understanding of the oAgora on its own terms and condemns oral traditions to permanent misrepresentation. To put it another way, tCitizens without dual oCitizenship may prosper in the textual marketplace, but they will struggle vainly to conduct verbal business in the oAgora.

Of course, this ideologically driven agoraphobia is hardly restricted to the medium that most of us know the best. Performers and audiences of oral traditions who lack dual citizenship in another agora will inevitably make corresponding errors because of their ingrained cognitive habits. One can't begin to imagine static text-objects if all one knows are networks of pathways. Likewise with monomedium eCitizens, of whom there must be very few right now but who will undoubtedly increase their numbers dramatically in the years to come. With the advent of cloud technology (Cloud and Tradition) and with ever-morphing networks of options increasingly available wherever you go, how long will it be before the hard-core, brick-and-mortar text is the exception rather than the rule? Even now, we hear early adopters of the latest electronic strategy demeaning the world of texts, just as citizens of the other agoras are so inured in their own marketplaces that they can't credit alternate media. Toleration for diversity (Responsible Agora-business) in media-marketplaces requires true understanding, and understanding can't proceed until we escape ideology.

How to apply for multiple citizenship

It can be a long and torturous process—if it even proves possible—to apply for dual citizenship in different nations. Among the criteria espoused by various countries is proof of parents' or grandparents' birth there, for example, something you can't just generate or apply for. Whatever the specifics, gaining membership in one nation-state often means relinquishing that same status in another. You just can't have both; you have to choose. And that choice is necessarily exclusive, because you can't have it both ways.

Fortunately, media-membership doesn't require that kind of exclusive choice. Citizenship in multiple agoras is quite possible, and it's highly desirable as well. Given access to the marketplaces in question and given a willingness to get beyond ideology to a responsible appreciation of diversity in media, dual and triple citizenship are available to all concerned.

So how do we apply? The answer, curiously enough, is essentially by tricking ourselves. We start by accepting the rules and environment of each of the three arenas as diverse in function but equivalent in value (Agora Correspondences). Yes, they operate differently; and yes, they present and enable different realities; and yes, we need to adjust our activities and expectations accordingly. But "different" doesn't translate to "better" or "worse." Tolerating nonidentical frames of reference (Leapfrogging the Text) is the key to starting the application process.

The second step is to understand exactly how we trick ourselves into fluency in each of the three agoras. In the OT marketplace it's a matter of code and networks, of oWords and oPathways. We need to be prepared to navigate systems rather than trek through texts (Systems versus Things), to use the tools we are given rather than complain about not having the (locally useless) tools that shouldn't be there. Effective tAgora citizens will largely forget about textual cues like white spaces, lines, paragraphs, and the like because these signals have become part of the way they think and express themselves, and also of how they receive texts created by others. In the eAgora we trick ourselves into forgetting the apparent artificiality of URLs and HTML code (neither of which is artificial at all in this arena) and using these coded interventions to create or surf through networked experiences.

Pull-down menus of options

Think of multilingualism, multiculture membership, and citizenship in multiple agoras as pull-down menus. Click on "language" and options appear. Pull down from "Culture" and take your choice. Choose "Agora" and three selections appear.

In practice it's a matter of code-switching to adapt to different languages or cultures. When you enter a communicative situation, you adjust to the nature of the discourse by making the applicable choice from the menu. Each language or culture is of course fundamentally equivalent to all the others; it's just a matter of matching the tool to the immediate job. If you're lucky enough to be a citizen of both Italy and the United States, and if you've lived long enough in both places to acquire true cultural fluency, then you have options—once again choosing from among equally viable but diverse possibilities.

What we can aspire to in the world(s) of media is a similar range of options for agora citizenship. When we're functioning within the arena of oral tradition, we select the oAgora option from the pull-down menu and operate according to the rules that govern that marketplace. The textual arena presents another click-option, in which case we enable a different set of cognitive procedures tailored to communication in the tAgora medium. Or we could select the eAgora, and enter yet another universe with its own powerful rules about code and pathways.

To emphasize the point, all three options always appear in this imagined pull-down menu, just as all three appear in every node of the Pathways Project wiki-website. None of them is absolutely preferred, and no hierarchy is either explicit or implicit. You make the choice as to which of your triple citizenships is to be in force at any given juncture, and in electing one of them you do not disparage or forever eliminate other possibilities. The King's English is not inherently better than kitchen French, and neither of these linguistic tools ranks higher than the specialized register of Tibetan used to perform Gesar oral epic.

Diversity means the rich and rewarding experience of options—and citizenship in more than one agora is just that.

Cloud and Tradition

To indulge ourselves in an inexcusable pun, the Cloud is poised on our near horizon. And it's headed this way.

Grids, shifts, and redefining "here"

Wikipedia defines the Cloud[13] as "Internet-based computing, whereby shared resources, software and information are provided to computers and other devices on-demand, like the electricity grid." But of course this new initiative hasn't made its appearance without causing ripples. No radical change in media ever fails to elicit a mix of excitement and resistance, and typically we hear both encouraging and worried pronouncements about what the Cloud means for the ongoing evolution of the eAgora. There are immediate prospective gains: universal accessibility, the unique power of the morphing network, the geometrically increased opportunities for innovation. On the other hand, textual ideology makes it very hard for predisposed tAgora citizens to grasp this latest trend in a marketplace already brimming with perceived reasons for culture shock (Culture Shock) and agoraphobia (Agoraphobia). Compare Plato's cautions[14] about the advent of then-new writing technology in early Greece.

But here's the key (if also counterintuitive) point. As the virtual world evolves, what's *not* physically on your machine is rapidly becoming as, or more, important than what actually resides on that machine. As tools for communicating with the unprecedented riches of the interactive web proliferate, we're beginning to shift allegiances—not only spending more time learning, sharing, and doing on the Internet but actually committing more and more of ourselves to the Cloud. This shift amounts to a trend toward disembodiment, toward a new concept of ownership (Owning versus Sharing), and it only promises to accelerate. In fact, with ready-to-click, always/anywhere access to whatever we want to learn, explore, or contribute to the ether, the question of "Is it here?" modulates from a spatial to a philosophical inquiry. Fundamentally, in order to make it "here" all that's required is an ePathway (ePathways).

IT-OT parallels

1. *Access and instances.* Rethinking the simple notion of "here" applies to the oAgora concept of tradition as well as to the eAgora concept of the Cloud. In both marketplaces access depends on pathways, and for that reason every navigation will be nothing more (or less) than a single cocreated instance (Distributed Authorship) of the network—and not "the thing itself." For at bottom there simply is no thing. Burdened as we are by the twin illusions of object (Illusion of Object) and stasis (Illusion of Stasis), we will initially find it difficult to understand how the Cloud can't be contained and an oral tradition can't be exhausted. But keep in mind that both IT and OT versions of this inexhaustible resource are far more process than product, that they are always under construction, and that their strength derives from rule-governed morphing (Variation within Limits).

2. *Recurrence, not repetition.* Navigation episodes undertaken in both agoras may very well recur—on successive days or weeks, or on a staccato schedule—but they can't ever truly repeat (Recur Not Repeat). Using your local machine to access and work within the Cloud involves a process that takes its meaning not from your last episode, but rather from the systemic network of linked ePathways that supports all activities. Since the experience in which you participate is emergent and ongoing (Reality Remains in Play), what you do isn't an instance until you complete the journey. And for those same reasons any later episode will necessarily amount to a separate, different instance that doesn't relate in a linear fashion to any other

episode—even though it may be similar or cognate and even though you may intend an identical journey.

Likewise, the oCloud that produces real-world instances of an oral tradition serves as a linked web of potentials that supports recurrence (of stories, or charms, or histories and genealogies, and so forth) but never repetition. Even those oral traditions that boast word-for-word transmission and performance are staking ideological claims that don't hold up to textual examination. Once again the strength of the OT process lies in its ability to morph as needed under applicable rules, using oPathways (oPathways) and oWords (oWords). From an exclusively tAgora point of view it's easy to see the common blind spot: we've often failed to understand oAgora and eAgora dynamics because we've focused linearly on comparing two products as wholly discrete artifacts, rather than as genetically related instances of an ever-variable process.

3. *Always immanent.* The Cloud makes the network and data we need ever-present anywhere, as long as we have a connection, authenticating codes, and the eFluency to navigate effectively. The riches we seek aren't (nor can they be) sequestered in a book (Getting Published or Getting Sequestered), which would at any rate perhaps be available only in designated, geographically remote libraries or uniquely on your laptop, for example. The Cloud makes these riches universally accessible and alive. And what you create, in partnership with website architects and other users, is accomplished across the limitless expanse and networked potentials of the eAgora. You start with your local situation—your ideas and your physical machine and its eTools—but with the Cloud you enter an "always-here" process of community sharing that profits immensely from being collective and individual at the same time.

   Just so with the traditions that provide networks for performances within the oAgora. The shared code of oWords and oPathways connects individual instances or products to an ever-present background resource that for fluent performers and audiences is always effectively online (Online with OT). It's that immanent tradition—an implied web of potentials—that fills out the momentary utterance via a characteristic part-stands-for-the-whole dynamic. So Homer's "green fear" expands to "fear caused by a supernatural agency" and the South Slavic epic singers' "jumped to his or her light feet" guarantees a heroic, life-or-death adventure to follow. Tradition provides an oCloud that turns literal into idiomatic.

4. *Moveable performance arenas. A Moveable Feast,* Ernest Hemingway's famous title, could well be applied to the Cloud and to tradition. Because these resources are always "here," always available and interactive according to applicable agora-rules, surfing performances aren't restricted to any

particular physical location(s). The arena of the web (Arena of the Web) and the arena of oral tradition (Arena of Oral Tradition) are anywhere and everywhere because they occupy virtual, not geographical, space. You can access the Cloud from your home or any foreign country where you can find a connection to the web. Once connected, the limitless vista of ePathways stretches out before you, independently of your (meaningless) brick-and-mortar site. Just so, performers and audiences make their own virtual marketplace and stage their own virtual event—wherever they happen to be physically—by shared reference to and dependence on the tradition that informs every instance of an oral tradition. Neither the oAgora nor the eAgora is confined to artifacts or physical spaces. Performance arenas connect to and are defined by Clouds.

5. *Homer's ancient Greek Cloud.* Testimony that comes directly from oAgora citizens is precious indeed, such as the information on oWords provided by the South Slavic epic singers. In this vein consider just a single hexameter line of Homer's *Odyssey*, the tenth verse of Book 1. It concludes the so-called prologue to the poem, in which Homer addresses the Muse and asks her literally to "sing in me [the adventures of] the many-turning man," the hero Odysseus. Here's how the prologue ends:

tôn hamothen ge, thea, thugater Dios, eipe kai hêmin.
Of these things from somewhere, goddess, daughter of Zeus, speak also to us.

"These things," conventionally understood as the Odysseus story, clearly exist "somewhere" else—within the epic tradition or oCloud. For that reason the singer must enlist the Muse's help in navigating the oPathways or *oimai* that Homer himself identifies as the performer's critical skill, taught specifically by the Muse. Let me emphasize that crucial point: the adventures reside in the oCloud, not in hard, memorized local form, and the bard is asking for help in clicking through a network of oURLs. He underlines that dependence on tradition by requesting that Zeus's daughter "speak also to us," indicating a shared resource that has been, is now, and presumably will remain available to other performers and other audiences. In essence, this single hexameter tells us that within the oAgora, and through its built-in strategies, the oCloud provides the performer-audience amalgam with a cocreated, emergent experience in which reality remains in play.

6. *The* Beowulf *poet's medieval English Cloud.* The anonymous poet of the Anglo-Saxon epic *Beowulf* also provides inside testimony on the cloudlike tradition to which any performance of an oral poem connects. His story-ethnography of another singer's oral performance takes place during the group expedition to the watery lair of Grendel's mother, which they reach by following her son's tracks to the edge of the mere. On the way back, initial wonder at the hero's achievement gives way to celebration, and partic-

ularly to Hrothgar's court bard considering what kind of king the youthful warrior will eventually become. To present embodied alternatives, the bard draws two example figures from the oCloud—called the "word-hoard" in several Old English poems—and presents them as options in his contingent narrative of the future. These figures are, on the positive side, Sigemund, a dragon-slaying and protective ruler revered throughout Germanic saga; and on the negative side the despised Heremod, who failed his people at battle and brought them only sorrow.

So tradition provides Hrothgar's court bard with ready examples of two possible futures drawn from the word-hoard or oCloud. But even more interesting than this navigation-based procedure is the language that the *Beowulf* poet uses to describe his surfing through the Germanic myth-web. Here's what immediately precedes the brief biographies of Sigemund and Heremod (lines 867b–74):

> Hwilum cyninges þegn,
> guma gilphæden, gidda gemyndig,
> se ðe ealfela ealdgesegena
> worn gemunde, word oþer fand   870
> soðe gebunden secg eft ongan
> sið Beowulfes snyttrum styrian,
> ond on sped wrecan spel gerade,
> wordum wrixlan welhwylc gecwæð, . . .

At times the king's thane, a man laden with proud words, mindful of stories, he who remembered many of all the old traditions, found another word bound in truth; the man began in turn to steer the adventure of Beowulf wisely, and to skillfully perform a fitting story, to exchange words; he spoke everything, . . .

To translate from Old to modern English and then to Cloud-speak, the king's bard is fluent in oWords and oPathways, and he remembers how to navigate through the tradition of the Anglo-Saxon and Germanic story-web. For his present goal—providing a double-vision of what kind of ruler the splendidly successful young Beowulf may eventually become—he finds another oWord bound in truth: another story (actually two) that are linked and accessible within the overall mythological network. By performing the stories of Sigemund (+) and Heremod (–), he foreshadows two possible outcomes for the promising slayer of Grendel, steering Beowulf's contingent future wisely (Contingency), choosing fitting tales (in telegraphic format, since they are well known to his cocreating audience). By "exchanging oWords" he takes advantage of the oCloud to suggest how the hero and his epic may ultimately turn out. And, although like any in-process experience it will reach completion only when the story is actually told, singer and audience play the dynamic uncertainty off against their prior knowledge of how events must evolve. Beowulf's biography will mirror Sigemund's, and decidedly not Heremod's. Tradition, or the oCloud, thus provides a nuanced sense of irony, dependent as much on shared oAgora dynamics as any individual contribution.

7. *Texts can't connect.* Texts don't interact with the Cloud or with tradition. Oh, you can store textual data in the form of static eFiles in the Cloud and then access that fixed material electronically, and even edit and redeposit the edited version. But when those materials tip toward interactive networks with potential for navigation via options and cocreativity, they aren't texts anymore. The tAgora doesn't support shared networks because it doesn't support pathways (Impossibility of tPathways) or variation within limits. It functions by amassing finite instances and then making them locally—not systemically—available according to the restrictive rules of that particular marketplace. Instances are all there is, as the fraught concept of intertextuality (Texts and Intertextuality)—which by nature and etymology cannot apply to either the eAgora or the oAgora—very clearly demonstrates.

Nor can texts interact with tradition. The common misconception that the advent of writing technology cues the immediate closure of the oAgora has proven time and again to be nothing more than blind tAgora bias. Writing is used initially for record-keeping and similar accounting procedures (Spectrum of Texts), most certainly not for preserving group and personal identity, remembering history, transmitting remedies for disease, and the myriad other social functions performed by oral traditions. Societies and individuals are quite capable of becoming and remaining citizens of more than one marketplace (Citizenship in Multiple Agoras), transacting some of their business in the oAgora and some in the tAgora. What's more, without a pathway-driven connection, there's simply no way for texts to enter or influence ongoing oral traditions—except through the agency of go-betweens or performer/readers who can communicate fluently in both the arena of the text (Arena of the Text) and the arena of oral tradition. As artifacts, texts don't connect to the oCloud anymore than they connect to the eCloud.

Contingency

It's all around us

Contingency is everywhere, if we're willing to look: in politics, in economics, in philosophy, in social identity, in the plans we make, even in the plans that others make for us.

Here is a brief but perhaps representative litany. Political successions often consist of a nest of contingencies. Home-buying is often made contingent on various related issues such as appraisal, loan qualification, home inspection, and so forth. Philosophers[15] define contingency as "the study of propositions that are not necessarily true or necessarily false." Some people understand the very bedrock of personal identity as a contingent social function subject to many variables both intraculturally and crossculturally. Every flight itinerary we arrange is, as we only too often discover en route, contingent on weather, traffic, and airline foibles. And the official organ of the American Association of Actuaries is named—what else?—*Contingencies* magazine.

So we can't escape contingency, and that's the most salient point. In truth we're always and everywhere negotiating potentials and possibilities, working through them in real time, not asynchronously (Real-time versus Asynchronous). After the fact, that process may get conveniently flattened into a lockstep, here's-what-happened narrative. But until that juncture we're far too caught up in the evolving story to recount how it went (before it happened). We're too busy living the events to manufacture the distance required to reduce them to a tidy, past-tense scenario.

What does contingency mean?

The adjective "contingent" reveals a familiar kind of family tree,[16] reaching back to Latin and moving through Old French before making its Middle English debut in 1385, roughly about the time Geoffrey Chaucer began writing his *Canterbury Tales*. In today's language the word has the general sense of "liable to occur, but not with certainty; possible," as when we speak of some favorable or hoped-for result as "contingent upon" some still pending action or development. The continuous availability of the Pathways Project website, for example, is contingent upon a number of factors: a connection to the Internet, a browser, smoothly functioning servers at the University of Missouri, the technological expertise of the webmaster, and not least electricity!

For our purposes—in this node and more widely—it's crucial to recognize that "contingent" doesn't quite mean "accidental" (though the two words are frequently used synonymously). A contingent outcome doesn't occur inexplicably, with no underlying cause; instead, it's dependent upon conditions or events not yet established; conditional.[17] At its core a contingency is always an evolving reality (Reality Remains in Play), an emergent process that hasn't yet generated a product. It names a possibility that may well occur but isn't yet "writ in stone."

Contingency most essentially means "What if . . . ?"

Web-networks are contingent

"Contingent" also names the evolving, emergent, process-oriented experience of navigating through OT and IT networks. Because of the links that empower your exploration of interconnected possibilities, where you choose to go next isn't by any means a willy-nilly decision (Not So Willy-nilly). Surfing options are certainly myriad, especially as they pile up one decision after another, but at the same time they're rule-governed and systemic (Systems versus Things). Every route leads to somewhere, or, more precisely, to many linked somewheres.

So negotiating a pathway-driven itinerary is by its very nature a contingent undertaking. It happens as it happens, unpredetermined, as you make one choice—one click after another. You can't see through to the end product because you haven't yet reached the end.

So what actually *is* contingent, anyway?

A fair question: just what is conditional, dependent, in the process of becoming in OT and IT? We can identify at least five features of responsible business in the oAgora and eAgora (Responsible Agora-business) whose contingency is central to their operation. Contingency keeps both marketplaces from collapsing into tAgora artifact-trading.

Here then are five trademark contingencies:

1. *The very next option.* OT performers and IT clickers remain in the present, continually confronted with options they may or may not elect. Storytellers and web-surfers conjure experience via serial decisions, each of which brings another decision—the next option—into play. As long as options exist, the journey is ongoing and under construction.
2. *The performance.* Because they create in the right-now immediacy of virtual agoras, both OT and IT surfers generate unique performances that are never true iterations of any other performance, either by them or by anyone else. Each set of choices is the result of weighing a great many alternatives, and weighing them serially, one after another, as you go. No two experiences, even if they're reduced after the fact to texts, will ever match because each one is individually contingent.
3. *The network.* Like performances, which amount to tours of the oAgora or eAgora network, OT and IT networks are themselves contingent. Each one can and does morph in and of itself, remaining forever under construction, whether under the influence of social developments, personal creativity, or some other life-giving force.
4. *Meaning.* If surfers are navigating through networks by making serial choices among the options that open before them, then they are cocreating the experience and cocreating meaning. Because OT and IT users are choosing among alternative pathways (rather than trekking through texts), they are fluently converting contingencies into (momentary, necessarily evanescent) realities.
5. *Authorship.* Agency in the oAgora and the eAgora is only partially in the hands of any network navigator. Much depends on those who have come

before, who have assembled the web of contingencies that supports an infinite number of individual configurations. And those who contribute afterward will reconstruct the shared system in unforeseeable ways. To a considerable extent OT, like the IT resource Wikipedia, is an open-source phenomenon. Authorship is distributed in both arenas (Distributed Authorship).

Contingency is an invitation

In other words, contingency, so often negatively construed as unmanageable uncertainty that threatens to undo our best efforts, is an invitation to participate and to create in the oAgora and eAgora. Contingency means that the process cannot go forward without your involvement—and not just a thumbs-up or thumbs-down verdict, but a continuing commitment to stay with the exploration until it's over (for the moment, for this performance, for this instance). If you accept the invitation, you're entering a web of potentials that will guide but not predetermine your activities. And as you make choice after choice, the individuality of your surfing will emerge as the jointly authored itinerary it is.

Of course, this "standing" invitation offers admission to an experience that develops as you go; there can be no foregone conclusions (Accuracy). oAgora surfers will adapt each of their performances to the existing variables (their own mood, the audience, the time of day or night, the physical venue, etc.), and eAgora surfers will find their way through complex, interactive constellations of electronic routes according to their preferences that day, week, or hour. Both kinds of navigators are invited not to a destination, but rather to a system of pathways through which they can jointly fashion an event.

Texts mask contingency

Historically, it's been the role of texts to mask contingency, to (seem to) remove uncertainty and replace the conditional with the factual. Never mind that the very origin of the word *fact* (Just the Facts) exposes the fantasy of exterior, free-standing truth. For many centuries we've been content to accept the inscribed as the permanent, as somehow immune to contingencies, as the "last word" on matters of real importance.

If you need evidence of how open-and-shut this ingrained attitude is, you need go no further than the old proverb, *Don't trust everything you read in books!* (Don't Trust Everything You Read in Books). If we weren't so blinded by our unexamined fascination with tAgora commerce, why in the world would we need such a warning?

But textual ideology (Ideology of the Text) is a powerful force, not least because it operates under the radar, deflecting our perspectives before we have a chance to consider other ways of managing knowledge, art, and ideas. It's demanding and extremely uncomfortable work to escape ideological bias, and a kind of culture shock (Culture Shock) inevitably attends inter-agora boundary-crossing. We count on texts as beacons of objectivity (Illusion of Object) and stasis (Illusion of Stasis)—as still points in the chaos of give-and-take argument, as the "true" story that never varies, the official and dependable source to which we can return to settle disputes and establish the acts of the matter.

Of course, texts only appear to have eliminated contingency, as contemporary philosophy and literary criticism have shown with great persuasiveness over the past couple of decades. Every word in any text is subject to interpretation by every individual who encounters it, and—certain political stances notwithstanding—the individual's prior life experience, always unique, will necessarily play a part in that interpretation. Texts as physical objects may themselves stand firm; how they are read does not (Reading Backwards).

And this isn't a liability: Shakespeare's redoubtable Hamlet wouldn't be nearly as intriguing or celebrated if the text that revolves around his world-view communicated with total objectivity in every time and place. Is Hamlet's character contingent? Yes, because our readings of the text—rather than the text itself—are contingent. Again, the artifact holds still; perspectives do not. That's a significant difference between operations in the tAgora on the one hand, and on the oAgora and eAgora on the other.

OT and IT actively *depend* on contingency

The oAgora and eAgora aren't merely venues where contingency is unavoidable or grudgingly tolerated. Neither marketplace could function without a system of openly acknowledged, dynamic "What ifs?"

Take the oAgora. As the performer and audience work their way along an ever-branching set of narrative pathways, both sides aware of the alternatives that lie before them, they're effectively playing within an interactive set of rules. The Basque oral improviser, or *bertsolari*, for example, is juggling several balls at once: responding to an assigned topic, answering a competitor's poem, singing along a melodic template, and fulfilling the requirements of one among many verse-forms. Within this rule-governed universe, there are many oPathways (oPathways) to choose among, many routes that the performer and the audience could follow, but contingency doesn't become reality until that pathway is actually chosen and engaged. And so it proceeds, step by step, not all at once but emergently. Only at the end of the stanza, when available options have converged to a single inescapable solution, do the *bertsolari* and the audience converge, singing the final two lines ensemble. Until that culminating point the negotiation, fueled by contingency, is ongoing. Contingency initiates momentum.

Likewise in the eAgora. You characteristically begin surfing with a plan in mind, but just as characteristically your itinerary will include ePathways (ePathways) and experiences you hadn't foreseen, that you couldn't foresee, when you started out. A Wikipedia entry on the medieval Irish manuscript called the Book of Kells[18] presents you with a host of "What if?" opportunities, among them an entry on vellum, the sheepskin medium of this and so many other manuscripts of the period, and Johannes Gutenberg, who introduced moveable type to Europe. If you choose the latter, a link within the section on Gutenberg's legacy may attract your attention; you might then click on Marshall McLuhan,[19] the media theorist, an interactive page that offers a gateway to the academic program in culture and technology at the University of Toronto that was established in honor of McLuhan.

Alternatively, you might be exploring the Pathways Project node on the eAgora and find yourself clicking through the various species that make up the genus IT. Suppose you fasten on the idea and example of the mashup, the digital meshing of previously freestanding works into a new synthesis. And suppose further that you follow the ePathway to remix (Remix), where front and center stands none other than Marshall McLuhan, the focus of *McLuhan Remix*. This site also does honor to the media theorist, by combining his very words with a host of others' words, all knit together with the aim of representing as well as articulating just what it is that new media can do and how we should understand them.

For the sake of illustration, let's agree that your navigation follows one of these two tracks and ends in one of these two places, either at the University of Toronto program or with the *McLuhan Remix*. Either series of choices, inherently logical in itself but nonetheless unpredictable, becomes a fact only after the matter. And what made "fact" possible was an open-ended, systemic series of contingencies.

The next move is up to you

In truth, of course, it's hardly just the next one; *every* move is up to you. Of the more than 40 links that occur within the web version of this node alone, you may have chosen to follow several, all, or none. Perhaps you didn't even get "here." Perhaps you're somewhere else. No one—not even you—can predict precisely where you'll go, what exact choices you'll make. All the oAgora or the eAgora can do is to create options for you to choose among, networks for you to navigate. But that's most assuredly not a liability; it's a serial opportunity to participate. OT and IT work only when you convert contingencies to cocreated reality.

So from this point on (if you're "here"), and from any point on (if you're "elsewhere"), you have a number of choices. You can pursue any or all of the four ways to navigate the Pathways Project, as detailed in the Getting Started node (Getting Started). At various junctures, whether in the morphing book (Morphing Book) or the wiki (Wiki), those four strategies may well lead you beyond the Pathways Project itself, and you may choose to return or not (today, at some future time, or whatever).

Or you may decide to explore other parts of the larger web, to Tweet, to check your Facebook page, to store a bookmark for later reading, or to pursue some other eActivity. Or you may decide to pick up a brick-and-mortar book, settle down comfortably with a cup of tea, and savor the offline pleasures of the tAgora.

Whatever pursuit you choose, this node will have succeeded as long as you see OT- and IT-based contingency as an invitation. And the Pathways Project at large will have succeeded as long as you recognize the particular dynamics (Agora Correspondences) of OT and IT on the one hand and of textual technology on the other, as well as the benefits of earning citizenship in multiple agoras (Citizenship in Multiple Agoras).

Culture As Network

Misgivings over "soft" media

It's a stubborn, recurrent, and seemingly unanswerable question. How can oral traditions, which live to morph and morph to live, ever provide suitable, sustainable support for the unimaginably rich and complex embeddedness we know as "culture"?

You know the objection: OTs just involve too much variation and not enough stability over time, too many nagging loose ends in an ever-fraying fabric. And of course there's the more recent version of what amounts to the very same complaint—namely the charge that the Internet just isn't stable or dependable enough to trust for really important cultural purposes. Again the specter rises: disabling fears associated with variation, instability, and loose ends. How do we cope if the eAgora goes down? What do we do if the electronic marketplace just isn't available, either temporarily or, perish the thought, permanently? Won't culture as we know it and as we image it simply vanish?

In both cases the root of the perceived problem is flux. We agonize over the intangible and putatively impermanent nature of these "soft" technologies, a species of agoraphobia (Agoraphobia) that never fails to enervate well-meaning, thingcentric denizens of the textual universe. From this parochial perspective, OT and IT seem fundamentally evanescent, insubstantial; they threaten to disappear any moment, and then where would we find ourselves?

We imagine losing access to the OT's untextualized tradition or IT's remotely based cloud, and along with them our ability to manage daily activities as well as long-term plans, to discharge our individual and collective responsibilities alike. The powerful illusions of object (Illusion of Object) and stasis (Illusion of Stasis) convince us that transacting business in either the oAgora or the eAgora means being cast adrift on a sea of uncertainty, desperately seeking the safe harbor of brick-and-mortar reality that only the tAgora can provide.

Texts in hand and always at the ready, we scratch our heads and wonder how OT- and IT-enabled cultures ever survived or ever will survive. We examine the core dynamics of the oAgora and eAgora and ask ourselves a chilling question: "How can such unfixed, ever-morphing systems of pathways possibly support the depth, complexity, and manysidedness of culture?" We're ideologically committed to the belief that culture requires a page, a book, a library, something substantial that we can count on (Ideology of the Text).

Escaping ideology

But wait just a moment. There's a hidden snare lurking in that shopworn formulation—the rhetorical equivalent of asking whether you're still cheating on your wife. Instead of falling victim to the built-in trap, let's try posing a counterquestion: "How could any technology *except* a system-based technology ever aspire to meaningful, continuous cultural support?" And here's another: "If textuality and its mythology of fact (Just the Facts) really were the holy grail we long for, why would we ever need more than a single book on any subject?" And yet a third: "Is there any human endeavor—in any area whatsoever—that doesn't demand serial adjustment and continuous rethinking and reinvention over time and across different contexts?" Aren't cultures more like the mercurial Proteus than even the most splendid and "timeless" ancient monument?

To get beyond the ideological impasse imposed by unexamined text-religion requires two steps. To start, we have to be willing to entertain the possibility and the value of pursuing citizenship in multiple agoras (Citizenship in Multiple Agoras); then we need to qualify for visas that allow us to work in the oAgora and eAgora without succumbing to culture shock (Culture Shock).

That is, we have to step outside the tAgora (reset its textual defaults) and consider—without bias—just how cultural business is transacted in each marketplace, according to the rules of each venue (Responsible Agora-business). Then we need to learn how to manage our activities in the two new environments. It won't do any good to lament the lack of tAgora-style "certainty" in the oral and electronic marketplaces, or the lack of fixed, paper pages in OT or IT. We need to apply what amounts to the Golden Rule of Comparative Media (Accuracy): ask what each medium does best, and accept the reality that other media may well support other functions more faithfully (Online with OT).

The cosmopolitan citizen

The Pathways Project is devoted to just such a multiple, cosmopolitan view of human communication and of the technologies we have developed as cognitive tools for carrying out our various cultural activities. Toward that end the Project itself—like the homologous technologies of OT and IT—mimes the way we think. In other words, it depends not upon a linear inventory of fixed, invariable items but rather upon the systemic potential of a linked, morphing network of nodes that can be navigated in innumerable ways. It explores the advantages of systems over things (Systems versus Things).

The navigability of the Pathways Project network is described in the node *Getting Started* (Getting Started). The reader/surfer can pursue multiple citizenship in four ways:

- by consulting the three extensive nodes on principal media types (oAgora, tAgora, and eAgora),
- by following predesignated routes called linkmaps (Linkmaps),
- by clicking on branches within nodes in whatever fashion one sees fit, or
- by reading "straight through" the contents of the morphing book (see Table of Nodes) or wiki according to the alphabetized list of node titles.[20]

Any and all of these navigation methods will open up an understanding of comparisons and contrasts among technologies of communication, and especially of the OT-IT homology.

Network versus text

Consider a few disarming observations, all of which lead to a simple conclusion—namely, that cultures are better understood through, and represented by, networks rather than texts:

1. *Text and network are antonyms.* Texts derive their actual and perceived value from resisting change. They can be forced to morph on a limited basis, as in the book component of the Pathways Project, but they aren't "wired" to do so. Unless we redefine cultural reality as a still photograph of one moment in time and space as experienced by a single observer from a unique perspective, texts will always remain partial solutions. They will always do their explaining via analytical fragmentation rather than holistic embodiment. So what's the upshot? Well, you'll need an ever-accumulating collection of texts—scores of them now and scores more in the future—to create even a staccato approximation of what a network can do. And no matter how many you have, still photographs are now and forever still photographs. Texts offer only an arithmetic of frozen, one-dimensional culture, whereas networks provide a calculus for change (Reading Backwards).
2. *oNetworks and eNetworks, but no tNetworks.* Networks can exist only where there is rule-governed variability. A one-way street cannot qualify

as a network; only a *route-system*, with built-in support for multiple modes of navigation, constitutes a network. For that reason the oAgora and eAgora support web-thinking and linked exploration. Texts can't do that.

3. *In other words, oPathways and ePathways, but no tPathways.* Because pathways are provided by networks, tPathways are by definition impossible (Impossibility of tPathways).

4. *Cultures, unlike texts, "remain in play."* Here is the most important point, and the most important response to misgivings about "soft" technologies and questions about their ability to support ever-morphing cultures. Simply put, cultures don't hold still: they are morphing now, even as you're reading and navigating the Pathways Project, even as you go about your mundane daily tasks, even as you withdraw to splendid isolation in your cabin in the woods, apparently far removed from the hurly-burly of on-rushing civilization.

And because cultures are emergent—changing right now and then changing again and again without ceasing—they are constantly in the process of becoming something else. You can no more stop that (life-giving and life-enabling) process than you can freeze language forever at an arbitrary date, time, and place as an exchange limited to a single ideal individual and a single interlocutor. Cultural codification, like linguistic codification, is a temporary, workable, mythic approximation at the very best, and in the long run simply an inevitable distortion. Cultures thrive not by reaching some evolutionary fixed point but by remaining forever in play (Reality Remains in Play).

The last word isn't the last word

In other words, cultures are networks and are therefore best represented and best supported by networks. To the extent that texts capture a well-focused photograph of a moving process, they can be useful in the overall project of explaining singular moments along an ever-evolving story line, isolated scenes from an ever-emerging narrative. Such quanta can help us imagine the flow of culture, but they can't really embody it, either statically or dynamically. Even the best editing involves deletions and can produce jump-cuts.

In the end, the relationship of culture and medium can be expressed as a simple theorem: *only rule-governed morphing can effectively mirror and support rule-governed morphing.* To chronicle and experience culture, as opposed to sampling it through items that become obsolete as soon as they're fixed, the oAgora and eAgora are the systems of choice.

It comes to this: tAgora's powerful mythology notwithstanding, you can't textualize culture.

Culture Shock

Three uncomfortable anecdotes

Three stories to start—the first of them generically true to life, the second adapted from personal experience, and the last an actual series of intertwined events.

Displacement 1: Tools   You're seated quietly in the corner of a cozy little brasserie in Paris. You've struggled through the menu (there's no English version available), lodged your order, and the food and drink you requested have been delivered. But there's a problem: you can't begin to eat because you're lacking a fork and spoon. Easy enough to remedy the situation if you could resort to your native language, but try as you might you just can't dredge up from your high school French the magical words you need to negotiate this "implement shortfall." No: *fourchette* and *cuillère* lie tantalizingly beyond your active vocabulary, lost in the mists of time—somewhere behind your teacher's smiling insistence on the familiar versus the formal "you." And there you sit, feeling quite powerless.

Displacement 2: Trains   Imagine yourself rolling through the German countryside, reading a favorite novel, sipping tea, and marveling at the coverage and on-time performance of the European train system. That Eurail pass that your cousin insisted on purchasing for you has made possible so many new adventures, and at such a bargain price. Now it's off to Greece and then Istanbul, and even your second-class sleeper seems like a luxury.

But suddenly the train begins to slow and then stops, curiously enough, with not a station in sight. Word circulates among the multilingual community onboard that because of rerouting (due to a washed-out bridge) the engine has exceeded its allotted time commitment and is presently disattaching itself from the twenty or so cars it's been pulling since Munich. With a promise to send a replacement, the engineer abruptly excuses himself and chugs off, leaving his passengers stranded in then-Yugoslavia with no alternative transportation.

The railway cars start to empty out and microcommunities begin to form, sorted out roughly by language and home region. Western European passengers are concerned about the unexpected development and earnestly discuss the engineer's parting assurances and the (lack of) options, while their American colleagues fret and argue angrily among themselves, outraged over the inconvenience and what they see as an abrogation of responsibility. Central European passengers, on the other hand, simply break out the food and drink that they have brought along with them, precisely in case something like this might arise. They offer bread, cheese, and smiles of bemused resignation to those whose cultural horizons have left them anxious, frustrated, and impatient for the kind of resolution they could accept. After a while, with melding promoted by wine, food exchange, and good humor, the microcommunities begin to merge, and everyone rests more easily until the substitute engine miraculously arrives the next day.

Displacement 3: Coffee Some years ago during a six-month stay in Belgrade I developed a decided taste for Turkish coffee, a kind of high-octane espresso with considerable sediment lurking at the bottom of the tiny cup. But although my language skills were in most cases serviceable, I seemed to have trouble effectively ordering my beverage of choice at cafés. A request for *kahva* (coffee) would produce only a very milky, lukewarm latte, while the more definitive *turska kahva* (Turkish coffee) or *crna kahva* (black coffee) would produce the correct result severely compromised by a disapproving grimace. Like the prospective diner in the Parisian brasserie, I felt powerless, and things only got more embarrassing with every visit.

In response, I made it a personal challenge to overcome the linguistic barrier and figure out what was wrong. First I tried more sophisticated grammar: *crnu kahvu*, the same phrase inflected as the direct object of an understood root sentence, "I would like to have. . . ." Surely this in-language agility would impress the person behind the counter and remove the telltale grimace. But no, his stare was just as withering, a sure sign that I hadn't yet discovered the right code. So the next step was to resort to fieldwork. By sidling up to other patrons who were both native speakers and local urbanites, I planned to eavesdrop on how they accomplished the miracle of culturally sanctioned coffee-ordering. And, sure enough, the third or fourth man—for men ordered differently than did women—solved my dilemma in a way I couldn't have anticipated. He used the phrase *crnu kahvu*, all right, but he absolutely growled it, clipping the second syllable off the first word and acting (from my extracultural point of view) with unforgivable rudeness. I felt badly about the apparently dismissive way he conducted himself, but no one else did.

So I stepped up to the counter, mustered my best dismissiveness, and growled the appropriately abbreviated code at the poor, undeserving attendant. Miracle of miracles, he responded not only with a precious cup of highly caffeinated nectar but with an open-mouthed, approving smile. The moral of the story? "Rudeness" was clearly expected and highly valued because in that cultural arena it was idiomatic.

It's easy to experience culture shock when we find ourselves in an unfamiliar setting, unequipped to manage its language and culture. But the same is also true when we find ourselves in an unfamiliar agora (Agoraphobia), unequipped to manage the local technology for communication. Nor is the phenomenon restricted to any one word-marketplace; it's just a question of where you're coming from versus where you happen to find yourself.

tAgora challenges   Finding yourself in the tAgora without even the most basic literacy skills leads to the most obvious form of text-based culture shock, and it's a dilemma faced by millions of people worldwide every day. But that's not the end of it, not at all, for "literacy" isn't a single ability or condition. More specialized transactions, such as writing reports or newspaper stories or romance novels or corporate memos, show that literacy "writ large" consists of an infinite collection of skills, many of them requiring substantial time and energy to learn and interpret. Those lacking the more specialized skills may feel fully as helpless as anyone trying to manage a foreign language or culture.

eAgora challenges   Pity the IT-phobic person who has to wrestle with an eAgora agenda of software installations, uploads and downloads, highly secure passwords, and indecipherable error messages; without someone who "speaks the language," they're in the same position as the tool-less diner. Almost always the IT version of culture shock results from unquestioned and unexamined immersion in the tAgora, from having one's cognitive defaults effectively set to "text only." With that set of built-in and unexamined expectations, the web will always seem treacherous and insubstantial, a will-o'-the-wisp that you can't quite get your hands on, an ethereal sort of experience that vanishes without the trace you need to credit its real existence. The very virtuality that makes eCommunication possible becomes unnerving and disorienting, not seldom prompting defensiveness and outright avoidance. You may as well be trying to get yourself some Turkish coffee without growling.

oAgora challenges   But culture shock isn't limited to the discomfort associated with underdeveloped tAgora skills or seemingly rudderless navigation within the eAgora. It can plague foreign visitors to the oAgora as well, leading to what we might call oAgoraphobia. Consider the generations of well-meaning scholar-fieldworkers who have sought to better understand oral traditions by entering strange new worlds. They opt to leave well-charted, already negotiated environments in order to live in societies that depend heavily or exclusively on the oAgora for their daily transactions. But what lies beneath this program for "foreign exchange"?

Well, it starts with cognitively predisposed scholars, people who spend their lives using texts as their primary communicative medium, who choose to enter a world that does nothing of the sort. As well prepared as they may think they are, they cannot leave their predispositions about reality (Reality Remains in Play) and its faithful portrayal (Accuracy) entirely behind. For many years the goal of such activities was to *collect*—that is, to record, isolate, and remove from social context—and then to *edit* and *publish* what they unearthed (and in part created). Editing allowed researchers to "clean up" their recordings, to "correct" what informants said, in short to remove the last vestiges of process and convert their captured quarry to acceptable freestanding products. Publishing essentially made those products shelvable and thus usable by tAgora consumers of static and complete-in-themselves items, objective things that qualified for canonization and deposit in the Museum of Verbal Art (Museum of Verbal Art).

And why was this obviously reductive paradigm followed, until recently at least? Quite clearly, because oAgora culture shock was too much for text-bound researchers. There simply was no other way for self-respecting tAgora citizens— at least those who were limited to single-agora fluency—to understand and explain an oral tradition. They did what we all do if we're not paying close attention: they translated the foreign reality back into domestic-agora terms, representing what they encountered as something it was not. In later years, and particularly with the advent of digital and Internet technology, that kind of translation has become more faithful (eEditions). There is newfound attention to social context, process, emergence, performance, and other features that make oral tradition a decidedly nontextual—and finally *nontextualizable*—medium. Multiagora fluency (Citizenship in Multiple Agoras), with attention to the rules that govern communication in each venue (Agora Correspondences), has mitigated this particular species of culture shock.

Thwarting recurrence

Culture shock once experienced can be hard to dispel. The only real cure—the only remedy that promises to help with future as well as immediate problems—is to learn the language or culture or agora well enough to cope, if still and forever as an outsider. This lesson is absolutely transparent for utensil-seekers, for example, and we all appreciate the practical reality that living inside a foreign community for a substantial period generally vaccinates a person against chronic recurrence of this dread disease. And traveling by train can prove not only a relaxing, rewarding pleasure, but an opportunity for continuing education as peers from other social orbits introduce us to viable contexts we never knew existed. Serial fieldwork such as that described in the Belgrade coffee episode can also go a long way toward not only solving specific problems but also coming to understand that an alternative and even counterintuitive way of doing things could exist. In all three cases, people outside the language and culture make an effort to interpret the new situation on its own terms, aiming toward a workable cultural fluency that exposes their own cognitive biases at the same time that it opens them up to new channels, new code, and new kinds of exchanges.

The displacement anxiety caused by "residence" in a foreign agora can of course be handled with a cognate solution: learn and apply the rules of the particular word-marketplace in which you find yourself, rather than those you unconsciously import from outside. No matter which agora you hail from (for almost all of us, at least for the moment, the tAgora), seek at least secondary citizenship in your new context. Pluralize your perspective; diversify your frame of reference.

Better coping through homology

In addition, the Pathways Project also offers another remedy, one born of the OT-IT homology that lies at its heart. To put it aphoristically, when as a tAgora citizen you find yourself working and communicating in the oAgora or eAgora, be ready to navigate through networks rather than trek through texts. Put aside the expectations that arise from the ideology of texts (Ideology of the Text)—that knowledge, art, and ideas can be converted to finite, fixed things—and embrace the truth that you are negotiating and cocreating reality through exploring pathways. Give up the intense tAgora pressure to own and to sequester and concentrate on sharing resources (Owning versus Sharing). In short, recognize the fundamental democracy of the oAgora and eAgora, which operate, and in fact prosper, by remaining forever under construction.

Distributed Authorship

For most of us who spend substantial time in the tAgora, authorship is an unambiguous term and idea. Hardly a mystery in common usage, "to author" means to create and thus to own a work-become-item. So deeply woven into text-making is this idea of sole, exclusive agency and ownership that we have trouble even imagining a text without an author. Look no further than our transparent attribution of uncertain creations to that prolific author "Anonymous," a practice that says much more about our desperate need to force a work into the default marketplace of the tAgora than about the luckless, apparently orphaned work itself. (I do not speak here of the Internet-specific meme Anonymous,[21] though it presents interesting comparisons.)

The unexamined tScenario

Here's what you do without thinking about it. You compose a text, whether a memo, a novel, a policy brief, or whatever, and identify it as your product by adding your name (Owning versus Sharing). And why not? It's an item you and no one else created; thus it belongs to you and to no one else.

There are of course small variations on this simplex model that effectively prove the rule. Scientific reports authored by your team of researchers might seem an exception, but here again the product is made and owned in real time by you and your colleagues, by a coherent team that serves as corporate author (not seldom with precise explanations of who contributed what to the document). The process of publishing your text may also enlist the help of nonauthors: assistants who put an administrator's text into proper, distributable format; reviewers of manuscripts who offer their expertise and suggestions; copyeditors, designers, and other editorial personnel who ready your novel manuscript for the bookstore; or an evaluation team who reviews your policy statement and makes politically savvy suggestions (which you may accept or ignore).

But in all cases there is no doubt about the central authorship of the text: the document is attributable to one or a coherent team of composers, and its fundamental content is the finished product of those minds and no others. Authored texts resist change. In other words, they resist reauthoring. It's nothing less than their communicative job.

The ideology behind (single) authorship

In order to ballast these premises with a few examples, let's take a quick peek inside one wing of the Museum of Verbal Art (Museum of Verbal Art).

European literature from the ancient world onward has always assumed individual authorship. We celebrate the achievements of Homer, Chaucer, Milton, and Shakespeare, happy to be able to affix their names to great works like *The Odyssey*, *The Canterbury Tales*, *Paradise Lost*, and *Hamlet*. But there's more to this unexamined assumption than first meets the eye.

The ideological pressure (Ideology of the Text) to identify verbal art as necessarily a tAgora phenomenon is extremely strong, so strong that we've regularly created pseudoauthors where no believable evidence for them exists. Thus the exalted place of Homer at the fountainhead of Western literature—even though Homer seems to be an anthropomorphic legend, a mythic figure who never existed (at least in the form we've imagined him). Thus the outsized prominence of the shadowy figures of poets Caedmon and Cynewulf in discussions of the earliest English poetry. Never mind that Caedmon the cowherd poet is also almost certainly legendary, or that the only evidence for Cynewulf is a group of poorly matched signatures in runic letters. As tAgora citizens we feel compelled to appoint individual authors for all verbal art, no matter what its origins.

Authorship outside the tAgora

The eAgora   Not so in the marketplace we've called the eAgora, where distributed authorship is the empowering rule. Speaking of increasingly nonsingular creations engendered by computer networks, Christiane Heibach[22] has described the current trajectory in terms of "the author function, which . . . due to networked environments will change from the original creator to the co-creative collective." We expect this kind of cooperative, ongoing, emergent product as characteristic of the electronic marketplace, especially in the continuous evolution of facilities such as always-updatable databases, wikis, websites, and open-source software. Such activities prosper by evolving, by resisting fixation and singularity, by fostering a reality that remains in play (Reality Remains in Play). They simply can't live and develop in any other way.

The oAgora   Likewise the oAgora, which at its root supports variation over time via different performers and performances. In this marketplace the concept of "the original" is meaningless and single authors are a dead end. Like language itself (as distinct from texts, which are scripts for language), no one person is ever wholly responsible for the invention or maintenance of oral traditions. Consider any of the world's oral epic traditions, such as the Gesar stories from multiple ethnic groups in central and eastern Asia, the wealth of Son-Jara and Mwindo sagas from western Africa, or the well-collected South Slavic and Albanian heroic tales. All of these traditional networks were surfed by hundreds if not thousands of "authors" over centuries, and remained pliable, rule-governed, and open to ever-changing variation within limits (Variation within Limits). In other words, Heibach's closing emphasis is as applicable to the oAgora as to the eAgora toward which she directs the following judgment: "We indeed face a revolution: not the disappearance of the author, but the metamorphosis of its notion from the individual originator to the distributed collective author as a result of social dynamics."

Pathways support distributed authorship

The Pathways Project aims to show that OT and IT are both by their very nature collective, shared enterprises, and that their collectivity and sharing extend over both space and time, involving contributions from many different individuals and their interactive audiences from many different times and places. Pathway-driven creation and re-creation represent community activities, the joint work of many hands. Distributed authorship cannot be forced into the tAgora without denaturing its core expressive dynamics, without making it into something it isn't and can't be. Even a video of a single oral performance is only a text that preserves an experience by converting something living to a fossil—by removing its ability to morph, severing its connectedness to its tradition, and thereby conferring a false sense of singularity and singular authorship.

If we succeed in becoming citizens of multiple agoras (Citizenship in Multiple Agoras), we will quickly recognize that the oAgora and eAgora depend crucially on *distributed authorship*, and that the tAgora depends on the twin illusions of object (Illusion of Object) and stasis (Illusion of Stasis) as epitomized in the ideology of *singular authorship*.

Don't Trust Everything You Read in Books

Let me get this straight—*Don't trust everything you read in books*, eh?

Curious phrase. And considering the thousands of libraries and bookstores packed with ton after ton of these apparently untrustworthy artifacts, a more than mysterious sentiment. So it's only fair to step back and ask: Why in the world did we invent such a dismissive, nay-saying proverb (Proverbs)? Although cliché-driven wisdom of this sort is famously anonymous, at least three credible explanations present themselves.

Three possible answers

First, many of us have personal experience of being scolded by family members or friends disdainfully rejecting an indisputable fact (Just the Facts) or well-grounded opinion we've summoned from a reputable printed source. We cite an unimpeachable witness, and they seek to impeach our witness. Second, some of us have overheard this caveat as we eavesdropped—third-party–like— on an argument in which one person seeks to impugn an opponent's text-buttressed position. *Au contraire*, in other words. Or third, we may well have been needled by a well-meaning (or maybe not so well-meaning) colleague who is querying the medium at least as much as its message. Here and now, so many years post-Gutenberg (Homo Sapiens' Calendar Year), some miscreants actually prefer word-of-mouth, preprint fantasies to solid, stolid, page-bound truth. Imagine that. . . .

The price of doing tAgora business

Actually, the "miscreant scenario" is very easy to imagine once we get past ideology. From the perspective adopted by the Pathways Project, the third explanation qualifies as the most fundamental and far-reaching of the group. Why? Because it addresses the unavoidable, built-in price associated with doing business in the tAgora. Because it exposes the usually unexamined, below-the-radar truth that there are some things (Reading Backwards) that books and pages (Texts and Intertextuality) just can't manage. And whatever they can't manage is by definition lost.

Call it the "operating cost" or "overhead" or "tax" exacted by textual transactions, an automatic debit that we make it a habit not to notice. It's an insidious situation, to say the least. We've grown so accustomed to paying this tariff that we overlook its damage to the medium-sensitive "bottom line" of creating and transmitting knowledge, art, and ideas. We ignore the damage, pretend it isn't happening. Sad, because if there ever were a hidden cost that threatens to bust a communications budget wide open, the heavy tax on tAgora business must be it.

But no complaints here. . . .

Stop and think for just a moment about the shortfall we accept without complaint. In place of a Wikipedia entry (Freezing Wikipedia) that—if well configured—can lead to you to manifold explanations, myriad linked topics, and the opportunity to shape your learning yourself, you're sentenced to a one-way, blinders-on minitour of the book-author's sole choosing. Alternate "takes" on a complex, many-sided subject? Not a chance. Related ideas? Only if they fit into the master recipe for the book-author's carefully delimited concoction. Reader input to the process? Sorry; that's well beyond the technohorizon, at least until another edition of the frozen, monolithic artifact can be assembled (and even then the likelihood of impinging on the book-author's personal franchise is small or nonexistent).

Exclusivity and economics

The tAgora is *exclusive*, in both senses of the term, and it has prospered in its exclusivity. It demands that everyone play according to its narrow set of rules. It tolerates little or no extracurricular activities in its tightly controlled arena (Arena of the Text).

Nonetheless, we happily accept these crippling constraints with every book we purchase, borrow, read, or write; with every paper page we track across or dog-ear; with every static virtual page we merrily scroll down through. And we do so because we've effectively accepted the ironclad agreement that governs tAgora business: in exchange for subscribing unreflectively to tAgora economics (and ignoring the economics of other agoras) (Citizenship in Multiple Agoras), we're provided with a radically diluted, utterly monomedium, but quickly digestible message. And experience teaches that it's easier to metabolize artifacts than participation. Sign the contract, forfeit what it declares null and void, and all will (seem to) be well.

Nor does the litany of built-in tAgora shortcomings end there, especially with regard to the oAgora.

The dire implications for OT

Pity the poor nontextual aspects of the OT phenomena we're trying to understand and represent. Clearly their acoustic and visual dimensions can't be housed between two covers; more basically yet, performer(s) become at best vicarious and any audiences (Audience Critique) are conspicuous by their absence. On these grounds alone we might as well forget anything but severely flawed representations of oral traditions. Add a DVD or CD? Only if you have a generous publisher, and then the add-ons are irremediably static: uncorrectable, un-updatable, unsupplementable, ever inert. Thankfully, eCompanions (eCompanions) and eEditions (eEditions) can help us move beyond this media impasse, but as yet they're not widely in play.

Most fundamentally, it's the quality of immutability, the very characteristic that we textual devotees so highly prize (Accuracy), that blocks our way. Whatever its (supposed) advantages, a commitment to (imagined) immutability deprives OT of its core identity. It guarantees distortion, precludes verisimilitude and emergence. Freeze the performance, reduce it to print and/or static files, and what happens? The life, the ongoingness, the right-now, event-centered nature that defined the performance's most essential reality all perish without a trace. And in their place stands an artifact complete in itself and yet empty—a cenotaph, a triumph of taxidermy (Museum of Verbal Art).

The moral? Oral tradition can't be captured in texts, no matter how strong our ideological motivation. You just can't trust an em-booked oral tradition—not least because it's an oxymoron and a bald-faced lie.

Counter-proverbs

So the proverbial phrase we started with—"Don't trust everything you read in books"—may not be so curious or mysterious a saying after all, it seems. We might even understand its subliminal message as an acknowledgment of the terrible price we unconsciously pay in doing tAgora business. It wouldn't be the first time that a culture cloaked its objections to the reigning orthodoxy in safely coded, arm's-length language.

At any rate, in the spirit of understanding the tAgora tax on oral traditions, let's close by indulging ourselves in a few counter-proverbs, made-up nuggets of media-wisdom whose function is to remind us of the hidden costs entailed and help us negotiate the ever-present threat of agoraphobia (Agoraphobia). In that spirit here are three freshly minted "old saws" to ponder:

1. *Don't trust living realities reduced to books.*
2. *Save some trust for what books naturally exclude.*
3. *Trust multimedia (Resynchronizing the Event) over monomedium, and systems over things.*

eAgora: Electronic Networks to Surf

An agora is a verbal marketplace (Agora As Verbal Marketplace)—a site for creation and exchange of knowledge, art, and ideas. The Pathways Project recognizes three agoras, or arenas for human communication (Three Agoras). This node is devoted to the IT arena, the eAgora.

The true currency of exchange in the eAgora is eWords (eWords)—coded, virtual, and linked words. Not typographical prompts, but an actual, clicked-on, in-context performance experienced at that moment and in that place by a present audience. You participate in the electronic marketplace via real-time,

Roman agora, Athens. Photograph by DerHexer. Courtesy of Wikimedia.

directly engaged transaction, not by swapping texts. Everything happens "in the moment"—right now, not at some convenient future time to be chosen by a detached, independent reader and forestalled until the time seems right. The eAgora event is all-consuming for webmaster and surfer alike. Why? Because in interactive format it is unmediated by texts, with nothing held at arm's length.

Agora-mirrors

Before proceeding any further, let's highlight a built-in structural comparison among the three nodes on principal media types: the oAgora, tAgora, and eAgora. From this point on—and across all three involved nodes—the section headings and organization will follow a mirroring logic. In other words, immediately below this paragraph you will find two sections entitled "Genus and species" and "Word-markets," followed by another with the subheading of either "Public, not proprietary" or "Proprietary, not public," depending on the agora in question. In fourth position you will encounter a brief discussion of "The evolutionary fallacy," and so on. The purpose of this organizational strategy is to help demonstrate the comparisons and contrasts (Disclaimer) that lie at the heart of the Pathways Project. For a complete list of the inter-agora parallels, visit Agora Correspondences (Agora Correspondences).

Genus and species

The virtual landscape is awash with newly evolved species that simply can't be understood through the default technology of the tAgora. We can speak of "pages" and "destinations" and "data," but concentrating on what seems thinglike (and comfortably familiar) misses the point. What makes the eAgora categorically different from textual items and repositories is its ability to morph within limits (Variation within Limits) and to support navigation and cocreation by surfers, and at the same time not to foreclose on alternate possibilities (Reality Remains in Play). What matters is the network of links and ePathways (ePathways), which distinguish systems from things (Systems versus Things). Even a few hours' experience on the web highlights the remarkable diversity and complexity of eWorld ecology and the futility (Freezing Wikipedia) of trying to reduce that world to the pathwayless tAgora (Impossibility of tPathways).

Within the IT genus, then, we can discern many different and fascinating species or types of IT, with many more types on the near horizon. Suffice it to say for now that this host of species varies by genre, social function, surfers, sites, and modes of interaction with other agoras. Some of these interactions are counterintuitive for tAgora citizens (Excavating an Epic), and the ever-increasing variety of IT types on the web shows no sign of diminishing. The watchword for species within the genus IT must always be diversity.

Word-markets

Consider the wealth of different word-markets in which IT users ply their trade, whether users of Internet browsers, Facebook, Twitter, open-source software, mashups and remixes (Remix) (all of which are discussed later), or some other IT option. There's little or no possibility—and in many cases no need—of copyrighting what surfers do via these eInstruments. And why? Because they are rooted in the public domain (In the Public Domain), where sharing and rule-governed morphing are the source of power and where fixity and stasis mean death. Public-domain roots are both nourishing for each immediate event (for each pass through the multiply linked network) and necessary for the continuing survival of IT as a whole. This last point may be difficult to grasp for those who aim to police the eAgora by trying to enforce tAgora rules, but citizenship in multiple agoras makes it only too evident (Citizenship in Multiple Agoras).

Public, not proprietary

Subject to specific legal and financial constraints, IT strategies can be deployed by multiple people without fear of violating any laws governing exchange in what amounts to an open-source marketplace. Those rules may limit eligibility by password-certified membership or financial constraints on access, for example, but no individual ever wholly "authors" a strategy in final, invariable form, any more than a single individual ever authors a language. Nor can any one person ever deliver the final, canonical, "best" navigation of the involved network until texts enter the picture and make this kind of dead-end concept of verbal communication imaginable and feasible. Such a monolith simply isn't either imaginable or feasible within the eAgora. Once the economy of the tAgora is fully in place, however, public gives way to proprietary, open-access gives way to object-exchange, and web-systems stop being web-systems. The difference is between downloading things[23] and engaging in emergent experiences within an arena that is forever under construction (Arena of the Web).

The evolutionary fallacy

With the variant dynamics of the oral, textual, and Internet arenas in mind, it's easy to see why "oral evolves to written" and "written evolves to electronic" are fallacies traceable to the ideology of the text (Ideology of the Text). If we model our understanding of all verbal commerce on a singular creation attributed to a singular author and consumed by a singular audience (one-by-one), then the necessarily plural identity of web architects, surfers, and IT strategies will appear primitive, underdeveloped, and in need of streamlining. Likewise, we'll fail to understand and credit the plural identity of architects and surfers with their shared but diverse experiences in the eAgora.

In either case, nonwritten, nontextualized communication will seem to lack something, to fail to measure up according to our ideologically imposed criteria. For example, how many times each day do you hear or read about people bemoaning the informality and impermanence of the web? Likewise, until recently collectors of OTs have unquestioningly subscribed to an implicit rank-ordering by converting the living webs that support oral traditions into freestanding objects suitable for display in the Museum of Verbal Art (Museum of Verbal Art). They too undergo a kind of medium-specific culture shock (Culture Shock) and feel compelled to "diss" whatever isn't text.

But of course it's not just a matter of one situation—one agora—evolving progressively and inevitably toward another. Each arena operates according to its own idiosyncratic economy. The oAgora uses a different currency of exchange than the tAgora—embodied versus entexted words, oWords (oWords) versus tWords (tWords). And the eAgora uses eWords, similar in many ways to oWords and far removed from tWords. The eAgora sponsors code—like URLs and HTML—that depends for its power and efficacy on its performative nature; eCode actually causes something to happen, and does so recurrently, not repetitively (Recur Not Repeat). None of the three currencies is inherently better, more valuable, or more advanced than the other two. Each is simply the coin of its particular realm.

This is not to claim that any arena is entirely homogeneous. Nor is it to contend that they never interact, or that hybrid agoras can't form; they do and they can, in fascinating ways. But it is a fatal mistake to posit a one-way developmental trajectory, to view verbal technology as working its way inexorably from a text-deprived Dark Age toward a thoroughly evolved and fully textual us, and on the way to a (fascinating though feared) virtuality. We need to resist the ideologically driven assumption that limits our imagination and citizenship to the textual arena.

Five IT word-markets

Of the many possible eFacilities and eTools we could examine, I have chosen five that are familiar to many if not most patrons of the current eAgora: namely, browsers, Facebook, Twitter, open-source software, and mashups and remixes. As the Pathways Project wiki (Wiki) develops, it is my hope that contributors will broaden the discussion, both by furthering our understanding of these five areas (and their inevitable evolution) and by addressing other (including yet-to-be-invented) facilities and tools.

Browsers   The most basic tool for transacting business in the eAgora, for navigating through networks, is of course the Internet browser. Those in common use include, in descending order of market share as currently reported, Microsoft's Internet Explorer, Mozilla's Firefox, Google's Chrome, Apple's Safari, and Opera, all of them offering different configurations, speed, and options and all of them except Explorer compliant with web standards.

Browsers open the network and make possible your active participation and cocreation. Using eWords in the form of special coding, they support your self-generated itinerary by revealing and making available the host of options that present themselves at any point in your journey. When you open to a start-page you enter a performance arena, a virtual space where sharing is accomplished by exchange in the specialized language of URLs and HTML, the *lingua franca* of the web. Because the website architect and browser-maker have "written" the enabling code deep into their facilities, the surfer is automatically fluent in web-speak: if you can click, and perhaps occasionally type in a pathway-word (a URL), you can communicate without a hitch. Select a link and a new set of choices appears; select one of those and another set of links pops up. Potential avenues for discovery and cocreation are everywhere, and it is inherently impossible to exhaust the network.

But *caveat lector*; let the reader beware. For all of the myriad actions and adventures they support, for all of the resources they put at our fingertips (literally so, with touch devices), browsers cannot offer permanence, fixity, or closure. In true eAgora style (and parallel to oAgora style), they operate by resisting textualization, by always opening another connection, another option, another encounter with knowledge, art, and ideas. A browser's strength resides in its open-endedness, which runs absolutely counter to the twin illusions of object (Illusion of Object) and stasis (Illusion of Stasis) so central to tAgora exchange. Think about it: just like oral traditions, and just like language in general, eAgora tools must do their job by means of variation within limits, by remaining forever under construction. If a browser were somehow to submit to textualization, it would lose its engine of rule-governed variation, and thereby its purpose. It wouldn't be a browser, any more than a text is an oral tradition.

Facebook   So you've signed up for a Facebook account, entered your information and photos, started friending, and are well on your way to becoming happily enmeshed in a shared matrix of electronic events, groups, causes, and other virtual relationships. What's more, you've set up apps on your iPhone and iPad so that either of these devices will keep you plugged into an ever-morphing scene chock full of correspondents' everyday remarks, deep thoughts, and inane patter—all of it precious and unthinkable without the Facebook prosthesis. So what does it all mean? What have you and your ePosse cocreated? What permanent cultural intervention has occurred?

Well, if your Facebook crew is anything like mine, it's an incredibly diverse lot, so diverse that there isn't the remotest possibility of their ever gathering anywhere nonvirtual for any reason whatsoever. And that's not merely because they happen to hail from 19 different countries and have interests so wildly nonconnected that most of them would have nothing to discuss with one another. Different languages would constitute one barrier, maybe different cultures as well, but different idea-worlds would be the principal obstacle. Put them in the same physical space and not much would happen—just puzzled grins, frustrated grimaces, and an early exit.

Nonconnected interests, nonconnected people in a physical, brick-and-mortar world. But notice that I didn't say UN-connected. Using the special eTool called Facebook, you somehow managed to connect them. YOU created this world. YOU linked it up. And of course you aren't alone: each of your friends did likewise—not by replicating what you did, but by assembling their own networked worlds according to their priorities and interests. What they and millions more have accomplished isn't repetition, but rather recurrence. Because Facebook offers a platform that supports the core eAgora (and oAgora) function of variation within limits, these millions could also preside over the miracle of creating their own communities that otherwise couldn't exist. And they did so by deploying a shared facility to do something unique, using an open-access, public-domain eTool in inimitable, individual fashion. From an oAgora perspective, they're using a shared tradition to tell their own stories. No tAgora tool could manage that.

And not only does Facebook make it possible to found new, never-before-realized, and otherwise impossible communities, it also supports their emergent, interactive ecology. Its various channels encourage connections by "writing on walls," for example, by leaving simple messages and observations that restore the everyday comments, ironic reactions, and unpredictable whimsy that bind communities together in just as important a way as the much more formalized (and severely limited) swapping of texts. You learn about trips, family members, food, films, political stunts, and a hundred other aspects of your friends' lives, all without having to combat the inertia of tAgora-appropriate communication. Just dip your digital toe into the online water and sample the ongoing conversation, wherever you enter it. Contribute something, react to a long-lost friend's post, share a photo, or just sit back and lurk, absorbing what your impossible virtual community is saying, thinking, and doing. Just as in physical communities, there is no single approved form of communication, and participation is always multisourced—rule-governed (by Facebook formatting and options) but multiauthored (Distributed Authorship). Such is the richness of chaos when reality remains in play (Reality Remains in Play).

Facebook supports eCommunity-building, and serves a crucial function in the eAgora, a function that depends upon recurrence rather than repetition, upon variation within limits rather than fixity, and upon the open-ended quality of remaining forever under construction rather than aspiring toward closure. Its survival as an eTool actively depends on resisting fixity and closure, on keeping its ePathways open and connected for the greater good of the overall network. For this reason we can only hope that Facebook's increasing trend[24] toward the commercially driven release of users' personal information is reversed. Nothing will bring down an eAgora facility more dependably than violating the eSharing compact that governs its fundamental dynamics.

Twitter   Public versus private is also a fascinating aspect of Twitter, where tens of millions of electronic correspondents cocreate a bewildering array of virtual communities—140 characters at a time. Via this eTool you can broadcast your verbal reflexes and tip-of-the-iceberg philosophies to anyone who signs up to "follow" you. The formation of your web village is considerably less formal than the invitation approval process in Facebook, but Twitter will allow you to block those you want to keep outside your networked circle. And of course you can follow anyone you wish—from friends and colleagues you see every day to voices from other chapters in your life to the previously untouchable celebrities who have turned their "@" observations into a viral species of PR. Once again we can form and join communities that could not exist outside the eAgora.

So we can easily grasp the importance of Twitter as a social networking tool powered by IT, and the trademark phenomena of rule-governed variation, recurrence, resistance to fixity and closure, and permanent under-construction status are clearly at its functional heart. But does this connection-engine offer us any discernible long-term cultural value apart from its immediate purpose?

The Library of Congress certainly thinks so.[25] They've begun to archive tweets by the million, and plan to make them available to qualified researchers on a timetable and under conditions that are still being formulated.[26] The idea is to offer future historians a glimpse into the everyday stuff of life, unfiltered by historians' chosen paradigms or perspectives—a peek into "Everysurfer's Chronicle of My Self-generated Virtual Community," multiplied almost infinitely.

From one point of view, this makes excellent sense. In recent years historians have begun to tap into unofficial sources in order to understand the age they're portraying, paying less attention to government edicts and more attention to what ordinary and sometimes disadvantaged groups and individuals have to say. Witness the burgeoning accounts of women's lives and influence, so often ignored in earlier years, as well as the slave narratives that have not only humanized but often entirely "rewritten" our understanding of that tragic and shameful period in U.S. history. What top-down, corporate, officially sanctioned sources ideologically weed out, Twitter may well help to reinstate as realities to be confronted and interpreted.

Open-source software   In what some would call the best of all possible worlds, open-source software would win the day in every situation and at every level. All software products would be open, the code that enables them would be open, and everyone would have the same, shared, malleable platform from which to innovate. All subsequent innovations would remain effectively in the public domain, and the momentum of development would be maintained on the principle of "many heads [or groups] are better than one." To an extent that's what goes on with the Mozilla Foundation and their popular "public benefit" browser Firefox, as well as with the Open Office productivity suite, which has seen over 100 million downloads. Open-source would conquer proprietary, to everyone's benefit, and ultimate democracy would reign.

But at this particular point in eAgora history we find ourselves embroiled, either directly or indirectly, with something considerably more complex than an either-or binary. The openness of a system will always matter, because without the key quality of variation within limits all acts of cocreation and innovation are limited or even impossible. The question has become not *whether* but rather *at what level* individual manipulation of software's rule-governed variability should take place. If a proprietary program or application, bought and sold in what amounts to a tAgora exchange, constrains the creativity of even the most inexpert user, then it isn't fulfilling the practical philosophy of the eAgora. Word-processing software that relies on tiered menus folded deep within its hierarchy, predetermining most of what one can do because of its effective pathwaylessness, are simply reifying the textual mindset. They amount to typewriters on steroids, machines designed to produce a limited range of fixed texts and little else.

On the other hand, to the degree that proprietary programs open up creative possibilities—promoting easy intermingling of multimedia using shared open standards[27] and aimed at producing new kinds of vehicles like interactive magazines and morphing books (Morphing Book)—they support a measure of openness more suitable to the average user's role in the eAgora. From this perspective, software that is strictly speaking not open-source (that is, you buy it and use it under copyright, and the code isn't available for retooling) can still foster a kind of "open" cocreativity. It can foster what amounts to unconstrained innovation for the end user, who isn't interested in (or capable of) reworking code. Such users, and they surely account for the huge majority of eAgora patrons, will actually profit from the decisions made at a lower level—often to optimize the hardware-software synergy, as in the Apple universe. In such cases "open" innovation can be enabled by providing a vehicle with many of the lower-level decisions already in place.

Mashups and remixes   What does it mean to use eAgora tools to merge two or more "things" into a third "thing"? What are the implications of that kind of merging—not just legally, but also socioculturally and artistically? For the oAgora such questions never arise, since true ownership of an oral tradition, always a never-finished process driven by distributed authorship, is patently impossible. You can't own language; therefore you can't own OT, which amounts to a special case of language. Sharing is not merely the norm but the mandate (Owning versus Sharing).

New-media cocreations such as mashups and remixes[28] problematize the OT-IT homology. They also demand that we acknowledge some disparities between the core comparison of the oAgora and eAgora that the Pathways Project seeks both to understand and to represent. Of course, this is hardly anything out of the ordinary: as the disclaimer to the Project affirms in the strongest possible terms, a homology is a parallel and an analogy, and most definitely not an identity. We intend no simplistic, reductive equation of marketplaces. Indeed, it's precisely the disparities between OT and IT that give the fundamental, baseline comparison its vigor and depth.

For the sake of ready reference, let's use the examples of eHybrids featured elsewhere in the Pathways Project: musical mashups and their ancient precursors on the one hand, and the McLuhan remix on the other. Many of the principles associated with these particular instances apply to the much wider range of eAgora cross-species.

In musical mashups, two, or potentially more than two, recorded songs are combined to produce a hybrid that is meant as a separate creation. But here the easy description ends and the challenges begin. If the hybrid could not exist without its sources, to what extent can it ever be understood as an independent entity? If, further, that "new" creation varies over different performances, never taking precisely the same form twice, does that demonstrable lack of fixity affect how we regard its status? Should we distinguish its rule-governed variability (Variation within Limits) from live performances of a single-authored, copyright-protected song? How do we characterize the authorship of these digital amalgams, which appears to be distributed over at least three individuals or groups?

At this juncture in rapidly evolving media history, it would be foolish to see these questions as anything more (or less) than heuristics, as points of inquiry, and I will not attempt categorical answers. Our concern here is to emphasize that these are questions being posed in the eAgora that could not have arisen in the tAgora. Let's also admit that in trying to untangle their complexities we have so far mostly applied tAgora rules. In a real sense, our very approach to mashups—legal, sociocultural, and artistic—has been decidedly agoraphobic (Agoraphobia), a study in culture shock.

Distributed authorship (and for that matter, distributed editorship) are also the cocreative force behind Jamie O'Neill/Kurt Weibers's highly suggestive remix of Marshall McLuhan's ideas with contemporary eAgora interventions. *The Medium Is the Mix*,[29] which portrays O'Neill/Weibers in a virtually constructed interview with McLuhan, examines how meaning is derived not through what we pretend is wholly original thought but through sampling the ideas of others and blending them into something new. During the faux discussion, the interviewer channels McLuhan with remarks like "originality isn't what it used to be," emphasizing the role of digital media in enabling previously inconceivable hybridization. In fact, he goes so far as to observe that "today we do not think; we mix other people's thoughts." Radical commentary indeed.

But in terms of the Pathways Project this bold reformulation should come as no surprise. If as citizens of multiple agoras we look beyond the ideology of text and its pretense of individual authorship and ownership of knowledge, art, and ideas, we'll recognize the fundamental principles and dynamics of the oAgora reemerging in the eAgora. Mixing other people's thoughts? Navigating networks and cocreating? Actually, that's what we've always done.

No real authors

Authors—in our modern and highly ideological sense of the term as individual creators of original, unique, objectifiable, and usually published works—simply don't exist (Distributed Authorship) in the eAgora. And if authors as such don't exist, then the burden of "protecting the work" can't fall to them. Most fundamentally, there's usually nothing to protect because the browser or Facebook exchange or Tweet-sequence or open-source routine or mashup usually doesn't belong exclusively and forever to any single individual. It can't be owned (Owning versus Sharing) in the way a freestanding text-object can be owned and therefore can't be used or transferred under carefully written and implemented guidelines. In most cases there's nothing to prevent another person, sooner or later, here or somewhere else, from performing the "same" work, although the next performer will inevitably make changes in the "original" (which of course wasn't really an original in the first place). Even when a surfer creates and re-creates a singular work (as with mashup artists), each transaction in the word-market—always involving multiple sources and open to reconstruction in multiple performances—is but one transitory instance of an ever-evolving process. Culture gets continuously mashed up and remixed in the eAgora.

Five nonauthors

The five word-markets mentioned above are alive and bristling with verbal exchange, but they all lack what we would call "authors." Consider the dynamics of each IT arena (Arena of the Web). With their navigational horizons spread out all over the endlessly expansive Internet, browser users can hardly be classified as authors in our tAgora sense of the term. Facebook friends likewise depend on and draw from a malleable common source, creating unique posts by performing within the designated rules that govern their eAgora. The situation is extremely similar with the legions of Twitter enthusiasts, who construct and share personalized miniportrayals of their private lives by working within a 140-character matrix. The ability of this kind of conversation to morph is well illustrated by the array of subjects and viewpoints it supports in emergent fashion. And though a degree of ownership does enter the picture with open-source software, every singular product derives its identity as much from the ongoing, fluid nature of its never-finished process as from its latest incarnation. Even the (re-)creators of mashups and remixes, who generate unique, never-before-uttered compositions that may well be fixed via the text of a recording, are also providing undeniable evidence of multiple authorship. How could we interpret their work as necessarily "the final step" if it actively depends on recombination and repurposing for its very existence? And when it may well be reproduced through a variant reperformance? Strange as it may seem, there are no true authors anywhere to be found in the eAgora.

eAgora sharing and reuse

As a first premise, let's start by observing a simple truth obscured by the powerful (yet almost always unexamined) ideology of the text. The welter of rules that govern sharing and reuse of tAgora materials, embedded in a long and intricate sequence of legal battles that shows no signs whatsoever of abating, are largely inapplicable in the eAgora. To put it as straightforwardly as possible, tAgora rules were fashioned for the tAgora and don't work in other verbal marketplaces. As long as we continue to apply the wrong rules for transactions and (re)creations, we will continue to be frustrated by the non-fit.

If we evaluate the situation from the perspective of diversity in media, we'll see why. In fact, it's nothing less than inevitable, whatever the other agora involved. For example, for many years we misunderstood the communicative features and resources of oral traditions because we proceeded by insisting on a textual frame of reference. We imposed irrelevant and frankly damaging concepts such as single authorship, epitomized versions, and silent, spatialized, one-way pages on the multiauthored, Protean, and networked identity of the oAgora. We denatured the living reality of oral traditions, and of their oral-derived progeny, in what amounted to a desperate attempt to bring their natural variability and responsiveness into line with our philosophy of verbal art as a singular, owned, and purchased/bought thing. We tried to turn ongoing, ever-emergent navigation into a single, authoritative map. And of course we failed. How could we do anything but fail? Does French serve its intended expressive function (or any expressive function at all) when we sweep aside its native character and impose Swahili vocabulary and grammar?

The long and the short of it is that conventional Copyright (aka "Big C") can't apply to the itemless word-markets of oral tradition or Internet technology. But maybe another kind of "little c" copyright might apply to these two nontextual agoras. Let's briefly consider two of the licenses offered by the Creative Commons website[30]—the most and the least restrictive of the six contracts—with a view toward determining whether either of them could help in governing surfing and exchange in the eAgora.

The most restrictive   The "Attribution, Non-Commercial, No Derivatives" license stands at the conservative end of the Creative Commons spectrum, that is, closest to the ideologically driven concept of Big C copyright that governs the tAgora. This contract "allows others to download your works and share them with others as long as they mention you and link back to you, but they can't change them in any way or use them commercially." Of course, since truly interactive transactions in the eAgora don't involve authors or static, finite works—not to mention tAgora definitions and rules—this license can have no utility for IT exchange.

The most open   At the other end of the spectrum lies the simple "Attribution" license, which "lets others distribute, remix, tweak, and build upon your work, even commercially, as long as they credit you for the original creation." This one sounds like a perfect fit for the business of our online word-market until we get to the final clause calling for acknowledgment of an original work by, we must suppose, an original creator. In other words, even the most liberal license offered by Creative Commons, an institution dedicated to enabling the remixing of culture, assumes a fixed, finite object eligible for sharing and remaking. Although this least inhibiting of licenses speaks cogently to the realities of distribution, remixing, tweaking, and building upon as we encounter them within the eAgora, it still doesn't recognize the radical morphing and objectlessness of interactive surfing. The ideology of the text—whether a book, a musical score, a painting, a film, or whatever—dies hard.

Variation within limits

It's counterintuitive for us, but continuous morphing in the eAgora doesn't lead to anarchy. Things don't fall apart, primarily because there aren't any "things" in the first place. IT in fact draws its strength from variation within limits, from its rule-governed ability to change systemically—just like language itself, only more so (Proverbs). Surfers always have a choice; they can select from viable, systemically arrayed options. They can follow multiple different pathways in realizing their emergent performances (Not So Willy-nilly), which will not be photocopies or diskcopies of yesterday's or last year's or any other "edition." They may choose one route today, another similar but nonidentical route next week, and so forth, depending on factors such as their own state of mind and the particulars of the occasion. Motion never freezes into stasis, the journey of discovery never devolves into the closed circuit of a daily commute, pathways never become ruts.

This dynamic is clearly visible (and for some users just as clearly nettlesome) in simple navigation of the Internet via the browser of your choice. Even if you're embarked on the same quest as yesterday, what are the chances that you'll navigate identically through the linked potentials that await you? Maybe you'll get "sidetracked" (Misnavigation)—though the meaning of that designation doesn't really work in the eAgora—or discover new facets of even the most well-defined topic or theme. Or perhaps the website architect has added new features that cry out to be explored or deleted some pathways you surfed along in prior expeditions. Did friends suggest what amounts to a linkmap (Linkmaps)? If so, were you able or willing to retrace their steps exactly, or did the natural subjectivity of confronting nontextualized reality lead you elsewhere? Only too quickly the twin illusions of object and stasis begin to break down.

Or consider how variation within limits fosters interaction within the eAgora. When a "citizen reviewer" rates and describes a new application online, that communication becomes part of the conversation that surrounds the app. When software engineers respond to suggestions or requests from users (sometimes acknowledged in subsequent reviews), for example by installing a new feature or making another kind of cocreation possible, that step forward is directly attributable to the architect-audience interaction. In a similar vein, eye-tracking[31] devices, which chart exactly how users explore electronic pages, offer another avenue for understanding eAgora itineraries and joint communication. Like the singer and audience in an oAgora performance, the key to success is continuous, fluent exchange, with shared responsibility for outcomes. Of course, even the term "outcome" textualizes the process somewhat, since the goal is not to finish but to continue innovating. Without rule-governed variation, none of these OT and IT exchanges would be possible.

The analogy to language

Think about living, spoken language—continuously mixed and remixed—rather than its reduction to the printed or pixeled[32] page. We don't resort each and every day to one of a limited number of fixed monologues or conversations, do we? Even similar pronouncements or exchanges on identical topics involve innumerable choices and adaptations, made in the moment and outside the scope of any fossilized, predetermined scheme. We depend on our human ability to generate rule-governed communication, we vary our speech-acts within limits, we suit our discourse to different situations. IT does the same.

A basic proverb   Consider this OT-to-IT modification of a homemade proverb: "Internet technology works like language, only more so." IT is anything but objectified and static. It morphs according to rules that provide guidance and stability, but which also promote—to different degrees depending upon the particular vehicle—creativity and individual realization. In that regard, IT is simply a special case of language.

But how about the "more so"? Everyday language is necessarily broad-spectrum; general conversational language, for example, supports a great many interactions, with optional adjustments for your relationship with your addressee or for the physical site of the exchange, the time of day, the weather, and so on. But IT code requires more rules. Superimposed on the broad-spectrum language are additional rules that identify the communication as a particular kind of coded expression—perhaps the HTML underlying website navigation, or the URLs that serve as the ePathways to get there. IT languages are narrow-spectrum tools; they serve fewer functions, but they fulfill those fewer functions much more economically than could more general languages.

This built-in focus in turn means that IT languages are more densely idiomatic, with designated parts standing for much larger and more complex wholes. Thus, and despite its literal meaning, *43 things*[33] carries the connotation of a social networking site when provided with the *http://* prefix and *.com* domain suffix. Similarly, enclosing a word or phrase within the HTML sequence ** ... **

changes the font to italic, while the sequence ** . . . ** changes it to boldface. None of these specialized meanings is reported in any conventional dictionary or lexicon. Because such textual resources gloss the broader-spectrum language of texts, they are formulated to serve the specific purposes of the tAgora. The codes employed to fashion the eWords that serve as currency in the eAgora operate under an enhanced set of rules and confer an enhanced idiomatic value. Like the oWords that we discuss in relation to the oAgora, they "work like language, only more so."

Recurrence, not repetition

What does it mean to say that something repeats? The scenario is familiar enough: a discrete and itemlike event happens once, then it happens again, and so forth. A best-selling novel, for instance, may be published one year and reprinted the next, so that the title repeats on the bookstore or library shelf. Or consider a poetic refrain that appears at the end of every stanza, so that each iteration echoes those that precede it. Or the chorus to a song, which will dependably repeat after each verse. All of these cases are clearly repetitive because subsequent occurrences derive their meaning primarily from earlier ones within a finite, limited context. The chain of meaning is linear and contained, deriving from direct correspondences from one item to the next.

But that isn't the way IT works. IT actively depends on *recurrence* rather than serial repetition. It operates via idiomatic responses that follow networked pathways. Consider two simple analogues. Perhaps you're a college student and you make a habit of greeting your friends with a wave of the hand and a ritualistic phrase like "What's up?" You react in this way regularly, every time you pass any of your friends on the street. Or perhaps you're a Navy airman and your daily routine involves saluting a succession of officers, using exactly the same motion on every occasion. But in neither case are you really repeating the greeting; instead, you're resorting to an approved, idiomatic signal that indexes your encounter and relationship. You're following an established pathway, using a recurrent action to accomplish your purpose.

To illustrate the nature of recurrence in the eAgora, here are two simple examples from our shared web-world: recurrent beginnings and recurrent performances.

Recurrent beginnings   Surfers within the IT marketplace initialize their performances by opening their browsers to a startup page. This is, of course, a page of their own choosing, and it can be changed at any time, but the point is that summoning that ePage—the function that puts idiomatic code to work in the service of navigation to come—is a recurrent and not repetitive action. You don't open your browser for the third or fourth time in an afternoon because you did so two or three times before. You begin your surfing by employing the equivalent of an OT prologue, a ritualized introduction that bears little if any relation to what follows outside of its core function as a designated ritual precursor. Startup pages are first-step ePathways that get things underway by convention. Surfers cannot know in advance how the specifics of the subsequent Internet session will unfold, but that brief idiomatic gesture unmistakably marks a pathway toward whatever emerges. Most fundamentally, then, the startup page fulfills its purpose not because it repeats (in this session or any other), but because it recurs.

Recurrent performances Just so with entire surfing performances. Unless you pursue the very same static eFile,[34] which is itself pathwayless (Impossibility of tPathways) and offers no further options, your navigation of the web today is highly unlikely to follow the very same set of pathways as yesterday's surfing. In other words, today's navigation will not *repeat* yesterday's. Instead, with every click you'll be presented with new opportunities, each of which will generate another new set of potential destinations, and so forth. Even the most assiduous of explorers will find it hard or impossible to repeat under such conditions. More to the point, in the web arena it will be difficult to find a reason to repeat, or even to conceive of such tAgora-based activity. The eAgora operates, as does the oAgora, via variation within limits—the antithesis of repetition.

Now let's examine your surfing performance in closer focus. When you click on a link, you visit the site that's indicated by the underlying code. Neither the choice to do so nor the result of having done so constitutes repetition. If you know where you're headed (in the sense of having visited the website beforehand), you may have a general idea of what the idiomatic convention will produce. But you can't know that the site will be a mirror image of what you encountered yesterday, and you certainly can't guarantee that you will make the same decisions once you get there. What did your college friend write on your Facebook wall overnight, and did she leave a link for you to follow? What about those reactions to your latest blog entry—did they contain any useful eAgora leads?

While many will worry over the openness and unpredictability of Internet-based navigation, we should remember the built-in comparisons and contrasts between and among agoras. The eAgora has its own rules and its own advantages, which run parallel to the rules and advantages of the oAgora but not those of the tAgora (Responsible Agora-business). To avoid the culture shock and agoraphobia associated with imposing the ideology of the text in all marketplaces, we must remember the importance of citizenship in multiple agoras. In IT as well as OT, reality remains in play.

Surfing performances don't repeat; they recur.

Built-in "copyright"

It will seem counterintuitive to us at first, but the Internet is powerful precisely because it can't be fixed, precisely because it morphs while you surf it. Because it isn't predetermined and remains open to innovation that is idiomatically driven and forever under construction, the Internet harnesses the cumulative energy and contributions typical of distributed rather than single authorship. Unless or until it gets textualized, the web never weakens into finite, fossilized, and therefore discardable items.

What's more, and again it will initially seem contradictory, the nonfixity of the eAgora guarantees a built-in kind of "copyright protection" for website-creating and -using activities by setting limits on variation. Rule-governed flexibility is of course the engine of recurrence and continuity, but too radical a departure from the implicit rules is impossible. Fluent performance (on the part of the surfer) requires both an inherent grasp of those limits and an ability to fashion a here-and-now, true-to-the-place-and-moment experience. Otherwise the "surfing story" can have no narrative shape, no discovery, no cocreation. It might as well be a text.

Survival of the fittest

To put it another way, the self-sufficient ecology of the web will naturally select which websites and surfing performances are to be understood as viable. No single site will be able to claim completeness, absolute independence, or permanence. Likewise, no single surfer will be able to claim—or have any need to claim—that he or she "owns" a particular navigation of the web, at least in our default textual sense. If it's not recognized as a freestanding, tangible item, you can't own it. And if you can't own it, you can't restrict it. There's nothing (no thing) to restrict.

In the IT arena, strength and continuity reside not in stasis but in ongoingness, not in fixity but in rule-governed flexibility. The eAgora is a word-market for living, embodied, systematic communication.

The eAgora works via pathways.

eCompanions

eCompanions provide support that can't be housed between the covers of a book, whether due to media disparities or to publishing priorities. They can contain audio and video files (whether streaming or downloadable), photographs, supplementary texts, databases, links to other pertinent Internet resources, and so forth. eCompanions are critical for the presentation and understanding of oral traditions because they promote the user's understanding of oral performance as a living event to be experienced in its traditional context.

How to read an oral poem

The first eCompanion to be built accompanies a general book on oral poetry, *How to Read an Oral Poem*. This online facility includes audio and textual examples of South Slavic oral tradition collected in the field, a video of a slam poetry performance, photographs of oral poets from various cultures, and other ancillary materials. The reader can experience some of the performances described in the book by clicking through the eCompanion.[35]

Oral tradition

As of volume 19 (2004), the journal *Oral Tradition* began the practice of providing eCompanions for some of the articles that appear in its pages. Audio, video, photographic, and database support are available for articles on Gaelic song, American jazz, Bosnian epic, Javanese dance, North Indian music, Japanese *kabuki*, Chinese drama, Appalachian folktales, and other traditions. With the migration of *Oral Tradition* to an online, free-of-charge periodical,[36] eCompanions are now embedded in downloadable PDFs.

eEditions

eEditions promote the resynchronization of oral performance by recombining the parts that appear only separately—if at all—in the book format. The audio or video of the performance plays alongside a transcription and translation, and the apparatus (commentary, glossary of idioms, and other contextual materials) is linked to the translation. Clicking on those links makes the relevant material visible in a scrollable box on the same page, so that audio/video, text and transcription, and multidimensional context are reassembled into an integral experience for the user. The first eEdition to be built accompanies a South Slavic epic recorded in the 1930s, Halil Bajgorić's performance of *The Wedding of Mustajbey's Son Bećirbey*.[37] A text, translation, and other (text-bound) aspects of the performance are also available as a conventional book.

ePathways

The idea of pathways

Pathways sport a double identity: individually, they lead from one node to another; but corporately, they constitute an interactive network with innumerable built-in possibilities. The idea and term stem from the oAgora, the arena (Arena of Oral Tradition) in which Homer describes the qualities that an ancient Greek

they collectively constitute. The isolated parts are meaningless unless they're melded together, in idiomatic sequence, with the other crucial parts of the larger whole.

URL syntax prescribes the malleable structure of the entire eWord. It provides the general format for web addresses, with rule-governed variation possible via substitution or addition. For example, the initial protocol may also be *https*, which enables a secure connection; or *rtsp* (Real Time Streaming Protocol), which establishes and maintains communications with real-time streaming media servers. Domain names show enormous diversity, of course, and suffixes can vary within well-defined limits. Just as oWords are validated by usage and function within oral traditions, so URLs as eWords are validated by registration and activation on the Internet.

Even more generally and more flexibly, HTML (HyperText Markup Language) provides a standard, specialized language that supports all aspects of webpage construction and usage. Through a system of tags and elements, webdesigners can configure navigable sites with designated structure (page setup) and content (text, objects, scripts, and interactive links to other resources). Because they are using eWords from within the specialized vocabulary of webspeak, and because these eWords can morph according to prescribed rules, the code supporting developers' websites achieves the desired effects. Architects build fluently in a performative language that works, and users navigate fluently through a network built on functional code.

Within the IT arena (Arena of the Web), an environment consisting of and depending on ePathways (ePathways), eWords contribute crucially to surfing the web. You start up the process and enter the marketplace and then choose the next pathway from among those available to you. That choice generates a new spectrum of options from which you make your next selection, and the process continues until you exit the eAgora. During that time you cocreate an experience that emerges as you go (Reality Remains in Play), and for that reason will never be wholly predictable or repeatable (Recur Not Repeat). Navigating through networks, users process a rule-governed and performative code. They find their way through a constellation of pathways constructed and used not by a single person but by a group (Distributed Authorship). Variation within limits (Variation within Limits), the stock-in-trade of eWords and oWords but a dynamic inherently foreign to tWords, underlies all transactions in the eAgora.

eWords work for the same reason that the Internet works—because they actively support morphing.

Excavating an Epic

Sometimes the oAgora—like the eAgora—presents us with puzzling phenomena that seem to defy ready explanation. Often the puzzle stems not from the phenomenon itself but from a misguided reflex. We try and fail to fit the new reality into our default frame of reference, based as it almost always is (for this historical moment, at least) on the deeply embedded ideology of the tAgora (Ideology of the Text). Sometimes, in other words, we encounter an event or situation that doesn't match our entrenched cognitive predispositions. We may be fascinated by the collision, or we may experience a mild case of culture shock (Culture Shock). Either way, the initially mystifying experience can eventually prove educational.

An anecdote

The real-life setting for the following anecdote, the story of just such a media-collision, was a conversation with Dr. Chao Gejin, Director of the Minority Literatures section of the Chinese Academy of Social Sciences, who was organizing a special issue of our journal *Oral Tradition* on the theme of minority traditions in China.[40] His method consisted first of arranging for contributions on Manchu, Mongolian, Tibetan, Yi, and other traditions, and then of commissioning the translation of these articles into English. Naturally, the translations required some editing, and so he and I sat together at my desk in Missouri's Center for Studies in Oral Tradition for many afternoons, he with the original-language texts in his lap and I with the English renderings in mine. Our joint aim was to make these rare and precious insights into sometimes little-known oral traditions as clear and understandable as possible for an external audience. In other words, we were trying to help potential readers find their way past both linguistic and cultural barriers, and they turned out to be barriers of imposing magnitude, as we were soon to discover.

A buried idiom   Within this general context we one day encountered the term "excavating" as applied by Zhambei Gyaltsho[41] to a Tibetan bard's performance of an oral epic poem. Not illogically, I had flagged the several occurrences of this curious term, assuming a misfire in translation and explaining to Dr. Chao that in English we'd probably say something like "delving into his heart or mind for the story." No, my colleague replied, the bard in fact *excavated* his orally performed epic. Presuming that we were now dealing with a disconnect in English idiom (as well as my own ignorance of Mandarin), I then offered a brief and homemade semantics lesson on the specific connotations of the term "excavation" in English—digging something out of the ground, disinterring it, as with a shovel. To avoid any possible misconstrual, I tried to distinguish this narrow and literal meaning from more metaphorical terminology for performance ("reaching deep inside" or "searching his inmost thoughts," for example). But my best efforts fell short of the mark. My colleague remained unmoved, insisting that the oral singer was in fact excavating the epic.

So there we sat, at a stubborn linguistic impasse with no obvious prospects for resolving the problem—that is, until Dr. Chao came to the rescue by providing a mini-ethnography of the larger process that the article's author had described only telegraphically. And here's where the story gets interesting and educational, as well as reveals an unexpected dimension of verbal commerce in the oAgora.

Geoethnography Remarkably for us citizens of the tAgora, what the Tibetan oral poet actually does is to make his way to a cave in the wilderness and physically dig up a tangible text. That's right; he disinters a manuscript—takes it out of the ground—as a formal, culturally idiomatic prelude to orally performing the epic. That text doesn't serve as a prompt-book or even as a skeletal aide-mémoire, never mind a full-blown script. It amounts instead to a ritual object, a talisman or charm, used to initiate the act of performance, much like the always-unread text that helps create the performance arena for Mexican folk drama.[42] So against all odds (not to mention against all our default assumptions within the tAgora), the original term turns out to be absolutely accurate. The bard *really does* excavate the epic.

When a page isn't a text

Just in case we might be tempted to regard this phenomenon as a unique aberration, a far-out exception to otherwise universal rules about texts and performance, consider another type of oral epic poet in Tibet: the so-called "paper-singer" who performs while staring intently at a white sheet of paper.

Grags-pa seng-ge, Tibetan paper-singer. Permission from the photographer, Dr. Yang Enhong of the Chinese Academy of Social Sciences.

Before you jump to conclusions, let me caution that field research has established a disarming and remarkable fact: the paper is absolutely blank. And when no blank paper is easily available, the paper-singer resorts to a sheet of newsprint. It doesn't matter because he can't read anyway.

When asked about what he was doing, Grags-pa seng-ge, a paper-singer interviewed by Yang Enhong[43] of the Chinese Academy of Social Sciences, responded that he watches the action of his story dynamically taking shape on the paper as he sings it into existence, apparently much as we view a film projected on a screen (with the difference that we aren't also creating the film as we watch!).

In effect, his "reading" of the "nontext" amounts to assuming the roles of screenwriter, director, cinematographer, and audience all at once. He (re-)creates the script, puts the actors through their paces, frames the visually realized story, and watches and listens to his original yet traditional work. In so doing he offers us another glimpse of the radical otherness of the oAgora.

The upshot

So what's the moral of these stories? Well, whether excavating or paper-projecting their epics, these two types of Tibetan bards have a lot to tell us about the oAgora. First, the process of creating and receiving is anything but textual—at least according to our customary understanding of what a text is and how it's used. Second, oAgora reality (Reality Remains in Play) can seem counterintuitive when perceived against our ingrained (and unexamined) set of default cognitive categories.

To put things another way, the oAgora proves virtual (Online with OT), rather than tidily enclosed in brick-and-mortar textuality. Like Internet-surfers, these epic singers are navigating through a web of possibilities, a contingent universe that they help to bring into being. They find their way with great accuracy (Accuracy), but without the familiar matrix of right-justified pages, indented paragraphs, dust-jacketed books, and static eFiles[44] on which we've come to depend as the necessary support for so many of our activities.

Both of these Tibetan oral poets are surfing pathways, branching this way and that, remaking experience by varying within idiomatic limits. They're not thumbing through pages or in any other way subscribing to the ideology of the book. They are citizens in good standing of the oAgora, not—all appearances to the contrary—of the tAgora.

No mistranslation here

In the end, then, the so-called problem in translation to "excavating" proved no problem at all, except within my own tAgora frame of reference. Still a prisoner of textual predisposition at some level, I simply got it wrong.

Default expectations aside, some preliterate bards actually dig up texts only so they can then perform nontextually. Others actually hold a blank sheet of paper before their eyes only so they can watch the story they're singing onto it themselves. The oAgora houses idiosyncratic and sometimes surprising performance arenas (Arena of Oral Tradition).

Freezing Wikipedia

An experiment in media

In July 2008 the German publisher Bertelsmann announced what has been called a first in print publishing history: a one-volume encyclopedia with 90,000 authors[45] made up of the 25,000 most popular articles from the German Wikipedia (*Wikipedia: Die freie Enzyklopädie*).[46] Published in September 2008 and planned as an annual series, it offers the inimitable riches of the online networked resource between the covers of a conventional book. Or does it?

Lost in translation

Conversion from web to book—a case study in the perils of agoraphobia (Agoraphobia)—has crippling implications for Wikipedia as a dynamic entity (that is, as it was meant to be). Translation to the brick-and-mortar medium may seem an attractive option, but substantial sacrifices are necessarily involved. We can identify at least five major discrepancies between the eAgora and tAgora forms of the project, five ways in which the textual artifact falls far short and markedly compromises the value and usability of Wikipedia. Here they are, arranged from most to least obvious:

1. *Limited number of entries.* The one-volume tAgora artifact reduces the presentation to about 3 percent of the German Wikipedia's current contents, already a very modest percentage that will only diminish further as more entries appear in the online resource. Issuing annual Wikipedia volumes will expand and update coverage somewhat, but the overall contents will still be curtailed severely.

2. *Limited number of authors.* Ninety thousand people sounds like a large collective of authors, and it certainly is—for a book. But how many authors involved in creating the other 97 percent of the entries have been denied publication in that thin slice of an ever-enlarging whole? And how many authors who will revise and augment existing entries as well as contribute future entries have been or will be excluded? In an environment of not only multiple but distributed authorship (Distributed Authorship), the game changes.

3. *Fossilized entries.* The lifeblood of the international Wikipedia project is an active, participatory community involved in continuous updating and ongoing improvement of online contents. The core advantage of eEntries, in other words, lies precisely in their nonstatic, nonfossilized character. They respond to change, they counter the foreshortening imposed through print fixation by keeping the discussion open. They morph along with discovery and maintain currency (as well as the promise of ongoing, future currency), a process that annual "snapshots" of a process always in motion cannot support. To mount once-living entries as exhibits in the tAgora museum (Museum of Verbal Art) is an exercise in taxidermy.

4. *No linked network.* There is text-reading and there is web-surfing, and they are categorically different. tEntries in the Bertelsmann volume are cross-referenced in conventional tAgora fashion, but the medium prohibits the kind of network one finds in the online Wikipedia. I emphasize two issues here: page-bound cross-referencing can't ever simulate electronic hyperlinking, and the field of possible references to other entries is shrunk by 97 percent, not to mention links to external sites. Though it goes against the grain of our cherished textual ideology (Ideology of the Text), networks of potentials are far more powerful investigative tools than fixed rows of print, no matter how authoritatively edited (and even that supposed authority must always be an illusion from the perspective of evolving knowledge). tAgora entries are and will remain freestanding islands of data with very short half-lives of usability because they simply can't morph. They can't evolve along with the ever-changing world of information and insights, the world where their creators and users actually live and learn.

5. *Dramatically diminished and markedly narrower audience.* The "other end" of any communication—fully as crucial as the creator/sender—is the user/receiver. No matter how effective the advertising, or how assiduous the acquisitions librarian, the real-world audience for a tAgora, brick-and-mortar Wikipedia will inevitably be restricted to a very small and parochial segment of the eAudience for the online resource. Most basically, the book is strictly a pay-to-play option, whether the financial enabler is an individual or a representative of an organized group. Just as importantly, all book distribution systems do their work by involving one or another highly selective and undemocratic demographic. In contrast to the web arena (Arena of the Web), where anyone with a browser and an Internet connection can readily access free-of-charge resources, commercial and university presses interface with relatively miniscule, and again highly parochial, segments of the human population. By translating an eAgora resource to the tAgora, the potential pool of users shrinks drastically in number and drastically in diversity. Information traffic drops off the table, along with usability and democracy.

"Good enough to sell books"

Notwithstanding these drawbacks, Arne Klempert, the executive director of Wikimedia Germany, waxed enthusiastic about the migration to the tAgora. While extolling the value of the free online encyclopedia, he also observed[47] of the monetized forthcoming publication that "it's a nice experiment to see if the Wikipedia content is good enough to sell books."

This comment, from an important and very knowledgeable eAgora administrator, reveals the subtle media bias that is everywhere at work in the information biosphere we currently inhabit. Somehow the core concern gets deflected—from how and to what extent online content can be transferred to a book (I would say only very, very partially) to whether web-reality is of high enough "quality" to merit enshrining on the altar of the page. If it is, Mr. Klempert seems to be saying, then tAgora dynamics (Accuracy) will take over: books will sell, money will flow, and Wikipedia will have graduated to print. Not a word about the 3 percent ceiling on entries, the wholesale loss of connectedness and networked power, or any of the other fatal flaws we've identified.

With these thoughts in mind, we might see our way clear to adjust the comparison and rephrase Mr. Klempert's comment. Recognizing the stark disparities between media-technologies, between the eAgora and tAgora, I suggest that we stop automatically privileging published texts as the Holy Grail, the one true and inherently superior goal toward which all communication aspires. Turn the logic around and cease defaulting to a manufactured fact (Just the Facts). Quality simply is not an absolute [textual] concept across agoras. The reality is that, like it or not, *the book will never be a good enough vehicle to house Wikipedia*.

From living reality to museum artifact

For the sake of argument, let's bend over backwards. Let's give the Bertelsmann project the benefit of the doubt and imagine that the 25,000 entries (culled from more than 750,000) are somehow representative of the whole, and further that the 90,000 authors who composed those entries amount to a creditable caucus of the much larger group. Even then, however, the selected eEntries are irremediably frozen: they can't evolve, they can't respond to change. And they remain forever singular and freestanding, spatially segregated: cross-referencing must proceed via page-turning and thumb-inserting, or indirectly via combing indexes—not via clicking on hyperlinks. What's more, the limited and parochial audience chooses itself by opening their pocketbooks or joining the membership of book-distribution systems. If you can't afford the book or it's simply not stocked in your bookstore or library, you're disenfranchised. You're not part of the privileged oligarchy that transacts its business in the text-marketplace. You're out of the loop.

Whatever else may be claimed, the plain fact of the matter is that most of the eAgora value of Wikipedia necessarily perishes with its conversion to a tAgora artifact. No matter how many authors and entries the printed volume boasts, it can never emulate the living, networked, democratically open, and universally available resource.

As a book, it may be an interesting and unprecedented experiment, but as Wikipedia it's dead on arrival.

Getting Published or Getting Sequestered

The only too lonely author

You've spent the last six years hidden away in a small, sparsely furnished walk-up in a dilapidated old brownstone in Brooklyn. You live alone, except for an elderly cat, and you don't go out much. Your friends and acquaintances are remarkably few; you seldom meet, phone, email, or text them, and you can't even remember the last time you Tweeted or checked Facebook. You clearly don't measure up to Aristotle's vision of a social being.

So why this reclusive behavior? Well, because you've been otherwise engaged, crafting an object for the ages. You've been deep into the splendidly solitary business of writing the Great American Novel, or Great Zimbabwean or Yi Novel if you prefer, and it's demanded your full, unwavering attention. No time or energy for socializing, ftf (face-to-face) or virtually. For as Herman Melville, John Gardner, Isaac Asimov, and so many other writers found, the Muse visits only when you entirely remove yourself from the human network and its built-in distractions.

Entering the tAgora to sell your wares

At any rate, now that your book is complete—all five hundred pages, or one megabyte—you're understandably eager for people to read it. So you do what novelists around the world have done for hundreds of years: you emerge grudgingly from your self-imposed exile, reconnect to society, and go about the process of getting published. In the modern world that means that you contact editors, agents, and whatever colleagues and friends you have left. In short, you formulate a strategic plan for enshrining your precious creation in humanity's Museum of Verbal Art (Museum of Verbal Art), that great canon of world literature situated snugly within the busy print-marketplace of the tAgora.

If all goes well with your plan—and that's a forbiddingly large "if"—a publishing firm will accept your manuscript and you can start down the road toward production of a suitably configured artifact. After evaluation, revision, reevaluation, copyediting, design, printing, binding, advertisement, and distribution, your Museum exhibit will finally be mounted and ready for viewing. And imagine the manifold possibilities that then present themselves! People can buy your book in their local bookstores or online, or they can borrow it from their local libraries. They can read well-placed, appreciative reviews that make it sound too irresistible to pass up, or hear about its merits from enthusiastic friends in a monthly book club. What was once merely a motley set of characters and a vague plotline might even gain admission to college and university courses on contemporary literature.

The sky's the limit. The world is your oyster. There's no ceiling on the growth and scope of your potential audience because, wonder of wonders, you're now an author with a real-life book. Savor the moment: you got published.

But hold on just a moment. Is this rosy scenario realistic? More precisely, does it tell the whole, unexpurgated story? In particular, are your novel's horizons truly limitless?

What "publishing" really means

Let's start from scratch. Literally, "to publish" means "to make public." Etymology[48] and everyday usage both indicate a significant, dramatic change of status: namely, moving something you've created yourself from the private to the public sphere, making that something generally available and consumable by others, placing it "in the public domain" (In the Public Domain).

And it's simple enough to understand how that easy definition gained and maintains currency. If we track your novel from the germ of an idea conceived in that Brooklyn walk-up through the five hundred pages of printout and on through the sequential stages of the publishing process, the overall trajectory is obvious and striking. It stretches all the way from an audience of one (yourself) to an in-group of a few (your agent, editor, etc.) to a postpublication audience of thousands, maybe millions (your national and international readership). Publishing your novel has ratcheted up its ability to communicate—and not just in crude numbers, but categorically; it's now a different kind of creature altogether. The brute power of the tAgora is undeniable.

But on closer examination, this scenario also begs a number of unsettling questions, questions that we customarily ignore as part of our unspoken ideological commitment to textual reality (Ideology of the Text). Here are a few of them. When we publish, do we necessarily—as etymology and usage insist—actually communicate with "the public?" Are we verifiably contributing to the public domain? Does what we create—whether knowledge, art, or ideas—truly become generally available? If not, why not? Even with every best intention and every possible effort, do novelists and their book-making collaborators simply release their precious progeny to the world? Just how public is that public, anyway?

tAgora publication

In reality, conveying your novel via the book and page is never a simple, unqualified act. Although in principle em-booking your ideas enables their consumption by a broad (we much too glibly suppose unlimited) audience, there are at least four nettlesome issues that rear their heads and spoil the media-romance:

1. *The issue of selection.* It might well be the Great American Novel, but that doesn't mean your stack of paper or collection of bytes will win acceptance by a publisher overnight, or for that matter anytime. Too many desk drawers harbor collections of recyclable pages that have been serially refused, perhaps by dozens of presses, whether for real or specious reasons. Publishers make their selections according to a wide variety of criteria, many of them strictly business-oriented, so the literary worth of your efforts may not receive full attention. Because rejection rates in many cases run over 90 percent, the very first challenge you'll face on the road to tAgora triumph is also one of the most forbidding and absolute. It's a sad fact that many, if not most, novels are never published at all.

2. *The issue of copyright.* Once a project is accepted, creators and their publishers negotiate and lock in the kind of access that prospective audience members can have to their joint product. But legal barriers, championed as a necessary means of protecting ownership (Owning versus Sharing) and avoiding misuse of the communication, keep many users out even as they provide access to a chosen few. If your novel is owned, then access will necessarily be governed by applicable tAgora rules, whether Big C or Creative Commons licenses. And that means your audience will just as necessarily be limited by those same rules.

3. *The issue of fees.* An exchange of assets, normally in the form of fees to be remitted, almost always stands between prospective audience members and their use of tAgora artifacts. In the most familiar case, we pay bookstores for their brick-and-mortar objects, and online access also characteristically involves payment. It's crucial to remember that anyone or any group who cannot afford that fee—no matter how "fairly" we try to price the commodity or user license according to our scale—is effectively ostracized by this procedure. Your Great American Novel simply cannot be read by anyone who cannot afford the tAgora entry fee. Given the way the world unfortunately works, this exclusion will disproportionately affect those millions of potential readers outside the moneyed, libraried, wired West.

4. *The issue of distribution.* Just as constraining as the imposition of fees is the highly problematic matter of distribution networks. Your novel not only has to be afforded by prospective third-world readers, in other words; it also has to physically reach them where they live. It's one thing for U.S.

readers to visit the local Barnes and Noble, or order their books online with the firm expectation of two-day delivery to their doorstep. It's quite another, as a Nigerian colleague recently explained to me, to try (and fail) no fewer than five times to have a particular title shipped from a U.K. publishing house to his Lagos address. Things are rapidly changing, and the coming years will see an improvement in book availability as eReader devices like the Kindle, Nook, and iPad play a larger role by leveraging eAgora delivery strategies. But financial as well as physical access to these groundbreaking devices, not to mention limited content even on Google Book Search,[49] will no doubt remain obstacles for some time.

oAgora and eAgora publication

Much of the Pathways Project addresses oAgora and eAgora publication in one way or another. For example, eCompanions (eCompanions) and eEditions (eEditions) were created to take advantage of the basic OT-IT homology in order to better understand and represent oral traditions. They serve as answers to the question, "Why not textualize OT?" (Why Not Textualize?). Other nodes, such as Online with OT (Online with OT) and those describing the stand-alone book and media suites, point out ways in which media can be productively combined.

But as a guide to general principles, consider how the four issues cited translate outside the tAgora.

In the oAgora The oAgora has of course had its own publication strategies in place for a very long time, ever since that marketplace opened for business sometime during the first month or two of Homo sapiens' species-year (Homo Sapiens' Calendar Year). In this arena, "to publish" has a far broader and far more flexible meaning than in the tAgora. Telegraphically put, when communication is emergent and demands an immediate and present audience, it cannot resort to asynchronous strategies. When performer and audience are cocreating the reality they share, that reality cannot be predetermined or owned. The participants are constructing an experience together, as they proceed, navigating through shared pathways in a joint, continuing effort rather than depending on a one-time, one-way transferal of brick-and-mortar items for later perusal. So, because they cocreate (Distributed Authorship), they effectively copublish.

The four issues associated with tAgora publication take on very different shape in this scenario. Selection, the first hurdle that your Great American novel had to leap, is at once a more mutual and nonfinite phenomenon in the oAgora. Stories, for example, will not survive if they lose their function for the audience, or, as was the case in our fieldwork in the Former Yugoslavia, if the audience disappears altogether as other activities become more crucial. Even critical audiences are important partners in what is always a mutual project (Audience Critique).

Over time, oral traditions undergo a kind of natural selection, with the key being the survival of the most functional and most enjoyed. Over the generations that these stories are told, they may well go in and out of societal favor and cultural usefulness, as the behavioral codes they teach, for instance, win, lose, or regain their currency for the teller(s) and audience(s). Selection isn't "once and done," and the decision on continued viability is a cultural decision that is made again and again through the generations.

Correspondingly, copyright, or legal ownership and protection against change, isn't in the cards in the oAgora. All other things being equal, publishing in the oral traditional marketplace is first and foremost driven by sharing, not by sequestering. Of course, different cultures attach a variety of rules about who can perform, who can attend, when the performance can happen, and so forth, but the essence of oral tradition lies in its ongoingness, its continuity. Enforced stasis amounts to discontinuity and death; absolute individual ownership means that the chain is broken, that the pathways are no longer viable. oPublication demands the antithesis of tAgora-type transactions, and for that same reason, the imposition of fees is also foreign to the oAgora.

The matter of distribution is especially interesting. In contrast to the barriers erected in the tAgora, oral traditions propagate themselves and spread throughout societies over generations, again subject to cultural constraints for the specific genre. Some people may be preselected or restricted on the basis of gender, age, or societal membership, but traditions actively depend for their continued vitality on being shared—and not just among existing members of the society at any one time but through the multiple generations that have collectively navigated their richness. Distribution is, in other words, preprogrammed to reach all who need to be reached. Small wonder, given that well-integrated network, that the impulse to textualize—to translate from the living reality of the oAgora to the museum of the tAgora—almost always comes from outside the society, from beyond the interactive network.

In the eAgora Self-publication provides an easy alternative to restrictive tAgora procedures. You ePublish your novel, so it's evaluated and accepted by none other than you. Very soon it will become available universally as an open-access, free-of-charge entity. On the surface this strategy looks promising: problems associated with selection, copyright, fees, and distribution vanish. In the simplest scenario, this means that the 90 percent rejection rate diminishes to zero, the built-in delay of months or years compresses to a mouse-click, and anyone in the world can read your novel without charge. In short, everybody and everything can get published in virtual space—right now and without further impediment.

Of course, the millions of blogs that are read by no one except their creators testify to the inherent liabilities associated with this kind of unchecked process. Even the most energetic surfers quickly find themselves awash in unfiltered content, and the usual measures of likely quality—publication by a reputable press, prepublication reviews, and so on—are entirely lacking. So you can certainly go ahead and publish your novel on the web without having to scale familiar tAgora barriers, but there are crippling complications. Who will actually want or be able to read it? Who will "hear of" or even find it? Your public will immediately and dramatically enlarge—more accurately, it will explode—to include everyone worldwide with a browser and a connection to the Internet. But that global, unfettered democracy introduces some awkward new challenges into the picture.

Happily, solutions are being developed that avoid the all-or-nothing dilemma. Many of these solutions cluster around what might be thought of as the Golden Rule of media deployment: use multiple media in an integrated suite, with each medium assigned to handle what it's best at facilitating. This rule advocates nothing more than common sense: use the right tool for the job, as Corey Doctorow has advised.

A simple example is the creation of a sponsored gateway or portal for eAgora publication, with gatekeepers representing an association or company or readership with some sort of independent standing. Instead of getting lost in a morass of undifferentiated material, your novel would bear the trademark or "imprint" of that portal, to which surfers could turn to locate vouched-for content. (One example of this kind of gateway is the open-access, free-of-charge website[50] for the journal *Oral Tradition*.) Once the gateway gained credibility, prospective readers could subscribe to its contents via an aggregator or feed-reader, receiving notice when new novels were posted. Much of the needle-in-a-haystack problem—ever a threat in our Digital Age of Plenty—could be solved in this way.

The difference between this kind of ePublication and the usual tAgora publishing arrangement amounts to what media critics have identified as the Long Tail.[51] Because eAgora products aren't priced on a per-pixel basis, any such gateway could potentially afford to house a theoretically unlimited list of publications. Costs, storage, and other brick-and-mortar challenges wouldn't scale in anything approaching the same way as in the tAgora. Even with adjudication and preparation (copyediting, design, etc.) standing between aspiring authors and that wide, wired world of readers, the selection filter could allow a great many deserving novels to pass through its hallowed portal, many more than conventional tAgora publishers could afford. (And of course the sponsoring group would be able to set the filter calibration as they saw fit, to control the size and focus of their site's content, as well as impose modest fees for their contribution to sponsorship and preparation.)

What's more, this model has implications not only for your novel, but also for the publication of expensive reference books, magazines and professional journals, and even the books and articles that support the awarding of tenure and promotion in our colleges and universities. And there are myriad other models, such as Project Muse at Johns Hopkins University Press, which eLicenses professional journals to libraries, folding multiple subscription fees into user licenses and leveraging the digital medium to put texts in the "hands" of readers without trafficking in bulky items. But whatever the model, the key is meshing media to best advantage, creating a hybrid, multi-agora system that optimizes the communication of knowledge, art, and ideas.

What's in it for you? Well, thanks to such a media suite you could reach beyond the tAgora and get ePublished, achieve sponsored eRecognition, and reach the international, nondenominational ePublic that only the Internet can offer. All by becoming a multi-agora citizen (Citizenship in Multiple Agoras).

Getting sequestered

So let's take stock. Congratulations are certainly due on the publication of your novel in the tAgora! But your emergence from the brownstone idea-factory into the celebrated world of print—the ritual ceremony of "getting published"—has also meant, counterintuitively, that you're getting sequestered. Why? Because in committing your novel to tPublication, you've automatically curtailed as well as expanded its possible audience, constrained as well as increased its availability. Ironically enough, you've made sure that a certain very large segment of the human population will never be able to read your epochal saga without extraordinary, out-of-agora intervention. Yes, by publishing you've engaged a public, all right, but conventional tactics have unavoidably narrowed that public to "the usual suspects": those who can gain admission to the tAgora.

. . . and getting unsequestered

But all is not lost. If you're willing to become a citizen of multiple agoras, to mix media in effective proportions, and to commit to communication beyond textual ideology, the way is open for your novel to make its mark in a much larger world. In the coming years entities that offer novels—and any other texts as well—via such hybrid channels will have the chance to combine the best, most useful features of the eAgora and the tAgora. They will have the opportunity to ensure that audience and communication are optimized without regard to geography, culture, demography, or other limiting factors. Just as eEditions have made oral traditions available in new and engaging ways, bringing oral performances back to life for a far more diverse audience (Leapfrogging the Text) by resynchronizing the event (Resynchronizing the Event), so the eAgora can promote increased participation by a truly international, nonpredetermined readership.

So we can hope that the eAgora eventually puts your Great American novel in the virtual hands of anyone in the world who wants to read it. That would be a boon not only for your novel but for myriad other texts as well. And in the process, who knows? We may succeed in engaging a suitably diverse and representative readership, something geometrically beyond John Milton's elitist notion of a "fit audience though few."

We may even manage to recover the root meaning of "to publish"—which is emphatically not "to sequester," but rather "to make [truly] public."

Homo Sapiens' Calendar Year

Sometimes it seems as though writing has been with us forever in one form or another. Pre-Gutenberg media such as the rich manuscript traditions of the ancient and medieval worlds, not to mention even earlier inscribed tablets from the Middle East, are commonly thought to offer evidence of writing systems coeval with the development of civilization as we know it.

But perhaps that's the point—just *how* do we "know it"? Our default notion of history is founded on *documentation*, that is, on textualized knowledge. And what precedes documentable reality? Although archeology can extend our knowledge further—albeit by resorting to interpreting objects (Illusion of Object)—its reach is necessarily limited. The pejorative label "Dark Ages," for example, regularly denotes pretextual eras, conventionally understood as periods when writing was unavailable to light the way.

Commitment to a textual definition of origins has blinded us to the technology of oral tradition that long predated writing and texts of any sort and which served as the principal communications medium through which predocumentary societies were built and maintained. By insisting on history as text-derived, we've artificially defined whatever preceded writing out of existence. We have foreshortened our species' history.

Given our unthinking faith in the ideology of the text (Ideology of the Text), we may be surprised to learn that writing is in fact a very recent invention. It most certainly wasn't there at the beginning, or even near the beginning for that matter. Just how much of the life span of Homo sapiens is implicated by this media chauvinism? What part of our history as a species is lost to the (indefensible) assertion that communication and culture-building begin only when the tAgora is founded?

Our species-year

As Carl Sagan often remarked when discussing the age of the universe, huge numbers can be very hard to grasp and therefore deceiving. The enormity of astronomical time and space is intrinsically difficult for most of us to imagine, and only made more difficult by the scale of measurement; a million or twenty million or a billion are figures that don't get much play in our every-day experience.

What's true of the story of the universe is to some degree true of the tale of media-invention. Taking a cue from Sagan, then, let's consider the advent of writing and related events on a calendrical rather than an absolute numerical scale.[52] Let's think of Homo sapiens' entire history as a total of twelve species-months spread over a single species-year, and then plot the various media-events on this more manageable grid.

We start with two preliminaries about the calculations that appear in the following table. First, they're based on a very conservative estimate of the longevity of Homo sapiens: one hundred thousand years. Many sources cite a much longer period of time. Second, the dates assigned to the media-inventions are taken largely from a major source entitled *The World's Writing Systems*; the most modern events, such as the emergence of the Internet, are plotted on the basis of commonly agreed-upon dates.[53] Lengthening our species' life span would make this demonstration more dramatic (moving all of the charted events later in the calendar year), while absolute date-shifts of even an entire millennium would move the invention only three to four species-days one way or the other. In other words, the table presents a conservative and reliable if rough chronological perspective on the origins of various landmark media.

The first real writing developed by humankind appears more than 11/12—or about 95 percent—of the way through our species-year. Another way to put it is that the tAgora has been open for communicative business for only twenty-one species-days, merely 5 percent of the time we've been creating and maintaining societies. Of course, the Internet and the eAgora it supports have been available only sixteen species-minutes, or .003 percent of Homo sapiens' life span.

The relative age of the oAgora

But for our purposes the most striking figure is the relative longevity of oral tradition and the oAgora that it makes possible. The ideology of the book not-

Media-Inventions and Our Species-year

Species-date	Invention
November 22	Numeracy
December 10	Egyptian scripts
December 10	Mesopotamian cuneiform
December 19	Greek alphabet
December 20	Mayan and Mesoamerican scripts
December 24	Chinese printing technology
December 27	Gutenberg's printing press
December 31, noon	Typewriter
December 31, 23:44	Internet

withstanding, OT far predates any other medium of communication. And it continues today, worldwide, supporting myriad activities and social functions.

Quite clearly, the documentary understanding of cultural knowledge comes up far short of the mark. The eAgora has been with us for a mere sixteen species-minutes, and the tAgora for not quite three species-weeks. But there is every reason to affirm that the oAgora was coeval with the emergence of Homo sapiens, from the very beginning of our species-year.

Although other technological prostheses may appear more prominent in today's Western world, OT alone has stood the test of time as a medium we have used continuously since the beginning.

How to Build a Book

Long before there were commercial or university presses, or even printing presses for that matter, there existed a highly developed technology for making texts (Texts and Intertextuality)—that is, for making manuscripts and for combining manuscript pages into collective codices. Of course, every step of this process—from finding and preparing the basic materials through actually writing out and gathering the texts—required enormous labor and know-how, and as far as we're aware there weren't any help desks[54] available.

In early medieval England manuscripts and codices were the products of monastic scriptoria, where clerical orders could devote the time and energy required to accomplish such an arduous task. With no manuals to guide them, medieval scribes presumably transmitted their craft person to person, in much the same way as apprentice musicians or carpenters still appropriate their trade from expert practitioners. In effect, and by default, book-building was taught and learned textlessly.

More than a simple enigma

One of the approximately ninety riddles[55] of the Exeter Book manuscript "remembers" this process of text-making in an interesting way, and with a particular end in mind. See whether you can solve *Riddle 24* below, which, as is customary for these enigmas, confers a human (and here a decidedly heroic) identity on a nonhuman object and process:

Riddle 24

A certain enemy robbed me of life,
snatched my world-strength, wet me afterwards,
dipped me in water, then took me outside,
set me in the sun, where I quickly lost
the hair I had. After that a hard-edged knife,

with impurities ground off, scraped me,
fingers folded me, and the bird's joy*
overspread me with drops, made frequent trips
over my dusky surface; swallowed tree-dye,
a stream-share, then stepped across me again,
traveled in black tracks. Then a hero wrapped me
in protective boards, covered me in hide,
girded me with gold, so that the smiths' splendid work
glistened on me, enveloped by wire.
Now my ornaments and the red dye
and my glorious dwelling widely honor
the people's protector—let no fool find fault.
If the sons of men wish to use me,
they will be safer and more victory-fast,
braver in heart and happier in spirit,
wiser in mind; they will have more friends,
beloved ones and kin, true and excellent,
good and faithful, when their glory and prosperity
increase in bounty and in benefits,
they will be covered in grace, and will clasp love
firmly to their bosom. Say what I'm called,
helpful to people; my name is famous,
useful to heroes and holy in itself.

Solving the technology

Understanding the description as "constructing a manuscript codex," the universally agreed-upon answer to the riddler's closing challenge, gets us most of the way to the solution. Pity the poor sheep, whose skin the "enemy" took to fashion the vellum writing-surface. Soaking that skin and curing it in the sun then led to scraping and folding before it was ready to write on. A quill pen, the "bird's joy," absorbed ink made from tree-dye and laid down tracks across the page, configuring ideas in tangible textual form and in good tAgora style. Next came the hide-covered boards that protected the manuscript leaves, and the gold and eventually the coloring that together indicate a precious (and possibly illuminated) manuscript, an extremely valuable text wrought for some special purpose.

To this point (about halfway through), *Riddle 24* follows what we might identify as a well-trodden oAgora pathway (oPathways), a blueprint for the larger genre. Typically for the overall form, which derives from Anglo-Saxon oral tradition, it portrays an inanimate object and process through personification.

---

*The kenning "bird's joy" means "feather"; here, a quill.

Thus the text is made to speak of severe and challenging heroic tests: mortal combat against an enemy, immersion in water and sunlight, losing its hair to a sharp blade, and—more curiously—being covered by drops. Some "hero" (a companion in a fight?) then effectively arms the text for battle: he wraps it in protective boards, "girds" it with gold, and arranges the work of smiths (usually armor and weapons) to help secure the whole.

But at this juncture we reach a pivot-point, as the riddle moves from secular book-making to activities associated with Christian worship. Not just any book, this codex now discloses its special purpose: to "honor the people's protector," using heroic language that names the lord of all peoples, God. What's more, the text offers a variety of beneficial effects for its users, their kin, and their friends. That unmistakably religious dynamic, along with the affirmation that "my name is famous," has led almost all scholar-solvers to narrow the solution to "constructing a Bible codex."

Merged marketplaces

So let's summarize what *Riddle 24* presents. First, we can plainly see that OT and textual technology are both in play (A Foot in Each World). Transactions are taking place in both the oAgora and tAgora, as the poet employs the OT form of the riddle to describe a textual practice. What we probably have in the riddle-text that has reached us in the Exeter Book codex is an evolving cultural memory of "How to build a book," a learned biblical spin on a folk manual for book-making. This kind of syncretism—between oAgora and tAgora, and between secular Germanic learning and Christian knowledge—is common throughout surviving Old English poetry, providing a distinctive hybrid vigor to verbal art from the early medieval period. Like *Riddle 45* (Indigestible Words), this tale of text-making images not one but two communications technologies, thoughtfully portraying the contemporary situation in its full complexity.

So how do you build a book? Let me tell you, says the riddler. And while I'm at it, let me also tell you about what it can do for you and the rest of humankind.

Ideology of the Text

What do ideologies do?

Ideologies preempt considered judgments. They short-circuit critical thinking by automatically defaulting to familiar, comfortable, predesignated positions.

Political ideologies provide perhaps the most familiar example in our everyday world. Instead of confronting social realities as the complex, many-sided phenomena they actually are, we often settle for honoring our subscription to this or that ideology. In the process we terminate open-minded consideration before it begins. We cast ourselves as Democrats, Republicans, progressives, or independents, and sign ourselves up as members of an ideologically based—and therefore dependably like-minded—group of adherents. In many cases, membership in such a group excuses us from grappling with the ins and outs, pluses and minuses, of alternative political positions. Instead, we let the ideological credo of the group do the work by overriding and dismissing natural complexity.

How do ideologies function?

Ideologies operate under the radar, invisibly for the most part. We usually don't notice when they blind us to otherwise challenging realities, when they reduce or even define them out of existence. Nor do we recognize how they funnel inherently contradictory phenomena toward a single, uncluttered (and carefully constructed) "truth."

If we're willing to embrace a given political ideology, for example, we may not be aware that our tidily monolithic view of the world doesn't take fair and equitable account of various segments of our society. We may not appreciate the full impact of a proposed regulation on small business entities, or of a copyright convention on file-sharing or artists' rights. Because ideologies do their work in the background—as unexamined templates for interpretation—we usually don't notice or credit their preemptive power. That's part of the game, of course. Once subscribed to an ideology, we seldom unsubscribe; there's just no real incentive to trash our trusty frame of reference and start all over again.

The power of textual ideology

Not all ideologies are political, of course. For example, how often do we stop to contemplate just what we're doing when we scan the lines and turn the pages of a book (Texts and Intertextuality)? Instead, we conventionally skip the preliminaries and get down to reading—all without giving much if any thought to precisely what we're doing. And for general, everyday purposes this is how it has to be; that's the default procedure, after all. Only because we subscribe to the ideology of the text, only because we have agreed to put aside extraneous concerns and adhere to the implied rules, can we use this tAgora instrument fluently and economically.

In other words, reading habits trump comparative analysis of media. It's precisely because we don't pause over how texts work, what they do, and most importantly what they define out of existence that we're able to use them so well. Like any medium, the book and page require that we categorically ignore other realities in favor of the reality they construct and represent.

Just what *is* a text, anyway?

One response to this demanding question is to investigate the history of the word. The Middle English *texte* enters our language from Old French *texte*, which in turn derives from Latin *textus* (fabric, structure). Since *textus* amounts to the past participle of the verb *texere* (to weave), a text is etymologically "something that has been woven." The larger family tree also includes a cousin in ancient Greek (*technê*, craftsmanship), with a common Indo-European grandparent **tekth*, a root likewise meaning "weave, build, join."

This root sense of something woven bears certain implications, among them the obvious connotation of a text as a finite thing. It's not in-process, emergent, or under construction; it's the tangible product of craftsmanship. In this respect such a product preserves and supports the twin illusions of object (Illusion of Object) and stasis (Illusion of Stasis), two tAgora principles that help to prop up the ideology of the text. The act of constructing such a thing—even the default cultural conviction that such an idea-container *could* be constructed— "speaks volumes" about our preemptive and unexamined commitment to the book and page.

Weaving and unweaving Contrast a famous weaving project featured in Homer's *Odyssey*: the celebrated burial shroud for Odysseus's father Laertes. It was, we recall, Odysseus's wife Penelope who used this never-ending process to hold her suitors at bay. For twenty years she wove by day and then unwove by night, cleverly delaying completion of the task she cited as a necessary preliminary to making any commitment to a new husband. Penelope's project was in effect designed not to reach completion but to remain under construction indefinitely.

Unlike Penelope's shroud-text, the texts we make and exchange can't be so easily unmade; once woven, they can't readily be unwoven. By their very nature our tAgora tools tend to persist in their unique, objective identity, impervious to revision until another edition or printing is undertaken. The whole point of creating a text—of weaving that finished product—is to eliminate the possibility of change, to foreclose on process, to prevent further adjustments, and in short to secure our ideas, arts, and knowledge in a finished tapestry resistant to unweaving. Such is the nature of our brick-and-mortar text, and such is its ideologically supported identity.

Or, rather, what *are* texts?

It's well to remember, though, that the common noun "text" has both singular and plural forms. We can speak logically (if somewhat abstractly) of a singular, overarching umbrella concept—"text" as a general category—but reality presents us with more than one type of weaving. An analogy to the natural world may help explain both sides of the phenomenon, both its diversity and its unity.

Genus and species We start with the observation that the genus we call text (tAgora) comes in various types or species. For Pathways Project purposes, we will distinguish three species: tablets and manuscripts, printed pages, and static eFiles (each with multiple variants).

By *tablets and manuscripts* I mean to indicate handwritten texts (as reflected in the etymology from *manus* and *scriptus*), whether on stone, clay, wax, papyrus, vellum (sheepskin), birchbark, notebook paper, or some other inscribable surface. The critical defining feature of manuscripts is that they are inscribed, sign by sign and in unique copies, by the direct agency of one or more human beings. *Printed pages* are of course the legacy of Gutenberg and now of computer-driven typesetting machines, and can be mass-produced in exact replicas without direct and continuous human agency. *Static eFiles*[56] live exclusively as binary code that translates to pixels on a screen, but their "text-ness" lies in their nature as fixed entities, as finished products posted to the web as freestanding artifacts. As such, they should be clearly distinguished from websites and other electronic entities that allow or even require ongoing interaction by users.

As a consequence of the history of technology, these three species show marked disparities in physical composition and usability. In the ancient and medieval periods *manuscripts* were produced only by great and sustained labor (How to Build a Book), and even then these fragile records were produced one at a time, stored in a single location, made accessible to few (a considerably smaller fraction of the already small fraction of society who could read), and were ever subject to loss or damage (Indigestible Words). In other words, they were hard to produce, hard to use, and hard to keep safe. *Printed pages* could be much more easily and precisely duplicated—"backed up," in a sense—because every copy (of hundreds or thousands) was precisely the same. Thus, the printing press and related inventions essentially pluralized documents, making it possible for widely separated readers to learn from what was for the first time precisely the same resource. With the advent of the Internet, such documents could be keyed in or scanned and then posted electronically as *static eFiles* for the benefit of a dramatically broader community, thus further distributing the readership and further democratizing knowledge, art, and ideas.

But as different as these three species are, they also constitute a single genus. Each of the three is an object (no matter what its particular physical makeup or dimensions), each is therefore tangible (unlike the experience of navigating through a virtual, interactive network), and each aspires to serve its users as a fixed, change-resistant medium.

The work = the text & The text = the work

What's more, the conviction that texts are objective, tangible, and static lies at the very foundation of our tAgora ideology. Over centuries we've committed ourselves to certain articles of faith, and we've made a tacit agreement to never look back (though the eWorld is currently starting to undermine our blind and long-unexamined faith in brick-and-mortar reality) (Reality Remains in Play).

tReligion   Here's how tReligion goes. If we believe that texts actually contain the works inscribed in them, and if we further believe that these textual containers are monumentlike edifices that keep their contents inviolate for as long as the medium survives, then the works have effectively *become* texts. Ideologically speaking, we've convinced ourselves that the texts we hold in our hands or scroll through on a screen actually *are* the works. There's no distance between encoding medium and encoded message. Knowledge, art, and ideas have been successfully mapped and stored.

Homer's performance-texts   Manuscripts provide myriad instances of how a work becomes embodied in a text. Consider the case of Homer's *Iliad*, circulating in OT well before the eighth century BCE, committed to papyrus in the seventh or sixth century BCE, fractionally sampled and remapped by other writing projects in the centuries that followed (as papyrus scraps testify), and "deposited" in the Alexandrian Library in no fewer than one hundred and thirty-one copies.[57] But scholars often submerge an embarrassing fact: namely, that the first whole *Iliad* that survives to our time appeared in a Venetian library manuscript[58] dated as late as the tenth century CE, roughly two millennia after its suggested "launch."

In the meantime, we frankly don't know and can't discover just how a long succession of editors cooperated to produce that tenth-century text. What earlier scraps of the poem we have—some in agreement and some in conflict with that first whole text—cover most of the preceding millennium, but there's no way to assemble the ancient shards into a single restored artifact. Primarily, of course, because the oAgora *Iliad* never was a single artifact to begin with; and that's to say nothing of the two missing millennia of tAgora history. Distributed authorship (Distributed Authorship) followed by distributed editorship. All in all, quite a messy text-story.

But that messiness has not prevented modern editors from sifting through the rubble and establishing what they claim is a single authoritative text. And how do they do it? By applying editorial principles and selecting preferred readings, they reduce an inventory of incongruous pieces to a hybrid artifact, a well-woven tapestry with no loose threads. Decidedly a compromise tailored to meet tAgora criteria.

The strength of the ideology behind this process cannot be overestimated. So pressing is our need for an object-text—fully as pressing as our modern cultural need for a singular author where none can exist—that we have been willing to indulge in radical reductionism, all in the name of text-making. And why? Because text-making amounts to cultural code for work-making.

Saul Bellow's *Herzog*   To take a much more modern example, we can speak of Saul Bellow's novel *Herzog* as the typed manuscript he submitted to the publisher, or the printed pages issued by that publisher, or a downloaded static file available online. Each of these texts exists in a different physical form, with different projected audiences, usefulness, access, and so forth. But those differences don't go to the real heart of the matter: the fact that all three forms are negotiable currency in the tAgora. At bottom, the variant physical identities—bond paper, bound paperback, or paperless pixels—aren't crucial. At bottom, the disparate audiences—Bellow's editor, buyers of brick-and-mortar books, or the web community—aren't crucial. What truly counts is that all three forms are "texts." Fundamentally, even if in variant guises, *Herzog* the work is *Herzog* the text(s).

So what do texts actually *do* to OT?

How about prima facie OTs that we can experience as live events and in person? What does textualization do to them?

First, and this is an obvious but inherently difficult preliminary, we must be willing to think outside the tAgora box. We have to get some distance, to suspend our default procedure of freezing reality into a spatialized, page-bound representation and ask how that ideological short circuit compromises our ability to understand OT. We have to credit the possibility—however unintuitive—that merely snatching a sequence of recognizable, dictionary-approved write-bytes severely distorts rather than fairly represents oral performance. Just as no drama worth the name can ever be fully realized within a silent, disembodied, unenacted script, so no OT worth the species label can ever be captured alive in a text, no matter how deftly conceived and executed the textual container may be. Proteus just doesn't submit that easily.

What gets lost?   With this cautionary tale in mind, let's start by enumerating some of what's lost when an OT performance event is reduced to the cenotaph of a text. It's a surprisingly lengthy and multidimensional catalogue.

We lose vocal features such as intonation, loudness and softness, and silence. We lose visual signals such as gesture and facial expression, not to mention meanings attached to costume, setting, and props. We lose the musical and rhythmical dimensions of performance. Critically, we lose the background of variability (Variation within Limits), the network of potentials out of which any single performance emerges. Just as importantly, we lose the contribution of the audience, real or implied, and any interaction that influences how the performer proceeds. And, not by any means least, we lose the historical and cultural context, as well as the general idiomatic content of the performance (dimensions that are segregated to other parts of the ruthlessly linear book even in the best-case scenario).

That's a lot to forgo in coming to terms with OT, a lot to eliminate in the name of textualization. If we're willing to settle for that degree of compromise—and we've long ridden the bandwagon of the book with few if any complaints—then the ideology of the text must be very powerful indeed.

A few projects have begun to address these shortcomings and to provide electronic solutions to the flattening of experience mandated by texts. One of these is the eEdition[59] of a South Slavic oral epic poem created by the Center for Studies in Oral Tradition, which combines the sounds of the performance with two parallel texts (in the original language and in English translation), a glossary of traditional idiomatic meanings, and a commentary. All of these parts are reassembled into a single whole on the same interactive electronic page, thus resynchronizing the event and helping the reader/surfer toward a fuller experience of Halil Bajgorić's ninety-minute performance (Resynchronizing the Event). Other eProjects with similar goals, such as the Homer edition[60] being undertaken by the Center for Hellenic Studies, are also underway.

Getting beyond textual ideology

Getting out from under any ideology is inherently a demanding task. In this case the process has to start with recognizing that our core beliefs in stasis and objectivity are nothing more (and nothing less) than a convenient, serviceable illusion. In a sense, the tAgora fosters a kind of cultural codependence, an uncritical loyalty to what we've convinced ourselves that texts can do. Restoring an unbiased perspective is hard work because it means pushing against the momentum of habit-driven behavior—in this case of note-taking, list-making, report-writing, and all of those other text-enabled activities that fill up and define our daily lives. To exit the well-mapped and familiar world of the tAgora—or at least to recognize that the worlds of the oAgora and eAgora exist—is to undergo a kind of culture shock (Culture Shock). And most people seek to avoid culture shock and agoraphobia (Agoraphobia) whenever they can.

A case in point   If you're reading "Getting beyond textual ideology" as printed pages in *Oral Tradition and the Internet: Pathways of the Mind*, you're well aware of the inherent constraints on text-processing. You know firsthand what it means to relinquish the chance to navigate a road-system and to plan your own itinerary in favor of obeying the traffic signs and proceeding down the one-way highway of the text (letter after letter, line after line, page after page, and always "just so"). The brick-and-mortar book is reassuringly and economically organized, to be sure, but that organization is purchased at a steep cost.

If you're reading "Getting beyond textual ideology" as a pixel-realized design on your screen, there's a radical difference in your experience. Oh, there's an organized and sequential text for you to read, all right, but that's hardly the end of the story. Now you have some choices to make, namely, about whether to keep following those letters and lines one after the next, or to exit by clicking on links that will take you elsewhere (but still within the universe of the Pathways Project). That "elsewhere" can be one of the three principal media environments (the oAgora, tAgora, and eAgora always available in the top menu-bar), another of the many nodes listed in the Full Table of Nodes (always available in the left menu-bar), one of the Linkmaps (also always available in the left menu-bar), or simply any branching link within any node. And of course you can always return to this very paragraph—or any other one, for that matter. Merely surfing through the Pathways Project, in other words, is a basic first step toward thinking outside that most restrictive box of all: the text.

Do's and don'ts

Somehow summaries and conclusions seem to go against the grain of the Pathways Project, which eschews linear sequence in favor of interconnected options. Instead, let me provide a few additional perspectives on the ideology of the text—none of them final or conclusive but all of them intended to be helpful. In eTerms, think of them as tags, as entry points to fundamental concepts.

I've chosen to present these tags in the form of "do's" and "don'ts," that is, as simple advice-bytes on how to avoid the pitfalls of blind and exclusive adherence to our default tAgora technology. In that sense they amount to another set of proverbs (Proverbs) that serve as easy pathways toward more complex ideas.

- *DO use each technology according to the rules of its home agora.*

For the oAgora and eAgora, this means navigating through pathways and co-creating a personalized, ongoing experience. For the tAgora this means spatializing and sequencing knowledge, art, and ideas in a fixed, linear format for consumption by text-readers. As a general principle, it means avoiding agoraphobia.

- *DO take into account the diversity of the genus "text."*

For the purposes of the Pathways Project, we have identified three major species, all of them highly variable, within this genus: *Tablets and manuscripts*, *Printed pages*, and *Static eFiles*.

- *DON'T settle for brick-and-mortar when virtual is the name of the game.*

Neither OT nor IT can be captured in a text. Accept that undeniable reality, and create and use networks that foster morphing.

- *DON'T insist on a single technology if a media suite works better.*

In representing an oral performance, exclusive adherence to a textual transcription or audio or video or photographs or other single-channel versions of the event will inevitably fragment the end user's experience and make for a necessarily partial understanding. Employ multiple media as a coordinated suite of tools to more faithfully represent OT and to improve the user's experi-ence—by resynchronizing the event.

- *DON'T reduce the multiplex road-system of networked pathways to a one-way highway.*

The oAgora and eAgora offer opportunities to explore and create. Defaulting ideologically to textual representation necessarily means relinquishing those opportunities.

- *DON'T collapse reality into an object.*

Converting an ongoing experience into a thing may seem to confer objectivity and stasis (of course, it doesn't), but the price is forbiddingly high: nontextu-alizable features of the experience are automatically eliminated before you get started. Call it an ideologically based handicap.

- *DON'T let ideology preempt understanding.*

Think outside the tAgora. Consider the dynamics and native technology of the oAgora and eAgora. To abuse Shakespeare, "There are more things in heaven and earth, Horatio, than are dreamt of in your [textual] philosophy" (*Hamlet*, Act I, scene 5).

Illusion of Object

When titles just don't work

Sometimes even the most basic assumptions prove illusory, and we can profit by taking a step back and reexamining what seemed like an utterly straightforward situation. Here's a case in point:

> Fieldworkers interviewing oral epic singers (*guslari*) in the Former Yugoslavia were often puzzled by the singers' failure to understand which stories they were being asked to perform. Citing titles like "The Wedding of Smailagić Meho" or "Alagić Alija in Captivity" usually elicited only blank stares, in spite of the fact that such designations were regularly associated with published versions of these narratives. Only when the investigators framed their requests in the form of what amount to oPathways (oPathways)—such as "Tell me the story of the young hero Meho coming of age, and the kidnapping of his fiancée Fatima, and the great battle against General Pero to reclaim her"—did the *guslari* recognize what was wanted. Titles, it turns out, were merely textual cues and thus meant little or nothing to them; only a key to active navigation would suffice.

The problem? Simply that the fieldworkers were proceeding by making tAgora assumptions about what was clearly an oAgora phenomenon. They were speaking the language of things rather than the language of systems (Systems versus Things).

Let's dramatize this disparity in marketplaces (Agora As Verbal Marketplace) by formulating two sets of questions.

Questions we expect to hear

"Say, hand me *Beloved*, will you?" "Have you downloaded the latest Coen Brothers film yet?" "I don't have that rendition of *Moonlight Sonata* by Vladimir Ashkenazy, do you?"

None of these questions—or the myriad others that we could pose about myriad works of art—seems strange or unusual. Why not? Because the presupposition that the work under discussion is a text, an item, a thing is the operating assumption, the ultimate tAgora bottom line. Someone constructed that thing, felt it had reached final form, and then made it available (under applicable rules, of course) as a fixed, immutable object for us to own (Owning versus Sharing) and then to interpret as we wish. Our interpretations will always vary, perhaps radically, but artifacts supported in the tAgora will not and cannot. And since we understand the work as contained wholly in the artifact, the work seems just as thinglike as the object. Nothing curious or suspicious here; just business as usual in the tAgora.

Now for the other side of the coin.

Questions we don't expect to hear

"So how did Toni Morrison perform *Beloved* last Thursday?" "How do you expect the Coen Brothers to adapt their latest film for showings in fifteen major cities over the next year?" "Do I understand correctly that Ashkenazy wrote some new material to insert in *Moonlight Sonata* for his European tour?"

This second set of questions, on the other hand, seems nonsensical. For Morrison to reconstruct her novel, by adding, subtracting, or substituting dialogue, for example, would be to collapse the "work = text" theorem that we take for granted. For the Coen Brothers to abandon their carefully edited film-text in favor of multiple variants would be to undo countless hours of fine-tuning and compromise its artistry. For Ashkenazy to "add new material" to the magical, immortal score created by Ludwig van Beethoven would be outright heresy. Such interventions, entirely typical in the oAgora and eAgora, represent serious violations of textual laws.

Ideology and the tAgora

Under the influence of textual ideology we conventionally make a number of automatic, unthinking assumptions about the creation, transmission, and reception of knowledge, art, and ideas (Ideology of the Text). But none of them is more fundamental than the illusion of object, the firmly held conviction that all serious communication can be contained in and transferred by a collection of unchanging items.

Take the example of the South Slavic singer requiring a network-based prompt rather than a title to understand how to surf his shared epic tradition (Online with OT), as described above. We can put it very straightforwardly: *for performers and audiences of oral traditions there simply is no such thing as a thing.* To recompose the story, which recurs without repeating (Recur Not Repeat), is to navigate a linked web of potentials rather than to trek through a book or CD or DVD (or their static eFile equivalents[61]). What the *guslar* does is being determined right now, in an ongoing fashion, and will take shape according to choices not yet made. Its ultimate form will differ from yesterday's or tomorrow's or next year's performance, just as one singer's performance will vary from another's. Variation within limits is the name of the game (Variation within Limits). To regard any single surfing expedition as globally authoritative raises the specter of agoraphobia (Agoraphobia) and culture shock (Culture Shock).

Correspondingly, the Internet offers us a vast route-system that likewise draws its strength from variability and connectedness. Just as Wikipedia can't be housed between two covers as a thing complete in itself (though some have tried) (Freezing Wikipedia), so the web in general depends on opportunities and choices that lie beyond the textual world.

Process first, products second

The oAgora and eAgora prosper by sponsoring processes that lead not to a single result but to an infinite array of products. As platforms for communication they are forever under construction, and their builders and users are always free— in fact, their builders and users are absolutely required—to cocreate whatever emerges. Communication is a shared dynamic (Distributed Authorship), and reality remains in play.

Ideology notwithstanding, the oAgora and eAgora don't trade in the illusion of object, nor for that matter in the illusion of stasis (Illusion of Stasis).

Illusion of Stasis

When stability and truth seem lacking

Sometimes even the most basic assumptions prove illusory, and we can profit by taking a step back and reexamining what seemed like an utterly straightforward solution. Here's a case in point:

> Fieldworkers interviewing oral epic singers (*guslari*) in the Former Yugoslavia were often puzzled by the singers' stubborn insistence that they told their stories exactly the same every time, "words for words" as they put it, and that

these stories were doubtless "the truth." Well, different performances of the same story—and even performances by the very same singer—varied significantly in length, detail, and sometimes in pattern and content (Misnavigation) as well. Their stories weren't at all fixed or static; and if they weren't static, then which of the variant versions do we count as "the truth"? Such apparent deviations led one scholar to criticize the epic poets for their inattention to precision, and to suggest that their poetry would profit from better awareness of what they were actually doing as they composed and performed! Only when investigators began to understand what their informants were really claiming—namely, fidelity in terms of oWords (oWords) and oPathways (oPathways)—did their seemingly misguided claims start to make sense.

The problem? Simply that the fieldworkers and the scholar were proceeding by making tAgora assumptions about what was clearly an oAgora phenomenon. They were speaking the language of things rather than the language of systems (Systems versus Things).

Let's dramatize this disparity in marketplaces (Agora As Verbal Marketplace) by formulating two sets of questions.

Questions we expect to hear

"Say, could you return that dog-eared copy of *Moby Dick* my father loaned you ten years ago?" "How long has it been since you rented *Godfather I* from Netflix?" "Don't you just love Michael Hedges's live cover of the Stones's *Gimme Shelter*?"

None of these questions—or the myriad others that we could pose about myriad works of art—seems strange or unusual. Why not? Because the presupposition that the work under discussion is static is the operating assumption, the ultimate tAgora bottom line. Someone constructed that thing, felt it had reached final form, and then made it available (under applicable rules, of course) as a fixed, immutable object for us to own (Owning versus Sharing) and then to interpret as we wish. Our interpretations will always vary, perhaps radically, but artifacts supported in the tAgora will not and cannot. And since we understand the work as contained wholly in the artifact, the work seems just as static as the object. Nothing curious or suspicious here; just business as usual in the tAgora.

Now for the other side of the coin.

Questions we don't expect to hear

"How has *Moby Dick* morphed during the past decade?" "Do you want the 1972, 1981, 1995, or current version of *Godfather* I?" "Is it true that Michael Hedges reperformed his December 12, 1990, performance at the Bottom Line?"[62]

The second set of questions, on the other hand, seems nonsensical. For Herman Melville's novel to have morphed in some fashion since your father first borrowed that well-worn paperback a decade ago is unthinkable: *Moby Dick* is forever *Moby Dick* precisely because it remains static, and the immutabilty of the artifact makes it so (remember the tAgora theorem of "text = work"). The *Godfather I* film that won an Academy Award in 1972 is frame-for-frame the same film you stream from Netflix, and not a reedited, supplemented, or otherwise tinkered-with subsequent version. Hedges performed his engaging cover in a designated place at a designated time, at which point it was recorded and frozen into textuality; its particular artistry thus stems from its very uniqueness and lack of changeability.

Ideology and the tAgora

Under the influence of textual ideology we conventionally make a number of automatic, unthinking assumptions about the creation, transmission, and reception of knowledge, art, and ideas (Ideology of the Text). But none of them is more fundamental than the illusion of stasis, the firmly held conviction that fixed, unchanging items are the necessary and exclusive basis for all serious communication.

Take the example of the South Slavic singer who relies on oWords rather than tWords (tWords) for his claim of accuracy (Accuracy) and truth, as described above. We can put it very straightforwardly: *for performers and audiences of oral traditions there simply is no such category as stasis*. To work through a performance of the same story, which recurs without repeating (Recur Not Repeat), is to navigate a linked web of potentials rather than to trek through a book or CD or DVD (or their static eFile equivalents[63]). What the *guslar* does is being determined right now, in an ongoing fashion, and will take shape according to choices not yet made. Its ultimate form will differ from yesterday's or tomorrow's or next year's performance, just as one singer's performance will vary from another's. Variation within limits is the name of the game (Variation within Limits). To regard any single surfing expedition as globally authoritative raises the specter of agoraphobia (Agoraphobia) and culture shock (Culture Shock).

Correspondingly, the Internet offers us a vast route-system that likewise draws its strength from variability and connectedness. Just as Wikipedia won't hold still (Freezing Wikipedia) but instead derives its authority from continuous updating and linking to other entries that are themselves always morphing, so the web itself depends on opportunities and choices that lie beyond the textual world.

Process first, products second

The oAgora and eAgora prosper by sponsoring processes that lead not to a single result but to an infinite array of products. As platforms for communication they are forever under construction, and their builders and users are always free— in fact, their builders and users are absolutely required—to cocreate whatever emerges. Communication is a shared dynamic (Distributed Authorship), and reality remains in play.

Ideology notwithstanding, the oAgora and eAgora don't trade in the illusion of stasis, nor for that matter in the illusion of object (Illusion of Object).

Impossibility of tPathways

tPathways don't and can't exist. They represent an impossible formulation, a nonconcept.

Why? Because in-text references can't foster instantaneous and continuous access beyond the text. Because textual citations can't engage a network; all they can designate are other static things. Because any strategy that breaks the spell of the textual experience (Ideology of the Text) by shifting the reader's attention away from that text must by definition amount to a counterproductive strategy. And it isn't only that pathways can't work in a textual environment. Even if we could somehow install them, they'd actively subvert tAgora communication.

A case in point

The tried-and-true tAgora strategy of footnotes can help us understand the impossibility of tPathways.

> Imagine yourself in a library, immersed in an anthropological study of migrant workers in the southwestern United States. As you follow the author's argument about the economic forces driving this phenomenon, you notice that he or she cites several prior books and articles on the subject, quotes from one of them, and adds a descriptive or "talking" footnote to an opposing view. Will you now immediately close the text you're reading and, leaving it behind, go find and read the "sources" enshrined in these footnotes? Or will you (at most) weigh the dependability of the supporting citations, which may either increase or diminish your confidence in the argument you're evaluating? Remember, since texts are objects, you can consult them at any time—subject to their tAgora availability, of course. What you can't do is fashion a continuous, meaningful tAgora experience by abandoning the cross-country highway in favor of a series of local dead ends.

If those footnotes documenting economic forces were truly pathways, an open-ended vista of alternate routes (Reading Backwards) would appear before you. What's more, those alternate routes would offer credible options because the overall experience of reading and understanding would be understood as partly self-constructed. But, both for better and for worse, the book presents a one-way street rather than a route-system, and so footnotes remain subsidiary dead ends.

In short, footnotes can't ever become tPathways because pathways don't exist outside of the oAgora and eAgora.

It's a simple matter of navigability.

In the Public Domain

Continuity and sustainability *through*, rather than *in spite of* innovation

To the book-bound mentality, such a strategy may appear at best unlikely and counterintuitive, at worst simply wrongheaded (Ideology of the Text). But it accurately (Accuracy) describes how oral tradition and the Internet operate in their versions of the public domain—the oAgora and the eAgora—the arenas in which each thought-technology thrives most naturally. Despite what our default cultural reflexes encourage us to believe, OT and IT prosper not via the textual program of fixation-through-capture, but via morphing (Variation within Limits) and regeneration. For both pathways-based media, it's rule-governed, ongoing evolution—rather than the dead end of tAgora fossilization—that promises continued usefulness and accessibility.

Two aspects of OT and IT, both of them foreign to the textual world, stand out as especially important reasons underlying this counterintuitive reality (Disclaimer). The first is a radical openness to change, and I mean "radical" in two senses: fundamental and innovative. The second aspect is an unprivatized community of makers and users, a cyberdemocracy if you like. These two qualities make for a creative scenario that favors access, exchange, and diverse contributions over ownership, licensing, and proprietary products. Instead of microsocietal restriction by legal instruments and entrenched resistance to shared innovation, so typical of the régime of the book and page, OT and IT offer an invitation to cooperate and jointly innovate across the broad swath of the macrosociety.

OT accomplishes its goals by opening the performance arena to all performers and (let's not forget) all audiences, subject to individual cultural rules. Likewise, IT's ever-emerging openness and ever-expanding community are sponsoring more and more open-source and open-standards sorts of activities. In short, if OT and IT operate like matched bookends, it's precisely because they flourish by not closing the book on sharing, by conducting their business very much in the public domain.

Let's consider a few examples of IT behavior along these lines, instances of eDemocracy that are changing the landscape of our daily experience.

Open software

In recent years the open-source movement has begun what some are already calling a major revolution in software design and development. The trend away from proprietary, vendor-regulated products and toward open-source software has meant that innovation of any sort can take place without the usual restrictions of licensing, commercial purchase, and penalties for modification. The source code is open, experimentation is open, and redistribution is open—all across the eAgora.

In the simplest scenario, this initiative fosters adaptation of freely available applications to any subsequent purpose without abridgment of copyright. Thus anyone can tailor preexisting "open" software to a particular purpose without monetary impediment or fear of legal repercussions. Would your business function more smoothly if you could tweak a particular application by adding or substituting modules, or even by rewriting basic code? Under open-source rules,[64] feel free to go ahead and tweak—no questions asked, no fees incurred, no laws broken. Likewise for the next innovator, and the next, as evolution goes on unhindered.

Complementary to the open-source movement is a commitment to open standards, such as the OpenDocument standard[65] adopted by the state of Massachusetts as a replacement for proprietary, nonconforming productivity applications. As of January 1, 2007,[66] all state offices were required to install software that supports this new standard, which in effect disqualified any proprietary software that didn't do the same. Initially that meant Microsoft Office was out, as were WordPerfect and Lotus Notes, none of which originally supported the standard. But the power of the eDemocratic movement has since brought many software companies around.

But this story has another, more far-reaching side. Technophiles and ordinary citizens of the cyberdemocracy stand to profit from decreased costs and increased access, as did state workers—once they mastered the new applications that were required when "open season in Massachusetts" began. Capitulate to broader, community-based rule or suffer the consequences, the Massachusetts folks were saying to software vendors, even as they warmly welcomed makers, users, and workers into an open, seamless eCommunity.

Open courseware

Add to these symptoms of a deeply rooted and growing commitment to sharing—as opposed to owning (Owning versus Sharing)—another remarkable phenomenon: MIT OpenCourseWare,[67] which makes public and available many hundreds of courses over dozens of departments and programs.

Here is how MIT President Susan Hockfield,[68] speaking to a new world of users, described the broadening and leveling of the educational eAgora: "There is no limit to the power of the mind. We encourage you to use OCW—learn from it and build on it. Find new ways not only to pursue your personal academic interests, but to use the knowledge that you gain—and that you create—to make our world a better place. In the spirit of open sharing, we also encourage you to share your scholarship with others, as hundreds of other universities are already doing through their own OCWs."

In other words, IT opens doors, and it opens them via shared pathways, just like OT (Online with OT).

So . . . the state government of Massachusetts and the MIT faculty—what do these groups have in common? Briefly stated, they've decided that the way forward is not to hoard ideas but to distribute them as widely as possible, not to try to corner the market but to trade with everyone else, and on as equal a footing as possible (Getting Published or Getting Sequestered). They see their best opportunity for sustained contribution as members of a radically open community of makers and users—indeed, a community wherein the (essentially proprietary) distinction between "makers" and "users" really doesn't apply in the customary tAgora sense. Instead, and again as in OT, all involved become in one way or another participants, actors or doers participating in a process of mutual exchange. And the strength of their joint work, as well as the richness of their joint experience, derives from morphing and innovation.

That's what's meant by a truly public domain—an eAgora, an IT-based community in which ownership has given way to sharing. And sharing is in turn a recognition that ideas just don't hold still, that they're ever-evolving. In such circumstances, is it really any surprise that open-source software and open courseware have begun to take on more prominence?

As with OT, people are once again starting to understand the advantages of pathways. All tAgora claims to the contrary, innovation and sharing help insure continuity and sustainability through growth. That's how you grow the public domain and keep it vital. Like the oAgora, the eAgora recognizes that reality remains in play (Reality Remains in Play).

Indigestible Words

Sometimes, curiously enough, textual words provide no nourishment whatsoever. We don't expect that, of course, since the dominant ideology insists that handwritten or printed or pixel-imaged content is always and forever "there," ever ready to be consumed and digested (Ideology of the Text). All cultural expectation to the contrary, however, texts and their tWords (tWords) can prove to be merely empty calories.

What can riddles do?

Consider one such scenario from early medieval England, from a period on the cusp of OT and textual technology. *Riddle 45*, as it's known, was probably composed and perhaps performed orally before being committed to the Exeter Book manuscript, the grand miscellany of Old English poetry compiled by Bishop Leofric before the end of the tenth century. There are about 90 of these enigmata[69] in the collection, covering a wealth of subjects, and they're much more than facile games or harmless amusement for children. The Anglo-Saxons seem to have used riddles as vehicles for storing and transmitting cultural observations and discovered truths, as well as for pondering such thorny matters as the interrelationship of Germanic paganism and Latin Christianity. To put it another way, riddles could serve as dynamic thinking spaces, as virtual arenas (Arena of Oral Tradition) for reflecting on important cultural issues.

No exception to that rule, the following six-line riddle (translated) poses a puzzle for you to solve, a mysterious phenomenon that the speaker is asking you to step forward and explain. Just one hint before you begin: Anglo-Saxon riddles typically disguise an animal, object, or natural process in human garb, playing off its eccentric or even inexplicable behavior against everyday human traits. See whether you can come up with the answer, which—here's a hint—involves both a creature and a process:

Riddle 45

> A moth ate words—that seemed to me
> a curious event when I learned about the wonder,
> that the worm, the thief in darkness, completely swallowed
> a certain man's song-poem, his glory-bound speech
> and the basis of his strength. But that thieving stranger
> wasn't a whit the wiser after he swallowed those words.

Did you guess "bookworm eating a manuscript"? That's the solution accepted by almost all scholar-solvers, understanding the "moth" and the "worm" as successive life-stages of one and the same animal. Of course, we're hardly surprised about the riddle's dénouement: no creature, bookworm or not, can literally digest words. Sheepskin and ink, yes; the wisdom they encode, no. Thus it is that swallowing words yields no educational boost for the hungry bookworm, who "wasn't a whit the wiser" for his manuscript-munching.

Nor does our riddle's commentary on communications technologies end there. Notice that the moth or worm was consuming tWords from a manuscript text, tWords that aspired to be—and ideologically were thought to represent—a great deal more than textual artifacts. They contained, as best they could, the oWords (oWords) of "a certain man's song-poem" (the Old English term is *gied*, which means an orally performed poem). They mirrored, once again as well as texts can mirror, his speech and his strength. So there was potentially a lot at stake here: the manuscript eaten by the bookworm seems to have been nothing less than a transcription of a performance from oral tradition. It amounted to the tangible, static, objective reflection of a living, engaging event—song, speech, and strength transported, however imperfectly, to sheepskin stained with tree-dye (How to Build a Book).

The fragility of texts

But the manuscript was also nothing more than that, and the bookworm shows us why. As precious as the text was, it also proved only too perishable. As carefully and artfully inscribed as its tWords were, they readily fell prey to a "thief in darkness." After all of the enormous time and energy expended in a medieval scriptorium on creating this wondrous record, along came a lowly bookworm and by itself shut down transactions in the tAgora. Perhaps, as Riddle 45 appears to be telling us, texts aren't as permanent as they may seem. Perhaps their treasured authoritativeness is more fragile than we thought. Perhaps they're not quite the unshakable pillars that the dominant ideology preemptively insists they are.

Perhaps in the end texts don't provide the last(ing) word.

Just the Facts

When we want to decrease or eliminate uncertainty or subjectivity, we often narrow our focus to "the facts." Instead of filtered reality, so goes the ideology (Ideology of the Text), these irreducible verities offer us the unfiltered version—the real story, what actually transpired as opposed to an interpretation. By removing human agency and the fallibility and inaccuracy that are its inescapable trademarks, we gain access to a universal, freestanding level of truth. That's what happens when we concentrate on *just the facts*. Or is it?

Facts are made, not born

Consider for a moment the etymology of "fact," which derives from the Latin verb *facere*, "to make, do, or perform." Our English word descends from the neuter past participle of that verb—*factum*, a thing which has been made. Facts, in other words, are not at all preexistent truths, but truths that are made, constructed, done, performed. At bottom, these treasured bytes of freestanding truth are much more contingent than contemporary usage allows us to recognize. All appearances to the contrary, facts are fundamentally provisional.

Q: So just what are facts, then, if they're not archetypal principles waiting to be unearthed? **A:** They're constructed reality, preinterpreted thought. **Q:** And who does the constructing and interpreting? **A:** We do—as participant-observers who perceive, express, codify, and then reperceive in a never-ending and interactive cycle. Our verities are as true as we can make them, no more and no less, but they are subject to revision from the very moment they're made.

Facts in the tAgora

Facts are, of course, the everyday currency of idea-exchange in the marketplace we call the tAgora. Working within the twin illusions of object (Illusion of Object) and stasis (Illusion of Stasis), we trade facts, bartering with one another and with the culture at large, seeking to acquire items to fill up our warehouse of cultural literacy (the customary and idiomatic deflection from cultural *fluency* to cultural *literacy* is naturally no accident). The premise of isolatable, concretizable (Accuracy), and therefore tangibly exchangeable ideas makes the tAgora run.

But let's reexamine the textual reflex that short circuits our more considered view of facts. Stripping away the ideological assumptions that mask the root sense of the word, let's ask whether facts can exist beyond the tAgora. If we step outside the prelapsarian illusion of complete textual objectivity, can the concept survive the translation?

Well, it depends on how much you're willing to buy into the fiction of fact. Strictly speaking, since all facts are constructed, the tAgora concept of immutable, noncontingent truth is nothing more than a convenient falsification from the start (Contingency). Only because we codependently agree to the lie that certain perspectives are impervious to context can we even posit the kind of fact on which the tAgora depends for its continuing function.

If, on the other hand, we are willing to face the contingent, provisional nature of facts—no matter what they purport to explain or characterize, then we'll see that the oAgora and eAgora are actually far better equipped to support and understand them.

Facts in the oAgora

A more-than-leading question   Only too often we're confronted with a question so skewed that it condemns OT technology to a lesser, inferior ranking on the totem pole of comparative media. The query usually goes something like this: "What facts can we trust OT to provide us with, and what aspects of OT should we disregard, in our search for 'what really happened?'" Sometimes the question comes from historians trying to use Homer's epics or the Anglo-Saxon *Beowulf* or contemporary folk drama to write their histories. Sometimes it comes from journalists, who are responsible for *fact-checking*, a metaconcept that heaps irony upon irony. You can come up with many more examples, I'm sure.

But whatever the source, the core implication is clear: OT isn't as dependable as a document. It's the text that delivers facts, and our task in dealing with the less accurate, less dependable medium is essentially to weed out the inaccuracies, to separate the wheat from the chaff.

Of course, there's a trapdoor lurking here: the unexamined assumptions embedded in the question, which automatically foreclose on discussion before it can start. By attempting to answer the question as posed ("What can we salvage from OT technology?"), we're already subscribing to a hierarchy of media. We're already placing the ideological program of the tAgora at the top and making it the sole standard by which other media-technologies are measured. In a sense, we're confronted with the media-specific equivalent of "Are you still cheating on your wife?" That's a tough spot to begin a fair-minded conversation.

OT as a contingent medium   OT provides a perspective; more accurately, it provides multiple perspectives for the media users it serves. And, crucially, the users themselves are necessarily involved in formulating those perspectives. They're the ones who navigate the network of pathways, who surf their way through a web of linked possibilities.

Consider the situation. There can't be any pretense of objectivity if the performance-event takes its character in part from the patterned and flexible language of OT, in part from the performer's mood, in part from the immediate surroundings, in part from the makeup and dynamic participation of the audience, and so forth. There can be and often is competition among performers, each one claiming implicitly or explicitly to be the best. But none of them can claim the final word, just as no performance is the final or optimal version. Utter finality in OT—as in IT—yields nothing but silence and the death of communication.

The most essential truth is that OT functions not *in spite of* but rather *through* the agency of its contingent, provisional nature. It adapts in rule-governed ways (Variation within Limits) to the moment in which it finds itself, and therein lies its strength and power.

Two examples   Our fieldwork team observed this kind of power-via-morphing in Serbian *bajanje*, or magic spells, orally performed by female conjurers for the treatment of their village clientele. No one form of the charm would cure every disease; no single performance would suit every patient; no practitioner would voice precisely the same sequence of words or syllables every time she performed. The "fact" of the medicinal matter proved contingent, adaptable, subjective—and, most crucially, constructed. Multiformity made the magic work.

Or consider the composition of medieval literature, such as Chaucer's *Canterbury Tales*, a work created in writing but with deep and nourishing roots in the oAgora. Chaucer and his contemporaries drew on various kinds of storytelling conventions to portray their characters, events, and situations. During the Middle Ages these conventions were collected in rhetorical handbooks, which in turn served as recipe books for creating literature. The Wife of Bath's gapped teeth and red stockings, for example, were telltale signs of a lascivious nature—not invented merely for her memorable character but rather applied to signal her sexual nature by much broader and more pervasive convention.

Of course, there is nothing inherent in dental features or hosiery that would unfailingly identify the Wife—or anyone else—as lascivious. The traditional meaning that accompanies these unsuspecting physical details is linked arbitrarily on the basis of usage, not on the basis of tAgora-type fact. To put it in the terms we've been thinking with, gapped teeth and red stockings are constructed signs. And Chaucer was hardly alone. Many medieval authors deployed such constructed facts to spin their stories fluently and idiomatically. Once again, the medium works precisely because these "facts" apply across multiple instances. They provide authors with a contingent language that comes alive in the oAgora experience of storytelling.

Facts in the eAgora

So how about facts on the web? We might be tempted to cite such bedrock items as dates, statistics, and static pages, and conclude that facts (as imagined in the tAgora) can and do exist in a virtual environment. But a moment's reflection will reveal that even these supposedly immutable objects were mapped, calculated, and built by someone according to an arbitrary convention. In short, they too were constructed (Reading Backwards).

Then there's the network of potentials itself, each node linked in multiple ways to other nodes. Very little if any tAgora-type fact can be found in that powerfully morphing, interactive medium at any level. Indeed, the Internet's function actively depends on the absence of fact as ideologically construed.

And we can take things a step further. The very notion of *absence* already misrepresents the situation, using a tAgora distinction to mischaracterize the eAgora. It's not absence or omission, but rather presence, plenitude, and contingency that enable the surfer to cocreate experience(s). Every individual surfer constructs a personal "factual" universe, a self-made cosmos, by navigating pathways and coconfiguring reality.

Until ideas collapse into things, until virtual diminishes into brick-and-mortar, until textuality stops the heartbeat of OT and IT, reality remains in play (Reality Remains in Play).

Leapfrogging the Text

Sometimes truth proves considerably stranger than fiction and serendipity more instructive than carefully wrought analysis. What follows is one of those cases: a real-life event that illustrates firsthand the close correspondence between oral tradition and the Internet, between the oAgora and the eAgora. In other words, it amounts to a parable on the confluence of OT and IT (Agora Correspondences) that, remarkably enough, really happened.

The backstory: From performance to book

Let's start with the OT background. In late 2004 a book entitled *The Wedding of Mustajbey's Son Bećirbey as Performed by Halil Bajgorić* appeared as volume 283 in Folklore Fellows Communications, then the latest in a lengthy series of books that began about a century ago in 1910. As its title suggests, this brick-and-mortar publication features a South Slavic oral epic performance by the bard (*guslar*) Halil Bajgorić, who despite not being able to read or write boasted a repertoire of some thirty oral epics. The performance in question was recorded on aluminum discs by Milman Parry and Albert Lord on June 13, 1935, in the small village of Dabrica in central Bosnia, and later converted to a digital audiotape by David Elmer in 2002.

Notice the culturally sanctioned trajectory from performance to book, fully in accord with the dominant ideology of the text (Ideology of the Text). The audio "capture" of Bajgorić's enactment modulates into a visual artifact, a voiceless cenotaph on the page. But of course there was a price: from oral tradition to aluminum records to digital tape to paper, the long journey into silence meant radical reduction at almost every stage. Presence gave way to echo, which in turn gave way to a documentary image of the echo. Culturally sanctioned or not, we'd have to admit that this trajectory traces a downward spiral of reality, with OT devolving from a living process to a static product (Museum of Verbal Art). Bajgorić's performance moved from its origin in the oAgora to another kind of existence in the tAgora.

Strategy 1: Reading aids

My initial attempt at reversing this serial reduction involved providing the book-reader as much of what was lost as the printed medium would allow. Toward this end the paper edition features a variety of "reading aids." In addition to a transcription of the original performance in South Slavic and an English translation, I added a biographical portrait of the singer Bajgorić and his craft, a performance-based commentary, a digest of traditional language and context, and a study of another singer's remaking of the original song. Two colleagues, Wakefield Foster and R. Scott Garner, contributed analyses of musical aspects and performance variables, respectively. Via these strategies, then, dimensions of Bajgorić's performance that had been lost during its journey from voice to paper were added back into the printed resource. All for the sake of creating a truer experience and, I hoped, a better audience.

But it was still a book. You still had to turn pages. You had to leaf through chapters and scurry back and forth to notes in order to knit these discrete, freestanding parts into some sort of facsimile unity. Ironically enough, the very act of using the composite paper edition underlined its built-in limitations (Reading Backwards) as a vehicle for reintegration. You chose which page and part to read, and once you made that choice you automatically disengaged from everything else—at least until you exited one particular page or part in order to consult the next one. And of course the experience was still wholly and unremittingly visual. In short, while the composite edition promised and delivered more than a simple text, it just wasn't enough. The performance was still only a book.

Strategy 2: Online audio

So I next tried to look (and hear) beyond the confines of the multidimensional text. With the aim of bringing more of the original performance back to life, the next move was to make available an online audio file of the entire 1030-line performance preserved in the Milman Parry Collection of Oral Literature at Harvard University. A few months before the published book appeared, you could both read and listen to the epic as a multimedia experience online. More to the point, that audiovisual experience was easily accessible and free of charge to anyone anywhere in the world via that most democratic of all media: the worldwide web (Getting Published or Getting Sequestered). OT was being "published" via IT.

Strategy 3: The eEdition, a performance facsimile

So far, so good. But there was another step to take in order to resynchronize the event, to reassemble the textually dismembered performance (Resynchronizing the Event). In other words, the challenge was to meld the edition's segregated parts into a more integral, interactive whole. Once again, an IT strategy came to the rescue, this time with the invention of the eEdition (eEdition).

What is an eEdition and how does it compare to the kind of edition we're used to making and using? In addition to the full transcription, translation, and audio at the website, I aimed to create a prototype electronic version of the performance. Designed to foster audience reception, the eEdition contains each of the parts that make up the composite paper edition, but with a major difference—you never have to turn a page to use them. Consider the implications for reader-listeners: instead of remaining exiled from the performance arena (Arena of Oral Tradition), an inevitable casualty of the spatialized format of the book, the reader-listener can tap into an experience. Here's how it works.

Open the home page[70] and you immediately encounter not simply the transcription and translation, but a set of interpretive tools. Click first on "Performance" to set the interactive process in motion. Now click on the links within the translation—as many as you like and in whatever order you wish—and a traditional glossary of specialized meanings will appear in a small box located just to the right of the translation. Click on the "C" at the end of most lines to consult the relevant commentary, which will pop up in the same small box. With the sound-file playing concurrently (click to activate the mp3 file), the reader-listener need never exit the multimedia experience of the performance. To a degree that freestanding books can never emulate, this facility reassembles and resynchronizes the event of performance and puts you "on the same page" as the original audience.

Taken as a whole, then, the eEdition integrates the sound, story, meaning, and context of the performance. It converts an item back into an experience and offers the reader-listener a chance to join the original singer's audience as an eParticipant—albeit in facsimile. OT is reconstituted, and with much increased fidelity, by IT. The oldest medium is reincarnated in the newest.

Keeping IT (and OT) in the family

But our "OT-and-IT Vignette" doesn't end there. You've heard the backstory; here comes the serendipity.

One day, quite out of the ether, I received an email from a certain Ćamil Bajgorić, who pronounced himself interested in reading *The Wedding of Mustajbey's Son Bećirbey*. It seems he'd discovered an online reference to the eEdition while surfing, and was contacting me because the URL wasn't working. (The problem was straightforward enough, as I quickly wrote back; he'd simply caught us at a point of transition between servers.)

Now as a rule, broken links are a dependable source of embarrassment, but in this instance the reported malfunction turned out to be a stroke of good luck. Think about it: if the URL had functioned smoothly and invisibly, Mr. Bajgorić could have silently accessed the eEdition without my knowledge, used it in whatever way and for whatever purpose he had in mind, and exited without much of a trace. I'd never have become aware of his interest, and I'd have no story to tell. And that, as will be explained in a moment, would have been a shame.

Why? Because Ćamil went on to mention that the *guslar* (or epic singer) Halil Bajgorić, the performer of the epic he wanted to read and hear, was none other than his own grandfather! He wanted to read and hear the story, of course, but part of his motivation was also, shall we say, genealogical. With the kin connection to spur us on, we rapidly finished migrating the eEdition to the new server and restored the link so that the singer's grandson (and you, if you so choose) could experience his grandfather's performance in multimedia. Thanks to the eAgora, OT remains virtually available via IT (Online with OT).

The OT-IT link embodied

Thinking back over this extraordinary sequence of events in the weeks that followed, I was struck by the fact that Halil's epic and Ćamil's request mimed the fundamental connection in the Pathways Project (Getting Started). The real-life episode synced OT and IT in a memorable way because it bridged oral tradition and the Internet, and did so booklessly.

Halil, himself preliterate, composed his epic without the cognitive prosthesis of the page, and Ćamil sought to attend that performance via the virtual reality of the Internet. The composite paper edition—the culturally sanctioned vehicle—never figured in the interface between grandfather and grandson (at least until I sent Ćamil a copy of the book!). Moreover, by reintegrating various dimensions of the song-performance into a single form reflective of the original event, the eEdition allowed the grandson a far more genuine experience of his grandfather's performance than a conventional paper edition could ever manage.

Halil and Ćamil Bajgorić lived in vastly different worlds. One was a preliterate farm laborer from a tiny village in Bosnia whose sole technology of communication was oral tradition. The other is a book- and computer-literate resident of Michigan interested in learning more about his familial and ethnic identity. Although their life experiences were starkly disparate (and although they apparently never met "ftf," as the jargon has it), each in his own way became a navigator of pathways. And in the final analysis it was precisely their parallel modes of navigation that brought them together, long after discontinuities in space and time seemed to preclude any sort of meeting.

OT as IT made that connection.

Misnavigation

Pathways (oPathways) permeate and define the oAgora. They constitute its expressive universe, providing rich opportunities to create individual performances within a rule-governed environment. But they can't guarantee success, or even intelligibility, any more than a knowledge of French guarantees unerringly fluent conversation in a Parisian café. OT, like language in general, sponsors surfing along multiply linked pathways, and such surfing can sometimes go astray.

After all, OT performance is a process that necessarily involves not only a flexible, idiomatic system of expression but also one or more individuals who actually do the oAgora work. To put it proverbially (Proverbs), "without a tradition there is no language; without a speaker there is only silence." Systematic, pathway-driven morphing is a powerful vehicle, but vehicles can't function without operators. Practically speaking, to do business in the oAgora is to accept the real possibility of occasional off-course navigation in order to preserve the possibility of living, interactive, creative performance. Networks aren't texts because networks aren't predetermined. Linked potentials support miming, not mapping.

Mujo Kukuruzović in the oAgora

A pair of linked performances by the South Slavic oral epic singer(*guslar*) Mujo Kukuruzović offers a case in point. First, a short sketch of the background.

During their 1933–35 fieldwork in the Former Yugoslavia, Milman Parry and Albert Lord often elicited multiple versions of a given song-performance through their interpreter and colleague, Nikola Vujnović (A Foot in Each World). Their goal was to study the variability (Variation within Limits) inherent in this oral tradition—from one instance to another, from one singer to another, and from one region to another. The Parry Collection of Oral Literature, the archive where these song-performances are now housed, thus presents a unique opportunity to learn how *guslari* surf the pathways of their tradition, how they fluently convert the potential of a shared network to the reality of parallel but nonidentical instances. As we shall see in the case below, multiple performances also illustrate how rule-governed flexibility can lead to outright misnavigation.

A discrepancy discovered

Kukuruzović twice performed the same epic tale, *The Captivity of Alagić Alija*, once on February 22, 1935, and again on June 10, 1935. Let's call them versions A and B, respectively. In both of these performances the singer arrived at a particular juncture in the narrative and veered off course. On both occasions he sent his hero off to seek the wrong foe in the wrong locale: specifically, to meet with General Pero in Kara Bogdan instead of Paun harambasha in Jezero.

But it's exactly this pathway-detour that shows us how he surfs. Notice how Kukuruzović reacts, differently each time. In version B he immediately corrects his error by adding a revised itinerary, while in version A no such revision takes place and he continues all the way through to the end of his performance—*via the wrong track*. The singer admitted as much during his postperformance interview with Vujnović:

NV: When we wrote down this song [version A], you told me that when Alija killed his wife, he went off seeking some ban and general [Pero].

MK: Uh-huh.

NV: And that they attacked the Lika.

MK: Uh-huh.

NV: But this morning [version B] you sang that he killed his wife and then met some harambasha.

MK: That's right—Paun harambasha. . . .

NV: There's a difference here, Mujo, I'd say, and I'd say it's an important difference.

MK: Then it's possible that I skipped over.

NV: What's that?

MK: It's possible that I skipped over.

NV: I'd say, by God, that it's some sort of important difference.

MK: Yes, it's possible; I began to set [version B] straight immediately, so it's possible.

NV: Then which is the true story? Tell me.

MK: I consider [version B] the true one.

NV: The one this morning?

MK: The one this morning, *because, you know, I've heard it done that way more times.*

The bottom line in this scenario? Version B gets corrected when the singer clicks on the correct link, chooses the right oPathway, and sends Alagić Alija where he's supposed to go—to Paun harambasha in Jezero. Meanwhile, Version A stands as an uncorrected error of some 1603 lines (of 2152 total lines in that performance!), as Kukuruzović fails to redirect his hero from General Pero in Kara Bogdan. We can't help but agree with the interviewer Vujnović: that's a major misstep (Reading Backwards).

A number of questions must then arise. How could the singer go so wrong for so long? What could possibly prompt such a basic error and, once it was committed, why did Kukuruzović make a midcourse adjustment to correct his mistake in one version but not in the other? From a tAgora perspective, this series of events looks like sloppy composition (Accuracy), the kind of oAgora activity so roundly condemned in the tAgora marketplace under the doctrine of agoraphobia (Agoraphobia). Certainly this isn't the sort of artistic malfeasance we expect in a responsible, articulate poet! Why doesn't the performer have better control of his performance?

The singer explains himself

But consider the situation from the point of view of the *guslar* himself, as expressed in the following exchange, another part of the conversation between him and his interviewer Vujnović. In order to understand Kukuruzović's explanation, it's necessary to know a couple of things in advance. First, they are referring to two epic tales: *The Captivity of Alagić Alija*, the story we've been considering here so far, and a second very similar story, *The Captivity of Ograšćić Alija*. Second, these two tales are in many respects mirror images of one another, from start to finish. That is, the names, places, and specific actions are different, but the generic narrative pattern underlying them—the story backbone, so to speak—is one and the same.

In brief, both tales feature a long-imprisoned Turkish hero who survives an *Odyssey*-like captivity and returns home only to find that his wife has been unfaithful, the very antithesis of Odysseus's wife Penelope. He takes his revenge by killing her and then treasonously riding off to join the Christian enemy, although he eventually comes to his senses, rediscovers his original loyalties, and participates in a Turkish rescue mission. Up to the point at which the hero departs for enemy territory, the two stories are virtually identical; at that juncture Alagić Alija heads for Jezero and Paun harambasha, while Ograšćić Alija seeks General Pero in Kara Bogdan (the proper destination for each hero in the given story).

With these generic correspondences in mind, listen to Kukuruzović's own commentary on his performances, a kind of oAgora "lit-crit" that responds to Vujnović's tAgora-type prompting:

> NV: Do you sing other songs, for example, with the same kind of variation as this song? The question really comes to this—do you know these other songs better, or do you know them only as well as this one?
>
> MK: Well, brother, whatever songs I learned from singers, those I know, do you understand? But the songs about Ograšćić Alija and Alagić Alija are enough alike, one to the next, that the verses carry over.
>
> NV: Yes, yes.
>
> MK: So it was in this way that I skipped over, so to speak, and leaned in another direction. And then I saw that I was mistaken, but I didn't stop to tell you.

Let's examine what the singer is trying to explain. If we translate his description of "skipping over" into tAgora terms, we can see that Kukuruzović's "error" is an unforgivable breach of performance only within a textual frame of reference. Within the oAgora, choosing the wrong route is simply the price one occasionally pays for using systematic patterning, for surfing through potentials instead of staying committed to a one-way street. By sending Alagić Alija to the place where Ograšćić Alija is supposed to go, the performer has simply headed down a parallel pathway.

In effect, Kukuruzović was operating online within his OT (Online with OT). It's as if he visited an incorrect subsection of the Returning Hero website and clicked on the nearby and similar URL "www.returninghero.org/ograšćićalija" instead of "www.returninghero.org/alagićalija." In version B he adjusted by reclicking on the correct URL; in version A he followed the alternate and parallel but wrong pathway all the way through.

The built-in cost of oAgora-business

On another occasion Kukuruzović might never have veered off; he might well have sent Alagić Alija to the "right" instead of the "wrong" place from the beginning. No adjustment for misnavigation would have been necessary because the *guslar* would have clicked correctly, choosing the more appropriate of two parallel routes. Of course, there are always myriad additional decisions to make along the way: how elaborately to describe the hero's disguise and testing procedures, for example, or how graphically to portray his wife's infidelity. These are smaller, less consequential choices, where outright *mis*-navigation doesn't really come into play. But they're options nonetheless, at every point and every level.

Like Pathways Project surfers, performers can "read" their oral traditions as they wish, navigating their networks within the limits that define those networks. Is it possible to go astray, to make a choice one might regret? Certainly. And is it possible to click on the "back" button to return and modify an itinerary? Yes, although we can also follow the new and uncustomary pathway without returning to the fork in the road. We can initiate a new performance. "Errors" can effectively—and in both OT and IT—produce untried, unexplored linkmaps (Linkmaps).

In any case, what these two real-life instances of performances by Kukuruzović reveal is the crucial importance of pathways as the fundamental cognitive basis of OT. Pathways provide the opportunity for fluent, artistic performance, but they cannot guarantee unqualified success. Precisely because they present the performer with built-in options, guiding the process at the same time that they leave plenty of room for individual contributions and situation-specific details, they will occasionally license what the tAgora will label "flawed" products. They will occasionally license misnavigation.

That's the cost of doing business in the oAgora.

Morphing Book

As explained in Getting Started (Getting Started), the overall Project consists of two parts: (1) a website,[71] technically a wiki with gatekeeping (Wiki); and (2) a book entitled *Oral Tradition and the Internet: Pathways of the Mind*. Both aspects share the central mission of analyzing and representing the fundamental homology between oral tradition and the Internet, and the basic contrast of the oAgora and eAgora, on the one hand, with the very different textual marketplace, or tAgora, on the other.

A book that morphs?

A book is neither an oral tradition nor an electronic web. It is a species belonging to the textual genus (Spectrum of Texts), a warehouse-able object (Illusion of Object), a static item (Illusion of Stasis). Its role is to serve as a bulwark against change of any sort, not at all to foster the kind of navigation through networks and pattern-driven variation that characterize and define OT and IT (Variation within Limits). On the face of it, "morphing book" would therefore seem an outright contradiction in terms, an oxymoron. Not unexpectedly, then, questions must arise.

Question 1: **So how can this brick-and-mortar artifact possibly morph?** Books do not naturally morph, of course; once "cast in stone," they resist morphing. But they can be forced to do so to a limited degree in order to illustrate three phenomena: to simulate nonlinear, cocreative "reading" (Distributed Authorship); to reveal the arbitrariness of their programmatic code (Not So Willy-nilly); and to underline their unsuitability for network-based dynamics (Systems versus Things).

In other words, books can to a limited degree support multiple different reading itineraries that do not slavishly follow the canonical line-after-line, paragraph-after-paragraph, page-after-page, chapter-after-chapter routine. To an extent they can be supplemented to support various routes through their riches, and thus different experiences. And opening up alternate routes through books not only provides us with new opportunities for making sense of the subjects they treat. It also exposes linearity and all of the signals that blaze the "linear reading trail" as no more (and no less) than a convention. At the same time, this exercise in using a pseudonavigational strategy in *Oral Tradition and the Internet: Pathways of the Mind* is intentionally meant as a demonstration of the tAgora's built-in inadequacy to support the network-based activity typical of the other two agoras. Call the morphing book both a partial oAgora/eAgora facsimile, and at the same time proof that a full facsimile can't be created within the tAgora.

Question 2: **So how can we defeat the primacy of textual code and cause the book to offer more than a single linear route?** There are four ways in which the volume *Oral Tradition and the Internet: Pathways of the Mind* can be read, with each of them mushrooming to myriad more possibilities in actual practice.

First, the book can be trekked through via the default method—"straight through" according to the sequentially numbered pages, just as you would read through a Shakespeare play or an Ellison novel. To emphasize this linear organization (and its arbitrariness), *Oral Tradition and the Internet: Pathways of the Mind* consists of usually brief nodes arranged in alphabetical order in a Table of Nodes (Table of Nodes). But *caveat lector*: one node very seldom leads to the next one in line, since order-by-alphabet is perhaps the most artificial of organizations outside the arena of dictionaries, lexicons, and encyclopedias. Furthermore, within each node are links that provide opportunities for (but do not require) visiting other nodes. Linearity is thus the initial trajectory of this default method, but you will almost certainly choose to abandon that strict and impertinent pagination-based track at some point between the first page and the last page of the book.

Second, *Oral Tradition and the Internet: Pathways of the Mind* can be read via the three principal media environments: the oAgora, the tAgora, or the eAgora. Most of the book's nodes are only a few pages in length, but these three discussions of the oral, textual, and electronic marketplaces, and a few other nodes such as the Museum of Verbal Art (Museum of Verbal Art) and the Ideology of the Text (Ideology of the Text), are much more extensive. From one perspective, the three principal nodes collectively offer a thorough overview of how the OT-IT vs. TT contrast works, and are filled with examples of each medium/technology that illustrate the broad spectrum of possibilities for each genus of communication. From another point of view, they are structured in parallel fashion, to emphasize similarities and differences. In addition, they are also filled with cross-references to other sections in the book, nodes that treat the immediate topic in more depth or connect to a cognate idea, even occasionally to sites outside the Pathways Project. Once again, how you proceed—how you cause the book to morph, even within the confines of this second, agora-driven approach alone, is entirely up to you.

Third, you may choose to follow one of several linkmaps provided within *Oral Tradition and the Internet: Pathways of the Mind* (Linkmaps). These predetermined sequences, none of them alphabetical, consist of strings of nodes unified by a central idea, such as "The eWorld," "The oWorld," "Broadening your Horizons," or "Textual Limits." In selecting a predesignated linkmap you abdicate your own cocreation and turn the process of discovery over to another person, following his or her "take" on how the book, or at least parts of it, can be construed. You follow in someone else's link-clicks, so to speak. But never fear: you can depart from that preset itinerary at any time, either by choosing another linkmap, by following a link within any node in the sequence, or by opting to pursue any of the other three global strategies. As usual, your experience is of your own making (Reality Remains in Play).

Fourth and finally, and most basically, you can follow branches from inside any node at any time. Through these frequently occurring links you'll discover cross-referenced material that you may find useful or provocative, and as a result you may continue to explore other connected nodes according to your own designs. Or perhaps you'll decide to backtrack, staying with the original node—at least until you encounter the next invitation to explore something else within the network (or, more rarely, outside).

Diversity of experience, but built-in limitations

Through these methods you can cause *Oral Tradition and the Internet: Pathways of the Mind* to morph and to engender different experiences every time you pick up the book for a reading session. Your friends and colleagues can do likewise, and you can confer with them to discuss and compare the various itineraries you've put together—all of them equally viable routes and none of them the single, exclusive, authorized route. As you cause the brick-and-mortar item to mirror network-navigation to the small degree that a tAgora artifact can, you'll also sense the limits of an inherently pathwayless medium (Impossibility of tPathways). In short, you'll gain another perspective on the homology of OT and IT and their contrast to textual technology.

Museum of Verbal Art: A Parable

Museum and canon

[*Author's/wikimaster's note*: What follows in this node is a story. It requires an effort of the imagination.]

Imagine a museum that houses and displays the core of the literary canon—literature as we know it, or, more to the point, as generations of scholars and students have established its scope and identity.[72] Visitors to this privileged edifice have the opportunity to trek through the most treasured of texts, to read and study what Western culture has identified as the very most important verbal art, from the ancient to the contemporary world. Admission is gratis, the stacks are open, and the ever-diligent library staff has even placed a suggestion box just inside the front door.

But there is trouble brewing: the Museum of Verbal Art (MVA) is under serious threat.

Losing accreditation

After a lengthy and painful process of evaluation, the verdict is in: our much-admired, elegantly appointed MVA—the cultural centerpiece and pride of the tAgora—has lost its accreditation. We've been duly notified, and the evidence is unfortunately compelling, that our collection is radically incomplete, even deeply biased in its parochialism.

It's true, alas. The relatively few cherished items chosen for public display have been gathering dust, undisturbed on their pedestals, for far too long. We've tried to upgrade by repackaging our exhibits, pasting on fresh new labels, shifting the viewer's perspective this way and that, but none of these increasingly desperate strategies addresses the accreditation team's most damning charge: that we've created an unrepresentative display of Homo sapiens' verbal art (Homo Sapiens' Calendar Year).

And the criticism goes on. We're told that generations of our curatorial staff have shirked their duty in assembling the museum collection. Relying on inherited and unexamined assumptions about what constitutes verbal art, they've foreshortened rather than broadened horizons. Sadly, an unblinking appraisal must admit that, until recently, our labors have all too often produced a circular result: we continue to celebrate what has always been celebrated, privileging those very artifacts from which we draw our criteria for selection. A kind of "subcultural narcissism," one evaluator observed.

Recent renovations

On the bright side, over the last few decades complaints from visitors and experts alike have begun to stimulate dramatic and rewarding gains in many areas. Where are the long-lost women authors, you ask? Nationwide, new generations of scholars labor to bring women's literature into plainer view. Where are the exciting new works by African American and Native American authors, you challenge? Again, the answer is gratifying: today's reader-visitors are often as familiar with Toni Morrison, Langston Hughes, James Baldwin, Leslie Marmon Silko, and Louise Erdrich as with William Shakespeare, Herman Melville, or Leo Tolstoy.

In these and other once-marginalized areas, boundaries truly are expanding. New voices are entering the discussion, new champions are joining the fray,

Herman Melville.
Courtesy of Wikimedia.

Toni Morrison. Photograph by Angela Radulescu; modifications by Entheta. Courtesy of Wikimedia.

and the wizened old guard of canonical authors and texts is also profiting from immersion in a revitalized context of human diversity. The Museum of Verbal Art is inarguably a much more interesting place to visit these days. Nonetheless, we've apparently lost our accreditation. How could that possibly be?

The silenced majority

Living oral traditions   Well, it turns out that the problem goes far deeper than our selection of tAgora texts, no matter how many and no matter how diverse. For even our most visionary curators have largely failed to tap potential resources of verbal art that dwarf even the MVA's recently expanded holdings in size and variety. We've taken such brave and important steps to acquire and display newly discovered and rediscovered treasures from the four corners of the known world (the literate and textual world, of course). How unfortunate, then, that we should have largely ignored the magnificent array of expressive forms that have but a single shortcoming: their preference for the spoken over the written word. By depositing in our museum only what we can collect from the tAgora, we've programmatically ignored the oAgora. We've excised the greater part of Homo sapiens' experience, past and present, as a creator of verbal art.

Even when we haven't entirely failed to credit the existence of oral tradition, we've done the next worst thing: banning all or most such works from the hallowed halls of literary studies, treating them like unworthy pariahs by lodging them "where they belong" in buildings adjacent to the museum. Finding other quarters for these textless kin may have passed for recognition, and within the Museums of Folklore and Anthropology unwritten verbal art—the proud issue of the oAgora—has certainly prospered. But the Museum of Verbal Art itself remains largely off limits to prospective donations that lack a lettered pedigree.

Works with OT roots   Nor has our beloved tAgora-driven MVA been much more receptive to rethinking the descriptions and interrelationships of its current holdings as new discoveries about their oAgora history and most basic characteristics have emerged. Not that substantial pressure for change hasn't been brought to bear. It just hasn't worked yet: old cognitive habits die hard.

The Curator of Antiquities has probably had the worst of it so far: with evidence for the influence of oral tradition on Homer, Hesiod, and other ancient authors accruing at an alarming rate, it's gotten harder to recycle the same tired old portraits of these figures as modern authors of original texts.[73] Never mind that Homer "himself"—probably a code name for the oral epic tradition rather than a fully historical person (Distributed Authorship)—doesn't agree. He "himself" celebrates bards not as *literati* but as masters of oPathways (oPathways). So far, however, the oAgora origins of the *Iliad* and *Odyssey* haven't appreciably affected the museum exhibit: curator and patrons still defer to the time-honored concept of these and related poems as the fundamentally textual cornerstones of the Western tAgora.

Nor has the Curator of Medieval Studies had an easy time of it as the rediscovery of oral tradition has spread from era to era and item to item. The

Homer. Photograph
by Marie-Lan Nguyen.
Courtesy of Wikimedia.

exhibit on the Anglo-Saxon *Beowulf*[74] cries out for radical refashioning, as do those on the Old French *Song of Roland*, the medieval Spanish *Poem of the Cid*, and the Old Norse sagas, all of whose identities as uncompromisingly literary monuments once seemed safe and secure. There have even been whispers that high-traffic museum exhibits featuring elite authors like Geoffrey Chaucer, long recognized for his mastery of texts in many tongues, require a bit of face-lifting to acknowledge oAgora dimensions of their artistry.[75]

Similar woes have beset the Curators of Eastern Art, whether Indian, Oriental, or Arabic. Not only do texts like the *Mahabharata* stem from oral traditions, it seems, but some of them also appear to have "lesser" kin still alive today in folk tradition.[76] And this is to say nothing of Middle Eastern Art, in particular the Judeo-Christian Bible—both Old and New Testaments—with its roots firmly planted in the realm of the spoken, embodied word.[77]

Textual authority   Still, even with the pressure exerted by reports from field-work on living oral traditions and by the rediscovery of oral traditions at the root of many canonical texts, the MVA has undergone no fundamental change, no major building program or renovation, no paradigm shift. And the reason isn't far to seek: the tAgora canon of literary, text-based art looms far above the fray, austere and practically unchallengeable. Boasting both historical depth and contemporary political power (Ideology of the Text), it selects and rejects with a faceless and final authority, supposedly objective but in reality self-fulfilling to the core. When it comes to verbal art from outside the textual marketplace, the chances for mounting a new installation are very slim indeed, no matter how urgent the need.

This is a critical situation. As it stands, the MVA *simply fails even to acknowledge the preponderance of the world's verbal art*: those myriad and vital oral traditions that dwarf written literature in size, content, and diversity.

How, then, can we begin to remedy this disappointing situation? How can we restore our lost accreditation? What sorts of curatorial programs and strategies for acquisition are necessary to fill the enormous and important gaps in our collection? How do we ensure that visitors to our cherished institution are exposed to an appropriately expanded and enriched canon? What we need is an MVA that realistically reflects the many faces and voices of verbal art, and especially the worldwide cornucopia of oral traditions and works that derive from and depend upon this nontextual medium.

We need, in short, to hear from the oAgora.

From the Alexandrian Library to the Internet

As a first step, let's attempt some revisionist history. Let's try to place our hoped-for new museum and its open, expanded collection in perspective. To do so, we'll compare it to two famous "depositories": the great and mysterious Alexandrian

Library, wonder of the ancient world; and its present-day analogue and wonder of the modern world, the Internet. These two imposing edifices, bookends to the waning age of inscription and print, represent watershed moments in the technology of storing and communicating knowledge, art, and ideas. Underlying their physical differences, however—the one a towering stack of brick-and-mortar maps, the other a networked web of electronic potentials—lies a more radical distinction. The Alexandrian Library consisted of things; the Internet consists of pathways.

A warehouse in ancient Alexandria   Although plagued by contradictory testimony from earliest times, enough of the history of the ancient library[78] has been reconstructed that we can be sure of its central, ongoing purpose: nothing less than to house under a single roof copies of all texts ever created. During its prime under the Ptolemies, reports were required every year on progress made toward what was considered an achievable goal. How many scrolls were presently in hand? Were there prospects for major new collections?

Behind this bibliographical imperialism lay an astonishing assumption, straight out of tAgora thinking. Since there must be a limited, finite number of items, so went the reasoning, let's find them all and make them our own (Owning versus Sharing). This policy may not sound entirely unfamiliar to a twenty-first–century culture of authors, readers, and objectified works of verbal art. In our era the same spirit has filled old-fashioned library buildings to overflowing, created the need for off-site storage facilities, and accelerated the advent of the digital library.

The Ptolemies had virtually unlimited funds at their disposal with which to pursue their dream of a universal library, of course. But more important to the project than their deep pockets were their most deeply held convictions about the necessary relationship between, for example, the author and works we call Homer and the numerous scrolls at Alexandria that wholly or partially recorded some version of the *Iliad* or *Odyssey*.

Twinned illusions   One of these convictions, the illusion of object (Illusion of Object), is still very much operative today, although evolving electronic media are daily forcing us to extend our definition of what constitutes a tangible object. Under the influence of textual ideology, the ancient librarians effectively equated Homer and the scroll; for the purposes of collection, the two were indistinguishable. This is all the more remarkable because oral composition, transmission, and performance were still ongoing in some parts of the Greek world during at least the early years of the Library. Nonetheless, the illusion that the work of verbal art was a tangible and therefore collectible object made possible the Library's foundation and its continuing existence—despite the irony of that assumption.

Hand-in-hand with the work-as-object fiction went the illusion of stasis (Illusion of Stasis). Only if the work of verbal art had the permanent value of a static, immutable object could it merit deposit in the library. This second illusion must have helped relieve the embarrassment of the hundred-odd versions of Homer at Alexandria. If something had attained the form of a tangible object, then its suitability for the library's collection was warranted and defensible. And if one item, why not many? If you're aiming at a comprehensive collection, then by definition you need them all.

The First MVA   Once again, the early stages of this process must have taken place even as what we attribute to the legendary "Homer" was being performed and reperformed—in different places, by different poets, and certainly with varying results (as variant manuscripts prove). But the most important purpose served by the static objects so assiduously amassed by the Ptolemies and their agents was to nurture that sustaining dream of an exhaustive material record, a treasure-house of thought-become-written-word, an archive complete in itself. In this respect the Alexandrian Library also housed the first Museum of Verbal Art, the original canon.

    And so was created the royal model that has reigned for two millennia and more, just as significant for what it excluded as for what it included. The collectible was defined as the written; everything unwritten was implicitly defined out of existence. The library could aspire to all-inclusive, universal coverage because that universality was restricted solely to objects, that is, to texts. A finite canon was conceivable only because of the twin illusions of object and stasis, which then and in years to follow also made possible librarianship, literary studies, and, not least, text-driven cultural self-definition.

    By the same token, these illusions entailed a built-in program of exclusion that was vast and far-reaching. Because performances of oral tradition were neither objective nor static (since in tAgora terms there was no real substance to them), they couldn't qualify as entries in the grand inventory of concrete items. Oral traditions were not so much unwelcome as simply unshelvable in the library (Why Not Textualize?).

A virtual inventory in cyberspace   Now we leap forward to the other bookend, to the incipient and ongoing construction of the Internet, the information superhighway that promises unprecedented access to theoretically unlimited knowledge. In its grandiose aspirations, this claim may seem to echo what the Ptolemies had in mind, and the two "repositories" do in fact have some features in common. Although no single site on the Internet can play more than a supporting role, the system in its entirety—as a "virtual library" without geographical or other physical limitations—aims at providing universal access to everything.

    And "everything" now means a great deal more than simply "books." Already colleges, universities, and other institutions specialize in and subscribe to electronic archives of texts, manuscript facsimiles, and other tools economically or technologically impractical to publish or own in conventional printed format. Already various organizations sponsor electronic journals in various disciplines, while citizen journalism moves Everyperson's thoughts and commentary into virtual newspapers available and updatable 24/7/365. Already those at home in the virtual environment write their very identities into the Internet card catalogue on personal home pages, blogs, and social networking sites. Already Internet-savvy readers subscribe via RSS aggregators to favorite sources, each other's updated podcasts, and other kinds of automatable feeds. Taken as a whole, this computer-driven system brings a heretofore unthinkable number of "volumes" into the electronic marketplace of the eAgora and under the same virtual roof. And of course the "holdings" only increase daily as more institutions and individuals join the network, as more of their often unparalleled facilities go online, and as those networks—unlike static books—themselves continue to morph.

But what makes the Internet much more than even an Alexandrian Library is neither the sheer number nor the remarkable diversity of its "eScrolls," but rather their unprecedented, hands-on accessibility and interactivity. What sets the Internet apart, in short, are the connections woven into its web—the hyperlinks that open up a universe of immanent knowledge via the surfing of pathways.

Visiting the Book of Kells   For example: how do you get a look at that incomparable medieval masterpiece of manuscript illumination, the Book of Kells? Start up your browser and click on your first destination—in this as in so many other cases, Wikipedia offers a promising start.[79] From that point of origin you encounter a cascade of information, powered by ePathways and organized in a network that you can surf as you wish. Public-domain color photographs of the splendidly illustrated pages sit alongside sections on history (origin, medieval period, modern period, reproductions), description (contents, text and script, decoration), use, bibliography, and other related sites. Everything is linked together—both intra- (within the Wikipedia entry) and inter- (to other Wikipedia and non-Wikipedia entries). In other words, you pass effortlessly, according to your own needs and designs, among different texts, authors, languages, and centuries, fashioning your own understanding of the Book of Kells against a panoramic background as you go (Reality Remains in Play).

Compare this procedure to physically visiting Trinity College, Dublin, where the manuscript itself is housed in a conventional university library setting, and where I once examined a single page or two in dim light at the end of a musty corridor.[80] Or perhaps you prefer the complete, freestanding facsimile printed on paper and bound between covers, which will allow you to pore over more than a couple of pages, as long as your library is privileged enough to own one

A page from the
Book of Kells. Courtesy
of Wikimedia.

of the 1480 copies of the volume available for $15,000 each.[81] Or, for the bargain price of about 30 euros, you could purchase the DVD-ROM[82] of the Book of Kells approved by Trinity College, with a full visual record (plus zooming) along with information on the manuscript's history and the eighth-century technology used to produce it.

But neither a journey to Dublin nor a research expedition to your local library nor even a personal copy of the DVD-ROM can offer the kind of immediate, proximate, multidimensional context that is a built-in staple of Internet study and research. And it is not so much that Trinity College or your nearby library or the latest disc merely lacks the requisite information (though that may be the case), but more that they lack the living web of pathways that make the information instantly and always accessible to everyone, and which allows for continuous updating and surfer-determined exploring via new and existing pathways.

A virtual journey These ePathways (ePathways) have other characteristics as well, salient features that categorically distinguish an interactive journey through the Internet from browsing the best-stocked library, even the Alexandrian Library. For one thing, any route taken through the electronic maze is inherently more than a standardized, repetitive tour of the facilities. Within the interests and according to the judgment of whoever constructed (and continues to reconstruct) the given site and its options, it offers automatic, institutionalized access to myriad related possibilities as an ever-present reality. What's more, your itinerary is never writ in stone, but always susceptible to change en route. After all, it's being assembled by you, as you go.

Correspondingly, each Internet session—whether to research the Book of Kells or any other topic—is a unique event and experience, providing a fresh perspective for each user each time he or she enters the virtual edifice. Even after many sessions on the same topic, the opportunity to try out new avenues or follow out the same links in a different sequence or at a different depth, branching here or there or even contributing to the communal network (as in the case of open-source facilities like Wikipedia) will always shed new light on the most familiar surroundings.

Indeed, the watchword for successive visits to the Internet library must be variation within limits rather than rote repetition (Variation within Limits). As the Pathways Project illustrates, with these same observations we could just as well be describing the oAgora.

Pathways versus canon

Homer's "inside take"   In explaining how the ancient Greek bard navigates through the maze of traditional story, Homer also speaks of pathways (which he calls *oimai*). During the great feast among the Phaeacians on Scheria, for instance, he portrays Odysseus as honoring the celebrated singer Demodokos with the choicest cut from the shining-tusked boar and with a fascinating tribute to oAgora technology:

> For among all mortal men the singers have a share
> in honor and reverence, since to them the Muse has taught the **pathways,**
> for she loves the singers' tribe. (*Odyssey*, Book 8, lines 479–81)

What the Muse teaches, we should notice, isn't texts—that is, items supporting the twin illusions of object and stasis—but rather routes, avenues, means for getting there. She is represented not as lending volumes from an immense story-archive, but as providing links for the performing bard (and his audience) to click on. Her repository of traditional oral epic consists not of scrolls shelved in an Alexandrian Library, but rather of a web of pathways that gives users access to the stories via a pretextual analogue to our Internet (Online with OT).

Let's pursue this analogy, historically counterintuitive as it may appear. We've already suggested that the Homeric *oimai* are parallel to links on the Internet, and therefore that a web or network of potentials is a more apposite cognitive model for OT than any model associated with the tAgora, even such influence-sharing theories as intertextuality (Texts and Intertextuality).

Some modern colleagues Modern-day oral traditions certainly bear this out. For example, South Slavic *guslari*, preliterate singers of epics who have been particularly well studied at close range, focus not on the thing but the process. For them the song exists in its doing, its performance—its movement from here to there, partially predictable and partially unpredictable (Misnavigation); for them the song has nothing to do with the cenotaph of the book. To be sure, by recording one of their performances we can manufacture a textual item, a durable good, a "scroll" fully fit for acquisition and deposit by the Ptolemies' librarians. But a second and third recording made the next day, or in front of a different audience, or even with the same bard in a different frame of mind will reveal inevitable disparities that quickly put the lie to the "authority" of any one version.

The OT poem lives outside any single performance or any single performer—never mind beyond the reduced medium of any recording or transcription. It lives and thrives as a series of potentials, a network of pathways that offers innumerable options at the same time that it connects with innumerable unspoken assumptions and implicit references. Any South Slavic oral epic is thus nothing more or less than a special case of language, and as such there can be no end to its morphing. There are limits and rules, of course, but they foster rather than prohibit change. Had we the patience to sit through a hundred performances by one or a hundred singers, we would simply reconfirm the same thesis a hundredfold: none of the recordings would actually be "the epic," but all of them would in their different ways *imply* "the epic." OT can no more be canonized than IT can be forced between two covers.

Exploding the canon Thus we come to the first of the major reasons why OT is fundamentally incompatible with the concept of canon. Although Petrarch's sonnets, Montaigne's essays, and Gogol's novels readily found a home in the Museum of Verbal Art, and even though the recently expanded museum now features new displays on works like Morrison's *Beloved* and Silko's *Ceremony*, we still find no space for oral traditions. More to the point, there can't ever be space, at least in the present building. And it isn't the curators who are at fault this time. The problem lies instead with the very nature of oral tradition as a medium for verbal art, with the incontrovertible fact that any one performance is just that—one performance. We can't file it, title it, edit it and translate it as we would a papyrus manuscript, first edition, or other artifact of the tAgora. OT exists only in its multiformity and in its enactment, and to reduce that living complexity to a single libretto for ease of shelving is to falsify its art. Proteus exists only in his shapeshifting, and will forever resist the captivity of canonical form.

Virtues of plurality To accommodate the world's oral traditions, our MVA will have to undergo more than cosmetic alterations. First and foremost, the staff must find effective methods for representing plurality, as well as what that plurality stands for. Singularity, authority, and epitome are useless criteria for living OTs; they continue the illusions of object and stasis, ignoring the oAgora realities of process and rule-governed change. The many faces of OT are what folklorists seek to expose when they insist on eliciting and publishing multiple performances of a given story or charm or riddle, and we can take an initial step in renovating the MVA by following their lead. Just as any single node pales in importance against the totality of the Internet—since by isolating even the most valuable such resource we sap its greatest strength: connectivity—so concentration on any single fossil from a once-living OT blurs the focus on its naturally dynamic context. Always different and yet always the same, OTs are most realistically understood as *immanent to* rather than *uniquely contained in* each separate yet related performance.

Ethnopoetics There are also many other strategies that can be engaged, some of them presently available and others on the near horizon of our updated "museum science." Take the approach called *Ethnopoetics*, which amounts to constructing scripts that allow for more faithful reperformance of OTs. How do we proceed? In a sense, by being nontextual: by reinstating the pauses, intonations, gradations of volume, and other performance features that text-making customarily levels out or silences. We can make a start by respecting the actual structural units that each OT employs, rather than translating the performance to our default concepts of verse, stanza, syllabic line, or whatever. In short, we need to restore the expressive life that textualization robs from performances. Then, when readers read, at least they'll hear some echo of the original performance in their heads. Some fidelity to the experience will survive the trajectory from the oAgora to the tAgora.

eArchives, eEditions, and eCompanions Additionally, electronic text archives, in whose ready resources web-surfers will eventually be able to experience many dimensions of a performance (sound, video, etc.) as well as probe many parallel performances, are coming online. Tools such as eEditions (eEditions) and eCompanions (eCompanions) are overcoming many of the hindrances imposed by spatial limitations inherent in the book format. No longer will editors be required to incarcerate the performance in one silent and epitomized version, unfairly consigning its sibling versions to secondary status in appendixes and footnotes. What's more, with the multimedia revolution, oral traditions can also be presented in more than one dimension concurrently, with the acoustic and even visual reality of the performance becoming an integrated part of its transcription. No longer will a reader/surfer have to be content with segregated edition parts; transcription, translation, commentary, glossary, and any other "chapters" can be meshed electronically, enriching the reader/surfer's experience by resynchronizing the performance (Resynchronizing the Event).

Texts rooted in oral tradition   Very importantly, these strategies also apply to an appreciable number of texts with oral roots, what we might call *voices from the past*. These Januslike items, chiefly from the ancient and medieval worlds, are already comfortably housed in the MVA collection on the basis of their presumably literary and textual merits. Recently, however, they've been shown to derive from OT and are therefore deserving of additional attention. In many ways these works are also more process than product, and thus not entirely "canonizable," even though they survive only as manuscripts (with limited contextual information) and may appear to belong strictly to the tAgora. Of course, our readiness to accept that either-or reduction is just another measure of how blindly we adhere to textual ideology.

In updating these exhibits, we must take care to convey what we can learn about the background and foreground of each oral-derived text. Is their textuality merely an accident of transmission (as is always the case with performances recorded in writing before acoustic and video media were available)? If so, Ethnopoetics can help by creating a script for reperformance. Or are there performance cues that survive their reduction to texts? In that case Performance Theory can assist our understanding. Or are there special contextual meanings—traditional idioms—that require explanation? We can turn to the approach called Immanent Art for a way to discover and convey such meanings.

Even when we're dealing with singly authored, oral-derived texts, much closer to what most of us have been trained to call *literature*, we still have a curatorial responsibility to discover what we can about the history behind the work, its possible multiformity (in part or in whole), and the nature and degree of its dependence on an oral tradition. Even singly authored texts often harbor more than meets the eye.

The list of MVA exhibits needing attention includes, as mentioned elsewhere in this node, Homer's *Iliad* and *Odyssey*, the Anglo-Saxon *Beowulf*, the Old French *Song of Roland*, the medieval Spanish *Poem of the Cid*, the Old Norse sagas, the Sanskrit *Mahabharata*, the Judeo-Christian Bible, and even the "literary" genius Chaucer. To these and many similar *voices from the past* we'll need to add still-living forms such as the ubiquitous and familiar ballad, which has long prospered as both oral tradition and text. In fact, mentioning the ballad offers the opportunity to emphasize how the worlds of orality and literacy, once thought to occupy mutually exclusive orbits, can and do coexist and interact in myriad fascinating combinations, within the same culture or region and even within the same person. Not only do OT features persist alongside and into texts, but a single individual may be fluent in both expressive media. We know from real-life observation that the very same individual can indeed manage fluently in multiple agoras (Citizenship in Multiple Agoras).

Conclusion: The challenge for the MVA

So why did our Museum of Verbal Art lose its accreditation? Because in paying exclusive attention to the tAgora it completely ignored the oAgora. In focusing on objects, stasis, and shelf space it failed to pay due attention to pathways, performance, and networks. What it managed to accomplish it did very well, but in the process the MVA unfortunately eliminated the larger part of humankind's verbal art from consideration. In a word, by confining its displays to texts, the institution just didn't live up to its title and purpose.

If our museum is ever to house a collection truly representative of human diversity, then we must accept a new challenge. As responsible curators we must step outside of the tAgora and take full account of what transpires in the oAgora. And because of the developments in media technology, we are better equipped to do just that than at any other time in history.

The key is to enlist the tools of the eAgora to do what the tAgora was unable to support. The Internet, with its web of links, built-in context, and ever-emergent dynamics, offers both an analogue to oral tradition and a blueprint for renovation of the MVA. Online electronic editions, as well as online companions to brick-and-mortar textual items, can bring the verbal art that is OT to new (and new kinds of) audiences. Wikis like the one used as a vehicle for the Pathways Project (Wiki) offer another avenue for multilayered and multimedia representation, and there are certainly many promising initiatives already underway or on the near horizon. The core of the renovation effort will lie in educating museum-goers about the broadened and much more realistic scope of its holdings and displays, to demonstrate that verbal art need not be purely and exclusively textual. In regard to the oAgora, texts cannot by themselves present verbal art without serious reduction and distortion, no matter how polished and gemlike the treasured documents may be. Whether publishing or reading OT, the eAgora offers unique opportunities.

In terms of the untold wealth of living traditions, verbal art inheres in the instance of performance and in what that performance-instance implies. As for oral-connected traditional texts—and, as we have seen, there are many crucially important works in this category from all over the world—our responsibility is to gauge the extent to which pathways, performance, and traditional meaning are still applicable when speech-acts take on or survive in textual form. In either case, a significant part of the context for any individual performance or text will always lie outside the most expansive, comprehensive canon, just as it lay beyond the Alexandrian Library and the most ambitious acquisitions program in history. The Museum of Verbal Art must acknowledge these vital realities and reconfigure itself accordingly.

Homer was right Homer had it right when, as he began navigating through the fantastic web of the *Odyssey*, he made this petition to a virtual resource undreamed of even by the Ptolemies:

> "Of these events from somewhere, O Muse, daughter of Zeus,
> speak also to us." (Book 1, line 10).

Of what events? All of Odysseus's adventures, from boar-hunt to Trojan War to perilous trials and back home to reunion with Penelope. From where? From within the untextualized mythic reservoir of the oAgora. By whose agency? Under the aegis of the Muse, patroness of pathways and the OT internet. And to whom? Why, to Homer, to her beloved tribe of ancient singers and their audiences, and now, we hope, to future generations of Museum visitors.

Not So Willy-nilly

Textual predisposition

For many the oAgora and eAgora are venues for indeterminacy, "anything-goes" behavior, and even outright chaos. As media-technologies they seem to license undirected, scattershot activities, with surfers free to blaze their own individualized, unpredictable trails through a maze with far too many options.

Here's the often-cited problem in a nutshell: if performers or users can proceed just as they wish—lacking the one-way, exitless highway that predetermines our trek through linear texts—then how can we credit such an itinerary as valuable or valid? Couldn't they just as easily (and at every step) have chosen differently, whether in the arena of oral tradition (Arena of Oral Tradition) or the arena of the web (Arena of the Web)? Wouldn't told and retold stories "diverge," perhaps beyond recognition? Likewise, isn't the web experience inherently inaccurate as well as helplessly contingent? Doesn't faithful, logical communication inescapably fall victim to willy-nilly surfing?

Routes, not ruts

The very act of posing such questions reveals our hidden media bias. By crediting the fixity-based fiction of accuracy (Accuracy), we fail to recognize the creative and expressive advantages of contingency (Contingency). Understood on their own terms, OT and IT aren't inferior technologies at all; they're just different, with different advantages and disadvantages. Consisting not of artifacts but of systems that require active, cocreative navigation by users, OT and IT tap into the power of networked alternatives (Systems versus Things). Functionally, the pathways that characterize the oral marketplace and electronic marketplace must by their very nature remain open for exploration and thus unpredetermined. They do their job by fostering innovative thinking and communication, and that means denying the foreclosure of finality or epitome. In these two nontextual agoras experience is emergent, reality remains in play, and the arenas themselves are forever under construction (Reality Remains in Play).

But let's be careful here—open systems most certainly don't translate to "anything goes." Within the virtual universe of OT or IT, every node is linked to a limited number of other nodes. You are presented with multiple options, to be sure, but they're far from innumerable. More to the point, the finite array of choices actually restricts and focuses surfing activity (productively, one hopes), leading not to indeterminacy or chaos but rather to the flexible, rule-governed environment of variation within limits (Variation within Limits). In a sense, links between pathways serve as an index of idiomatic meaning in the oAgora and eAgora alike. Whether in oral tradition or on the Internet, you can't go just anywhere, can you? Just like language—only more so (Proverbs), these networked media provide a platform for idiomatic exchange, for creating and maintaining a patterned logic at the same time that they fully support ever-morphing reality. Pathways connect, but they don't fossilize.

First, imagine a storytelling event. . . . Every navigation depends on variables such as performer, audience, and the individual setting. Teller and listener(s) work their way through the story-network in tandem, with both sides reacting to the specificity of the moment against the much larger backdrop of linked alternatives. No two events can ever be "the same" in the sense that fixed texts are the same because that's not the way the OT medium works. In the oAgora rule-governed flexibility, variation within limits, and cocreation are the operative rules of the game.

Now imagine a web-surfing event. . . . Every navigation depends on variables such as web-designer, user, and the individual setting. User(s) work their way through the site-network, reacting to the specificity of the moment against the much larger backdrop of linked alternatives. No two events can ever be "the same" in the sense that fixed texts are the same because that's not the way the IT medium works. In the eAgora rule-governed flexibility, variation within limits, and cocreation are the operative rules of the game.

Escaping ideology

A forthright examination of the oral and electronic marketplaces yields a simple truth. It's only our ingrained tAgora prejudice (Ideology of the Text) that makes OT or IT surfing seem willy-nilly. If we can agree to set aside the demonstrable fallacy that portrays nontextual communication as flawed or second-rate, and if we can expand our single-medium model in favor of citizenship in multiple agoras (Citizenship in Multiple Agoras) and responsible agora-business (Responsible Agora-business), the picture will come clear. Navigable networks aren't texts, and they can't support textual communication. But they license equally valid and valuable—if fundamentally different—ways of creating and exchanging knowledge, art, and ideas. We need to grasp their inherent potential and surf them in search of new perspectives on human communication.

oAgora: Oral Networks to Surf

An agora is a verbal marketplace, a site for creation and exchange of knowledge, art, and ideas (Agora As Verbal Marketplace). The Pathways Project recognizes three agoras, or arenas for human communication (Three Agoras). This node is devoted to the OT arena, the oAgora.

The true currency of exchange in the oAgora is oWords (oWords)—spoken, heard, and embodied words. Not typographical prompts or even audio or video facsimiles, but an actual, voiced, in-context performance experienced at that moment and in that place by a present audience. You participate in the oral marketplace via face-to-face transaction, not by swapping texts. Everything happens "in the moment"—right now, not at some convenient future time to be chosen by a detached, independent reader and forestalled until the time seems right. The oAgora event is all-consuming for audience and performer alike because it is unmediated by texts, with nothing held at arm's length.

Agora-mirrors

Before proceeding any further, let's highlight a built-in structural comparison among the three nodes on principal media types: the oAgora, tAgora, and eAgora. From this point on—and across all three involved nodes—the section headings and organization will follow a mirroring logic. In other words, immediately below this paragraph you will find two sections entitled "Genus and species" and "Word-markets," followed by another with the subheading of either "Public, not proprietary" or "Proprietary, not public," depending on the agora in question. In fourth position you will encounter a brief discussion of "The evolutionary fallacy," and so on. The purpose of this organizational strategy is to help demonstrate the comparisons and contrasts (Disclaimer) that lie at the heart of the Pathways Project. For a complete list of the inter-agora parallels, visit Agora correspondences (Agora Correspondences).

Genus and species

Early investigations of the oAgora assumed a binary model, with literature on one side and oral tradition (OT) on the other. This exclusive taxonomy helped to make a place for studying communications that didn't use the default technology of the tAgora, but it grossly oversimplified the media involved. As studies in oral tradition expanded, and especially with the advent of widespread fieldwork in living cultures, investigators came to realize that their models needed to reflect the remarkable human complexity of verbal technologies.

Within the OT genus, then, we now discern many different and fascinating species or types of oral tradition. Suffice it to say for now that this host of species varies by genre, social function, performers, sites (both physical and virtual), and modes of interaction with the textual world. Some of these interactions are counterintuitive (Excavating an Epic) for tAgora citizens, and comparative research has established that OTs show enormous variety around the world and from ancient times to the present. The watchword for species within the genus OT must always be diversity.

Word-markets

Consider the wealth of different word-markets in which oral poets ply their trade, whether performers of Central Asian epic, Basque contest poetry, South African praise-poetry, Serbian magical charms, or North American slam poetry—all of which are discussed later—or some other oral tradition. There's no possibility of, or need for, copyrighting what they do. Why? Because of all forms of verbal art, oral tradition is the most firmly and naturally rooted in the public domain. And those roots are both nourishing for each immediate event and necessary for the continuing survival of OT as a whole.

Public, not proprietary

Subject to specific cultural constraints, OTs can be performed by multiple people without fear of violating any laws governing exchange in what amounts to an open-source marketplace. Those rules may limit eligibility by gender, age, kinship, status, or calendar, for example, but no individual ever "authors" a tradition, any more than a single individual ever authors a language. Nor can any one person ever deliver the final, canonical, "best" performance until texts enter the picture and make such a dead-end concept of verbal art imaginable and feasible. Such a monolith simply isn't either imaginable or feasible within the oAgora. Once the economy of the tAgora is fully in place, however, public gives way to proprietary, open-access gives way to object-exchange, and traditions stop being traditions.

The evolutionary fallacy

With the variant dynamics of the oral, textual, and Internet arenas in mind, it's easy to see why "oral evolves to written" and "written evolves to electronic" are fallacies traceable to the ideology of the text (Ideology of the Text). If we model our understanding of all verbal commerce on a singular creation attributed to a singular author and consumed by a singular audience (one-by-one), then the necessarily plural identity of performer(s), OTs, and audience(s) will appear primitive and underdeveloped. Likewise, we'll fail to understand and credit the plural identity of web architects and surfers with their shared but diverse experiences in the eAgora.

A web

In either case, nonwritten, nontextualized communication will seem to lack something, to fail to measure up according to our ideologically imposed criteria. After all, until recently collectors of OTs have unquestioningly subscribed to an implicit rank-ordering by converting the living webs that support oral traditions into freestanding objects suitable for display in the Museum of Verbal Art (Museum of Verbal Art). And how many times each day do you hear or read about people bemoaning the informality and impermanence of the web? They too undergo a kind of media-specific culture shock (Culture Shock) and feel compelled to "diss" whatever isn't text.

But of course it's not just a matter of one situation—one agora—evolving progressively and inevitably toward another. Each arena operates according to its own idiosyncratic economy. The oAgora uses a different currency of exchange than the tAgora—embodied versus entexted words, oWords versus tWords. And the eAgora uses eWords (eWords), similar in many ways to oWords and far removed from tWords. The eAgora sponsors code—like URLs and HTML—that depends for its power and efficacy on its performative nature; eCode actually causes something to happen, and does so recurrently, not repetitively (Recur Not Repeat). None of the three currencies is inherently better, more valuable, or more advanced than the other two. Each is simply the coin of its particular realm.

This is not to claim that any arena is entirely homogeneous. Nor is it to contend that they never interact, or that hybrid agoras can't form; they do and they can, in fascinating ways. But it is a fatal mistake to posit a one-way developmental trajectory, to view verbal technology as working its way inexorably from a text-deprived Dark Age toward a thoroughly evolved and fully textual us, and on the way to a (fascinating though feared) virtuality. We need to resist the ideo-

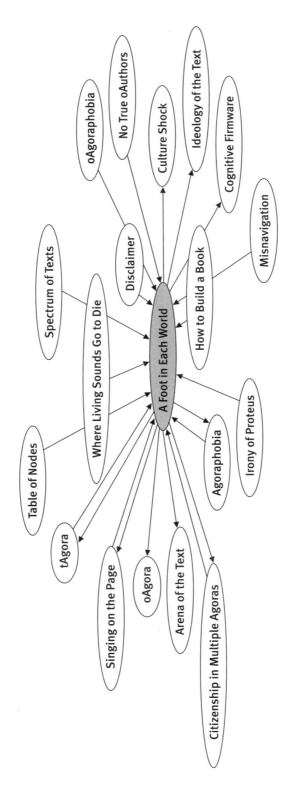

A web. Webpage by the author and Mark Jarvis.

logically driven assumption that limits our imagination and citizenship to the textual arena (Citizenship in Multiple Agoras).

Five OT word-markets

Let's start by visiting five modern oAgoras to investigate who "shops" there (both performers and audiences) and how their economies work, at least in general terms. For this purpose I've chosen an Asian, an African, a North American, and two quite disparate European word-markets, with the varieties of verbal art ranging from epic to praise to contest to magic to social protest. These examples are intentionally highly diverse, engaging different geographical areas, ethnic contexts, performance styles, and cultural functions. But they also have something vital in common: they depend upon several key features of all oAgoras—continuity, emergence, rule-governed morphing (Variation within Limits), roots in the public domain (In the Public Domain), and pathway-navigation.

Central Asian epic   The stories and story-cycles of Turkic oral epic stretch across a huge area of central Asia, and can be traced back to before the fourteenth century. Some of the principal "owners" of the epics are the Uzbek, Karakalpak, Kazakh, and Kirghiz peoples, who collectively range over large sections of Afghanistan, Uzbekistan, Turkestan, and northwestern China. When we add that many of these same heroic tales are told in Mongolian, Tibetan, and Tuzu languages unrelated to the Turkic tongues, it becomes clear that the oAgora for this tradition of oral epic is enormous and multidimensional geographically, linguistically, and chronologically. Singers, variously named in various areas, must have numbered in the thousands, each with scores of audiences over time. Within this complex and multifaceted scenario we will search in vain for individual authors and authoritative works. We will find multiple performers telling and retelling tales involving Gesar, Janggar, and other heroes by surfing the web of story shared throughout this oAgora. We'll find performers and audiences enmeshed in a continuous process of re-creation, navigating the linked pathways of their story-net.

No strategy for fixation and copyright—the core, defining activities of the tAgora—could ever begin to capture and protect even a fraction of the ever-morphing wealth of Turkic oral epic. Nor could such book-intensive strategies serve any purpose within the oAgora, since they work against the continuity typical of (and necessary to) OT by transforming living pathways into lifeless objects. While text-objects may constitute the official medium of exchange in the tAgora, they are nonnegotiable in the oAgora.

Basque contest poetry   This genre of improvised verbal sparring, called *bertsolaritza*[83] by its practitioners and enthusiasts, permeates Basque society at all levels. Communities sponsor after-dinner duels between hired *bertsolari*, and local and regional competitions lead to a national event that culminates

Basque Oral Poetry Championship, 2006. Permission from Nere Erkiaga Laka of Bertsozale Elkartea.

in an overall championship[84] every four years. In all cases a competitor must extemporaneously perform a short poem on an assigned but unpreviewed topic, using a particular traditional rhyme-scheme, melody, and verse-form, and his or her opponent must then counter with an immediate rebuttal composed within the same set of structural conditions. While each poem is unique and unprecedented, each one is also embedded in the web of *bersolaritza* tradition that is owned not by an individual singer or even a designated group of singers, but by the Basque community as a whole. In actual performance, audiences often sing the last few lines (of this original, never-before-heard poem) in unison with the *bertsolari*, a practice made possible by their fluency in the specialized poetic language and coapplication of the compositional rules. As the rhymes, music, and verse-form converge toward an inevitable climax, the audience joins the extemporizing poet in mutual performance. Collectively, the Basque people as an ethnic group support this contest poetry through an organization called Bertsozale Elkartea.[85]

South African praise-poetry   In earlier years Xhosa and Zulu praise-poetry served as an oral résumé for chiefs, a way to "document" and "publish" credentials and reputation via the oral traditional network. Composed for individual chiefs and based on well-defined rules for versification and performance, these poems celebrated the accomplishments and lineage of the tribal leader.

In more recent times praise-poetry, which always could be used to criticize as well as praise the figures in question, has been employed as a vehicle for social and political commentary, both positive and negative. One of the most famous positive uses is the many "praises" of Nelson Mandela[86] on his emergence from long-term imprisonment.

Serbian magical charms   In a Serbian village, medical treatments for skin disease and various other maladies take the form of incantations whispered by *bajalice*, or conjurers. As specialists in healing, these women learn their traditional remedies before the onset of puberty but don't actually perform them until their fertile years are concluded. Charms are considered part of the bride's dowry, and are passed from grandmother to granddaughter as a living inheritance, joint property of the natal extended family from which a woman derives and the affinal extended family into which her descendants will be born. The audience for these healing performances is the single patient, into whose ear the conjurer speaks the spell, even though the treatment may well take place quite publicly, with other people well within earshot.

In order to study and analyze Serbian magical charms, collectively known as *bajanje* in the local idiom, our fieldwork team quite naturally sought to record multiple performances on audio tape. Especially because this highly focused genre employs an often arcane vocabulary, with numerous archaisms and other rare forms not found in everyday language, and also because it is spoken so rapidly and *sotto voce*, we needed recordings that we could play again and again as we struggled to transcribe, translate, and understand the nuances of *bajanje*. We had already sought and received permission to make audio recordings of performances of other oral genres in the same village, so we anticipated no objections.

But objections there most certainly were, right from the moment we brought out the audio equipment, providing us with an instance of how a generally open-access medium can be culturally restricted. Our initial explanation—that we were studying the charms "kao poezija" (as poetry)—did little or nothing to dispel peoples' fears. It soon became apparent that our proposed text-making activities threatened to disrupt the traditional ecology of *bajanje*. By creating what amounted to objects that could be circulated outside their prescribed ritual environment in an unlicensed fashion, we were threatening to extend knowledge of the precious remedies beyond their "owners." In other words, a charm that constituted a valuable asset in one woman's dowry (and for which she had established a village clientele who recognized and paid for her particular expertise) might become another woman's property as well, to do with as she pleased. What we regarded as harmless recordings for research purposes ran the risk of collapsing "proprietary" distinctions among women who practiced individual specialties within a common, shared tradition. Far from being an advance or an evolutionary next step, texts were potentially a uniquely destructive medium, a short circuit that practitioners of these healing remedies wanted very much to avoid.

The solution? Effectively, to install another living node in the web of oral transmission, but one that would pose no danger to the overall charm ecology, and to entrust the charms to her safekeeping. For this purpose Barbara Kerewsky Halpern, mother of two teenage (and, strictly speaking, marriageable) daughters, was designated an honorary *baba* (grandmother) and identified as the recipient of the *bajanje*. By age and status she was deemed eligible to practice the healing arts, but as a Western anthropologist rather than a village *baba* she of course would never do so. Once this "dead-end" node was in place, and after pledging not to play the audio recordings for anyone in the village or the tradition at large, we were cleared to textualize the performances—for our non-proliferating, outside-the-circuit use only. From the perspective of the charm tradition as a village intranet, I presented no threat whatsoever to the process; as a male, I was automatically segregated by gender outside the set of pathways that constituted the tradition, and so I was allowed to be present at the various performances in order to run the tape recorder. What really mattered was maintaining control of the pathways among those who could participate, and this in turn meant keeping texts out of the loop. Overall, we learned a valuable lesson about how texts—our default medium in the tAgora—could present a dangerous threat to oAgora dynamics.

North American slam poetry   Step into a café in any large or medium-sized North American city, especially on a weekend night, and chances are you'll encounter an increasingly popular oral tradition known as slam poetry. Often a vehicle for social commentary or protest, this tradition arose in the mid-1980s in Chicago and has quickly evolved into a popular, well-attended activity with local, regional, and national levels of competition. In its purest form, slam lives solely for performance: although poets compose their verse in writing, they do so strictly for live presentation, ignoring or even discarding the script after the poem is initially committed to memory. A text has no status or function in this oAgora, and as a result the poetic performance morphs naturally over time. According to the rules for both individual and team contests, the scores awarded by judges allot 50 percent to the poem and 50 percent to its performance. In practice, the two are indistinguishable.

In any given competition the oAgora for slam can involve either individual competitors or teams, supported by highly engaged audiences who also play a significant role in their word-market transactions. Guidelines prohibit the use of scripts or props, as well as set time limits on each performance. Although experienced experts evaluate the results at the level of the national championship, the customary local arrangement is to select as judges people who are new to slam—in order, as it was explained to me, to keep this activity a "people's poetry." Audiences enthusiastically enter the fray both during and immediately after each performance, shouting their approval or disdain in the hope of influencing the scores awarded to their favorites. Except at the national level, the prizes are usually nominal: $25 to the winner, for example. As Allan Wolf famously put it, "The points are not the point, the point is poetry."

No real authors

Authors—in our modern and highly ideological sense of the term as *individual creators of original, unique, objectifiable, and usually published works*—simply don't exist in the oAgora (Distributed Authorship). And if authors as such don't exist, then the burden of "protecting the work" can't fall to them. Most fundamentally, there's usually nothing to protect, because the story or lyric or eulogy or charm usually doesn't belong exclusively and forever to any single individual. It can't be owned in the way a freestanding text-object can be owned, and therefore can't be used or transferred under carefully written and implemented guidelines. In most cases there's nothing to prevent another person, sooner or later, here or somewhere else, from performing the "same" work, although the next performer will inevitably make changes in the "original" (which of course wasn't really an original in the first place). Even when a performer creates and re-creates a singular work (as with slam poets), each transaction in the word-market—always involving a different audience, time, place, and set of conditions—is but one transitory instance of an ever-evolving process. Culture gets continuously mashed up and remixed in the oAgora (Remix).

Five nonauthors

The five word-markets mentioned above are alive and bristling with poetry, but they all lack what we would call "authors." Consider the dynamics of each OT arena (Arena of Oral Tradition). With their stories strung out across enormous geographical tracts and throughout both Turkic- and Mongolian-speaking populations, central Asian epic singers can hardly be classified as authors in our sense of the term. Basque *bertsolari* likewise depend on and draw from a tradition, creating unique poems by performing within the designated rules that govern their oAgora. The situation is extremely similar with South African praise-poets, both Xhosa and Zulu, who construct personalized poetic résumés by working within a traditional matrix; the ability of this kind of poetry to morph is well illustrated by its application to political leaders for both praise and criticism. And though a degree of ownership does enter the picture with Serbian *bajalice*, they all intone their healing charms using the octosyllabic, rhyming language of their shared genre. Even slam poets, who start by composing their verses on paper or a computer display, do so only in order to ready themselves to perform it. They typically do not seek publication, since their poems are meant specifically and strictly for the oAgora of live performance. Strange as it may seem, there are no true authors anywhere to be found in the oAgora.

oAgora sharing and reuse

It's primarily an issue for the eAgora, but we might pause for just a moment to weigh some alternatives to conventional copyright (aka Big C), which as we've seen can't apply to the itemless word-markets of oral tradition. But maybe another kind of "little c" copyright might apply to the oAgora. Let's briefly consider two of the licenses offered by the Creative Commons website[87]—the most and the least restrictive of the six contracts—with a view toward determining whether either of them could help in governing performance and exchange of oral traditions.

The most restrictive The "Attribution, Non-Commercial, No Derivatives" license stands at the conservative end of the Creative Commons spectrum, that is, closest to the ideologically driven concept of Big C copyright that governs the tAgora. This contract "allows others to download your works and share them with others as long as they mention you and link back to you, but they can't change them in any way or use them commercially." Of course, since transactions in the oAgora don't involve authors or static, finite works—not to mention tAgora definitions and rules—this license can have no utility for oral tradition.

The most open At the other end of the spectrum lies the simple "Attribution" license, which "lets others distribute, remix, tweak, and build upon your work, even commercially, as long as they credit you for the original creation." This one sounds like a perfect fit for the business of our oral word-market until we get to the final clause calling for acknowledgment of an *original* work by, we must suppose, an *original creator*. In other words, even the most liberal license offered by Creative Commons, an institution dedicated to enabling the remixing of culture, assumes a fixed, finite object eligible for sharing and remaking. Although this least inhibiting of licenses speaks cogently to the realities of distribution, remixing, tweaking, and building upon as we encounter them within the oAgora, it still doesn't recognize the radical morphing and objectlessness of OT. The ideology of the text—whether a book, a musical score, a painting, a film, or whatever—dies hard.

Variation within limits

It's counterintuitive for us, but continuous morphing in the oAgora doesn't lead to anarchy (Responsible Agora-business). Things don't fall apart, primarily because there aren't any "things" in the first place. OT in fact draws its strength from variation within limits, from its rule-governed ability to change systemically—just like language itself, only more so (Proverbs). Performers always have a choice; they can select from viable, systemically arrayed options. They can follow multiple different pathways (Not So Willy-nilly) in realizing their emergent performances, which will not be photocopies or diskcopies of yesterday's or last year's or any other "edition." They may choose one route today, another similar but nonidentical route next week, and so forth, depending on factors such as their own state of mind, the nature of the audience, and the particulars of the occasion. Motion never freezes into stasis, the journey of discovery never devolves into the closed circuit of a daily commute, pathways never become ruts.

Variation within Homer   We know the *Iliad* and *Odyssey* only through manuscripts from the ancient world. Nonetheless, even these silent, static remains show evidence of the systematic remixing typical of verbal art in the oAgora. We can describe three kinds of recurrent patterning in these oral-derived poems.

At the level of poetic lines, traditional *formulas* provide pathways within the network of Homeric epic language. For example, such predicates as "Then [he/she] answered him/her" combine with a broad array of subjects, such as "much-suffering divine Odysseus," "grey-eyed goddess Athena," and numerous other stock names, in order to produce a large array of introductions to speeches. There is variation, to be sure, but it's limited—and that double-edged dynamic makes the remixing strategy useful, effective, and evocative, not willy-nilly, overdetermined, or clichéd.

Likewise, *typical scenes*, such as the frequent ritual of the Homeric feast, operate by meshing individual, situation-specific details with a recurrent series of actions, that is, by placing unique moments in a larger, resonant (because traditional) context. The systematic nature of these recurrent scenes provides a recognizable frame of reference even as unprecedented developments occur within them. Thus the aberrant behavior of the usurping suitors at the opening of the *Odyssey* stands in stark contrast to the standard, expected series of feasting details, and the composite portrayal gains depth from the powerful juxtaposition of disorder and order. Once again, the traditional is creatively remixed.

Finally, the *Odyssey* as a whole is but one version of what may be the oldest and most widespread *story-pattern* in the world, distributed as it is from Ireland to India and Pakistan and witnessed from ancient times to the present day in many hundreds of examples. The gist of the tale involves a hero summoned away to war just before or after his wedding (or the birth of his first child) and forcibly detained in foreign lands for many years. After a series of life-threatening adventures he returns in disguise to find his wife or fiancée besieged by suitors.

He then defeats his rivals, tests the loyalty of his family and servants, discovers his mate's fidelity or treachery, and either reassumes his place (if she is faithful) or starts another adventure (if she is not). The identity of the hero and heroine change, along with geographical and cultural particulars, but the tale-type remains recognizably the same, varying within limits. The return pattern, a highly generative story-system, simply gets remixed.

The analogy to language

Think about living, spoken language—continuously mixed and remixed—rather than its reduction to the page. We don't resort each and every day to one of a limited number of fixed monologues or conversations, do we? Even similar pronouncements or exchanges on identical topics involve innumerable choices and adaptations, made in the moment and outside the scope of any fossilized, predetermined scheme. We depend on our human ability to generate rule-governed communication, we vary our speech-acts within limits, we suit our discourse to different situations. OT does the same.

A basic proverb   Consider this homemade proverb: "Oral tradition works like language, only more so." OT is anything but objectified and static. It morphs according to rules that provide guidance and stability, but which also promote—to different degrees depending upon the particular genre—creativity and individual realization. In that regard, OT is simply a special case of language.

But how about the "more so"? Everyday language is necessarily *broad-spectrum*; general conversational language, for example, supports a great many interactions, with optional adjustments for your relationship with your addressee or for the physical site of the exchange, the time of day, the weather, and so on. But OTs require more rules. Superimposed on the broad-spectrum language are additional rules that identify the communication as a particular kind of speech-act—perhaps there's a melody, for instance, or a rhyming constraint or a particular rhythm. OT languages are *narrow-spectrum* tools; they serve fewer functions, but they fulfill those fewer functions much more economically than could general languages.

This built-in focus in turn means that OT languages are more densely idiomatic, with designated parts standing for much larger and more complex wholes. Thus Homer's phrase "green fear" carries the connotation of a fear that has its origins in a supernatural source. Similarly, the South Slavic poets' idiom "black cuckoo" takes on the traditional sense of a woman who has been widowed or is about to be widowed. Neither of these specialized meanings is reported in any dictionary or lexicon, since such textual resources gloss the broader-spectrum language of texts; they are formulated to serve the purposes of the tAgora. The oWords (oWords) employed as currency in the oAgora operate under an enhanced set of rules and carry with them an enhanced idiomatic value. Like the eWords that we discuss in relation to the eAgora, they "work like language, only more so."

Recurrence, not repetition

What does it mean to say that something repeats? The scenario is familiar enough: a discrete and itemlike event happens once, then it happens again, and so forth. A best-selling novel, for instance, may be published one year and reprinted the next, so that the title repeats on the bookstore or library shelf. Or consider a poetic refrain that appears at the end of every stanza, so that each iteration echoes those that precede it. Or the chorus to a song, which will dependably repeat after each verse. All of these cases are clearly repetitive because subsequent occurrences derive their meaning primarily from earlier ones within a finite, limited context. The chain of meaning is linear and contained, deriving from direct correspondences from one item to the next.

But that isn't the way OT works. OT actively depends on *recurrence* (Recur Not Repeat) rather than serial repetition. It operates via idiomatic responses that follow networked pathways. Consider two simple analogues. Perhaps you're a college student and you make a habit of greeting your friends with a wave of the hand and a ritualistic phrase like "What's up?" You react in this way regularly, every time you pass any of your friends on the street. Or perhaps you're a Navy airman and your daily routine involves saluting a succession of officers, using exactly the same motion on every occasion. But in neither case are you really *repeating* the greeting; instead, you're resorting to an approved, idiomatic signal that indexes your encounter and relationship. You're following an established pathway, using a *recurrent* action to accomplish your purpose.

To illustrate the nature of recurrence in the oAgora, here are two kinds of examples from South Slavic oral epic: recurrent beginnings and recurrent performances.

Recurrent beginnings   Epic singers within this OT start their performances in one of two ways—either with or without a prologue (called a *pripjev*). If they opt to use a *pripjev*, the first few lines of the song might go something like this:

> Ej! Where we sit, let us make merry!
> Let us make merry and have conversation!
> Let us sing a little song of times long past;
> Long ago it was and now we are remembering.

What this short introduction does is to set the stage, to establish the performance arena, to admit performer and audience to the oAgora. It doesn't prescribe the specifics of the story to follow, and in fact any epic tale can then ensue, regardless of story-pattern, characters, action, or whatever. In their overall function such prologues resemble the "Once upon a time" of Grimm brothers' fairytales, recurrent but nonspecific cues that a story is beginning. Prologues are first-step pathways that get things started in an idiomatic way.

The epic singer, or *guslar*, may also choose not to use a *pripjev*, and to plunge directly into the story (usually after an instrumental prelude to signal the performance arena). If this is the case, he has the option of following a broad, multipurpose pathway or a focused, single-purpose pathway. For example, many performances begin with a line such as "Mujo of Kladusha was drinking wine," which can signal a wide variety of story-types, involving weddings, sieges of cities, or other subjects. But if the oral poet starts his performance with the phrase "[Someone] was crying out" (*Pocmilije*), there can be only one result: a Return Song. That is, if the *guslar* sings "Pocmilije X," where X names any of the dozens of heroes in the Moslem tradition of the South Slavs, he is alerting the audience to expect an *Odyssey*-type story about that hero. Of course, they cannot know in advance how the specifics of the narrative will unfold, or even whether the hero's mate will prove faithful or treacherous, but that brief idiomatic phrase unmistakably marks a pathway toward a single generic story-pattern. And it does so not because it repeats (in this performance or any other), but because it recurs.

Recurrent performances Just so with entire performances. Each version of a South Slavic epic tale is equally "the work"; no one of them repeats any other, or depends for its meaning on any particular prior rendition. A *guslar* may perform "The Captivity of Alagić Alija" on a Tuesday, for example, then again later that week and again two weeks later—all without repeating himself. How is that possible? Because these performances are not first, second, and third editions of a book, nor do they constitute a draft followed by a series of revisions. Each of these epic songs is a individual realization of the story, a singular navigation (Misnavigation) of the multidimensional pathways that—as a composite song-web—collectively make up the story-system. The epic tale doesn't repeat; it recurs.

Built-in "copyright"

It will seem counterintuitive to us at first, but oral traditions are powerful precisely because they can't be fixed, precisely because they morph while recurring. Because it isn't predetermined and remains open to innovation that is idiomatically driven and forever under construction, the Internet also harnesses the cumulative energy and contributions typical of distributed rather than single authorship. Unless or until they get textualized (Freezing Wikipedia), OTs never weaken into finite, fossilized, and therefore discardable items.

What's more, and again it will initially seem contradictory, the nonfixity of the oAgora guarantees a built-in kind of "copyright protection" for artistic activity by setting limits on variation. Rule-governed flexibility is of course the engine of recurrence and continuity, but too radical a departure from the implicit rules will turn an intelligible performance into gibberish. Fluent performance requires both an inherent grasp of those limits and an ability to fashion a here-and-now, true-to-the-place-and-moment creation. Otherwise audiences will complain or simply stop attending, and performers (or at least their performances) will be marginalized (Audience Critique).

Survival of the fittest

To put it another way, the self-sufficient ecology of oral tradition will naturally select which performers and performances are to be understood as viable. No single member of that ecosystem will be able to claim—or have any need to claim—that he or she "owns" a particular work, at least in our default textual sense (Owning versus Sharing). If it's not recognized as a tangible item, you can't own it. And if you can't own it, you can't restrict its use. There's nothing (no thing) to restrict.

In the OT arena, strength and continuity reside not in stasis but in ongoingness, not in fixity but in rule-governed flexibility. The oAgora is a word-market for living, embodied, systematic communication.

The oAgora works via pathways.

Online with OT

OT and IT don't provide us with things; instead, they offer us pathways.

Let's start with Corey Doctorow's neat, succinct contrast between old and new media, taken from a talk on digital rights management[88] he gave to Microsoft's Research Group as early as June 17, 2004: "New media don't succeed because they're like the old media, only better: they succeed because they're worse than the old media at the stuff the old media are good at, and better at the stuff the old media are bad at."

In other words, success derives from doing what each medium is meant to support. It's not about competing media; it's about using the right tool for the job. As Doctorow goes on to explain how conventional paper books and eBooks contrast in their goals and delivery systems, it's hard or impossible to disagree with his "different agendas" dichotomy.

Different tools for different jobs. Different tools for different agoras.

Disjunction between media

In fact, we can extend his argument a step further by noting that the once-new medium of page and book originally succeeded for precisely the same reason:

disjunction between media. The tAgora innovation offered a better way to accomplish certain tasks (emphatically not *all* tasks) than did oAgora strategies. Separate vehicles, separate agendas—at least in the most straightforward cases.

And how does that separate-but-equal arrangement work? Well, the page was (and remains) unarguably "worse" than oral tradition for transacting oAgora business, but far "better" at accomplishing the program of the tAgora. As emphasized and illustrated throughout the Pathways Project, we won't ever be able to compress the living reality of OT into even the most elaborately configured book. They're simply different animals—or rather one is a living animal and the other a taxidermist's museum-ready reduction of the now-dead beast (Museum of Verbal Art).

And what does the page have to offer? What can it do for us that OT can't manage? History, partnered by the ideology of the text, teaches that the cognitive prosthesis of texts can freeze (or appear to freeze) performances into conveniently spatialized items that can then be copied, stored, transported, and consulted at leisure (Ideology of the Text). Simply put, the book converts online OT surfers into offline text-consumers (Freezing Wikipedia). So not only does Doctorow's theorem apply to the book versus IT disjunction, then; it also accurately characterizes the role-segregation of OT versus the book.

OT and IT versus the book

On the surface it may seem as simple as two negatives yielding a positive match—OT and IT resembling one another because of their contrast to the book. In terms of core dynamics, however, the fundamental similarity between OT and IT (and their difference from the book) stems from their shared, trademark activity of navigating pathways.

As we observe, the oAgora and eAgora actually have a lot in common, all superficial appearances to the contrary. Both technologies thrive on morphing, on variation within limits (Variation within Limits), on open sharing among a broad-based community; and they both lack the concept of the freestanding, complete-in-itself item that's at the very heart of the book-and-page medium. OT and IT don't provide us with things; instead, they offer us a system of pathways (Systems versus Things).

Books are offline, OT and IT are online

Or, to reframe the relationship in a version of Doctorow's helpful theorem, *OT and IT are worse at the stuff books are good at, and better at the stuff books are bad at.* Furthermore, they succeed because they're good at the same stuff—namely, promoting interactive, alternative experiences (Reading Backwards) via a network of options. It's in this sense that books are offline, while both OT and IT are online.

Media recursiveness

On the face of it, then, we're confronted with a rather striking phenomenon of media recursiveness. OT contrasts diametrically with the book, which in turn contrasts with IT—making OT and IT similar to each other and distinct from texts (Agora Correspondences). Could it be that with the Internet we're returning to a way of representing and communicating that is more fundamental than the default medium of the book and page? Could it be that we're casting off what some philosophers have called "logocentrism" (a fixation on the myth of objectivity) and exposing the ideology that supports the tAgora (Illusion of Object)? Could we be returning to the kind of medium that mirrors the contingent nature of reality (Contingency) even as it mimes the way we think?

After so many centuries of offline activity, are we now getting back online?

oPathways

The idea of pathways

Pathways sport a double identity: individually, they lead from one node to another; but corporately, they constitute an interactive network with innumerable built-in possibilities. The idea and term stem from the oAgora, the arena in which Homer describes the qualities that an ancient Greek oral epic singer must possess in order to be a successful bard (Arena of Oral Tradition). Here's a hint: he doesn't mention a loud and clear voice, a fine memory, or a large repertoire:

> For among all mortal men the singers have a share in honor
> and reverence, since to them the Muse has taught the **pathways,**
> for she loves the singers' tribe. (*Odyssey*, Book 8, lines 479–81)

What the Muse teaches,[89] in other words, is the ability to navigate the web of OT, to surf through the shared riches of the story-hoard and shape a performance that is intelligible to and enjoyable for performer and audience alike. What the Muse imparts is knowledge of system or process, not of things or products (Systems versus Things). She teaches not "what," but rather "how to get there."

What do oPathways support?

Individual oPathways route an oral performance from one point to another as the surfer/cocreator initiates the event, generates a constellation of linked options, chooses one of those options and generates another set, and so forth. Watch the Pathways Project animated logo at the top of every node of the website and you'll see how options lead to more options. Stories or other oral traditions will follow roughly construed linkmaps (Linkmaps), with alternatives available at every node in the network. At every node in the network, there will always be multiple opportunities for cocreation: light or heavy development of characters, lengthy or brief descriptions, detours (Misnavigation) from the principal story line, and different kinds and levels of response to the partnering audience.

This flexibility and generativity—rather than the twin illusions of object (Illusion of Object) and stasis (Illusion of Stasis) at the heart of the tAgora—are the lifeblood of communication in the oAgora. And everything is accomplished by leveraging a system of linked oPathways and a vocabulary of oWords (oWords).

South Slavic oral epic singers, or *guslari*, provide us undeniable evidence of this dynamic of variation within limits (Variation within Limits) when they express puzzlement over fieldworkers' identification of songs by titles. OT-fluent citizens don't conceive of their performances by attaching labels suitable for fixed, brick-and-mortar products. Instead, they think in terms of sequences of pathways that reveal the oAgora communication as a kinetic, emergent, in-the-making process. It's a matter of cognitive predispositions. An item like "The Wedding of Bećirbey" meant little or nothing to them, whereas linked oPathways such as "When General Pero kidnapped Fatima, and Mustajbey of the Lika raised an army, and Tale of Orašac arrived, and they all journeyed to Zadar in order to rescue her, and she married her fiancé Bećirbey" speak in pathway-language, indicating what amounts to a sequence of clicks. It's simply a matter of how the oAgora mindset works.

Homology and difference

Pathways are the essence of the oAgora and eAgora, where surfing through networks of multiple possibilities is the core process that underlies all communication. Even though it will seem counterintuitive to readers of fixed, warehouse-able items, constellations of oPathways and ePathways (ePathways) boast a dynamic strength and diversity of expression and reception that texts cannot match. The tAgora, which depends on an ideological commitment to spatialization and storage of knowledge, art, and ideas as inert things (Ideology of the Text), is for that very reason pathwayless (Impossibility of tPathways).

oPathways work for the same reason that oral traditions work—because they actively support morphing and insure that reality remains in play (Reality Remains in Play).

Owning versus Sharing

What does it mean to *own* something? How do we come into possession of an item or idea, and what are the rules for *sharing* it with others? There's probably no hotter issue in today's digital, Internet-enabled world, and yet it's also an issue that has deep roots in the long history and prehistory of media (Homo Sapiens' Calendar Year).

An analogy to IT

Consider a hypothetical parallel. Imagine a time and place where and when there is no such thing as copyright—either "Big C," Creative Commons licenses, or any other such arrangement. And the reason such instruments wouldn't and couldn't exist is that the very concept of ownership of ideas, performances, and works of verbal and musical art didn't exist. Embroiled in a litigious society where patents and copyrights and intellectual property seem more and more the topics of everyday conversation, we might well find such an imagined time and place almost unfathomable. It just doesn't seem realistic.

But in fact this is far from a fantasy (Agora Correspondences). The oAgora, the verbal marketplace in which oral traditions have long flourished, was and is just such a place (Disclaimer). According to the basic dynamics of exchange, OT is most fundamentally an open-source phenomenon. It circulates widely and freely, with the only universally observed constraints being the capacity to perform and the ability to enlist an audience with a corresponding capacity to participate. (Of course, particular cultures may impose other constraints, such as the gender or age of the teller, the season during which a story may be told, and so forth, but these are localized rules and have little or nothing to do with the nature of OT as a shared event.) It's a matter of getting online in the oAgora (Online with OT).

The impossibility of oOwnership

In other words, people can't "own" OTs any more than they can individually and exclusively own the everyday languages they speak. Notwithstanding the long-established policy of the famed Académie Française,[90] no single person or group can absolutely prescribe or determine language use, which will always remain a rule-governed free-for-all that operates via natural selection. Likewise, no single person or group can prescribe or determine the precise content and trajectory of an oral tradition, which lives not by fossilization but by varying within limits.

OTs that function without support from text-based media show that this kind of open sharing—as opposed to our default tAgora concept of owning—isn't just grudgingly or tacitly permitted. The world of the oAgora isn't crippled by "primitive technology" or by "missing something." It doesn't have a monumental media handicap to overcome. To put it most directly, sharing is not in any sense a liability or weakness; on the contrary, it's absolutely the lifeblood of the continuing tradition. Unless OTs are free to flow across a culture without hindrance from a centralized authority, the tradition will simply die. The tradition belongs to the people who make and remake it, who navigate its pathways together. The performer and the audience engage in a collective enterprise that simply has no room for our brand of ownership.

Ownership is a tAgora-based illusion

So where does that meddling centralized authority come from? First and most basically, it's resident in the ideology of, for example, the work of verbal or musical art as a thing, a commodity, an objectified item that is subject to ownership and therefore to oversight and control (Ideology of the Text). Second, that kind of authority can emerge only with the conversion of an idea or work to textualized form (and here we include texts of audio and video recordings as well as the book and page). This transformation operates under the radar, as it were, via an unexamined, unacknowledged alchemy. Once made tangible by transfer to the book or page, so goes the unstated assumption, the idea or work effectively *becomes* that book or page. This is just the same kind of (faulty but ideologically powerful) assumption we make when we decide that what appears—spatialized and dead—on the page is language itself, rather than a script for language. We're only too ready to create new exhibits for the Museum of Verbal Art (Museum of Verbal Art). Unfortunately, such exhibits are necessarily dead on arrival (Freezing Wikipedia).

And there's another step, along with an accompanying trapdoor. Contrary to what some claim, it's not simply the introduction of a writing system that makes the difference. Writing systems need the attendant tAgora technologies of cheap reproduction (easily available copies) as well as broad literacy and mass readership before centralized authority can emerge and the commodification of ideas and works of verbal or musical art can take place. Thus the medieval European arena, in which authorship was often inchoate, emergent, and distributed (Distributed Authorship). Medieval works were regularly created, copied, and translated without attribution and depended for their "publication" upon manuscripts and reading aloud in public forums. No cheap reproductions or mass readership there. Authors and consumers were set up for sharing, and so the advent of ownership and all that it brought with it was to prove gradual, even halting.

In retrospect, the shift appears cleaner and neater than it was. But once the idea-to-page conversion was accomplished and became the reflex action of modern Western culture, the way was clear for our default concepts of authorship, publication rights, protection of intellectual property, and other text-dependent forms of ownership (Accuracy) to take hold. We've chronically ignored the history and continuing importance of this evolution in pursuit of our own agenda, but the truth is that the open sharing that fuels oral tradition preceded and in many quarters exists alongside the agreed-upon illusion of legally defined owning. It's been our conventional practice to foster that illusion without examining its roots or, just as importantly, its consequences (Illusion of Object).

Present-day challenges

So perhaps it's not just serendipity that the hot-button issue of ownership of ideas and works of verbal and musical art is rising to the top of our cultural agenda right now. Perhaps it's no accident that it's happening just as another "thing-less," non–item-based medium begins to take firm hold. Once again we find ourselves traveling along pathways, this time in the eAgora rather than the oAgora, and once again the medium we're using exposes the notion of ownership as a convenient and powerful but finally baseless ideology. Navigating along pathways means movement in and out of digitized, morphing environments. It's forever kinetic, emerging, and incomplete. It makes sense by changing rather than remaining (supposedly) static.

So what's the upshot? The Internet and digitization have bluntly put the lie to our comfortable assumption that ideas and works of verbal or musical art can ever truly become immutable items, things, or commodities. If this exposure seems enervating to individuals, groups, and corporations, their discomfort doesn't stem from the new media. That culture shock (Culture Shock) or agoraphobia (Agoraphobia) is the result of modern Western culture's ideological commitment to what's always been a falsehood. Small wonder that post-Gutenberg societies are essentially alone in locating the idea and the work within the palpable reality of the document. Faced with this dilemma, which is truly of our own making, we should resist the urge to blame the media-messenger.

And how do we know for certain that this claim of ownership has always been a falsehood? Because for many millennia—long before writing systems of any kind arose—owning ideas and works of verbal and musical art just wasn't possible. Ownership was simply not a category. Sharing was the rule.

Sharing and open-source IT/OT

With this perspective in mind, let's pose the following topic for discussion. Could the open-source initiatives now threatening to displace commodified, proprietary software in some areas be another symptom of IT sharing? Is the open-source movement a manifestation of sharing inspired not by anticompetitive or counterculture forces but by the natural ecology of the eAgora? Put another way, is OT an open-source process? Can we in effect get online with OT?

oWords

oWords are the designated means of exchange in the oAgora, the default currency of the OT marketplace. More to the point, given the performative power of this special code, oWords are customarily the only currency that OT surfers hold and spend. On the other hand, given the control exerted by textual ideology in most aspects of our daily lives (Ideology of the Text), it can be difficult to imagine any medium other than tWords (tWords). Agoraphobia (Agoraphobia) is so powerful that it's hard even to conceive of a nontextual communicative unit for our verbal transactions (Culture Shock). But we need to reset our tAgora default and open ourselves up to other possibilities for words.

How are oWords defined? Instead of crafting a definition from outside the arena of oral tradition (Arena of Oral Tradition), let's hear from an actual OT practitioner, an experienced navigator of OT networks. In the following excerpt from a conversation about the performance of South Slavic oral epic, the non-literate poet (or *guslar*) Mujo Kukuruzović explains to his interviewer, Nikola Vujnović, the real nature of oWords versus tWords. The opening topic in their exchange is a poetic line that amounts to four dictionary words in the original language of the Former Yugoslavia. I leave the term *reč*, the conventional designation for "word," untranslated:

> NV: Let's consider this: "Mustajbey of the Lika was drinking wine." Is this a single *reč*?
>
> MK: Yes.
>
> NV: But how? It can't be *one*: "Mustajbey of-the-Lika was-drinking wine."
>
> MK: In writing it can't be one.
>
> NV: There are four *reči* here.
>
> MK: It can't be one in writing. But here, let's say we're at my house and I pick up the *gusle* [accompanying instrument]—"Mustajbey of the Lika was drinking wine"—that's a single *reč* on the *gusle* for me.
>
> NV: And the second *reč*?
>
> MK: And the second *reč*—"At Ribnik in a drinking tavern"—there.

Consider the facts. Mujo Kukuruzović couldn't write himself, but he nonetheless recognized the difference between oWords (in the original language each is a whole decasyllabic line in length) and tWords. He knows and appreciates the disparity in marketplace currencies (Citizenship in Multiple Agoras). Further on in this conversation and in similar interviews with other poets, it becomes apparent that there are two additional levels of *reč*, or units of utterance, in the oAgora of South Slavic oral epic: both scenes and even entire stories are understood as single "words."

Nor is this particular OT unique in that respect. The same notion of an oWord as an indivisible unit consisting of many tWords informs numerous oral traditions, including ancient Greek, Old English, Finnish, and Mongolian. And this cognitive discrepancy between oAgora and tAgora communication is significant and telling. To reduce an oWord to its component tWords is to fracture a meaning-bearing word into meaningless syllables, to segment an integral unit into gibberish. If (unlike the nonliterate but still media-savvy Kukuruzović) we fail to recognize this fundamental discrepancy, we will inevitably misconstrue the real expressive unit and thought-byte.

Within the OT arena, an environment consisting of and depending on oPathways (oPathways), oWords contribute crucially to surfing the web of oral tradition. You start up the process and enter the marketplace, and then choose the next pathway from among those available to you. That choice generates a new spectrum of options from which you make your next selection, and the process continues until you exit the oAgora. During that time you cocreate an experience that emerges as you go (Reality Remains in Play), and for that reason it will never be wholly predictable or repeatable (Recur Not Repeat). Navigating through networks, performers and audiences process a rule-governed and performative code. They find their way through a constellation of pathways constructed and used not by a single person but by a group (Distributed Authorship). Variation within limits (Variation within Limits), the stock-in-trade of oWords and eWords (eWords) but a dynamic inherently foreign to tWords, underlies all transactions in the oAgora.

oWords work for the same reason that oral traditions work—because they actively support morphing.

Polytaxis

Clive James and the rich chaos of experience

Here's how Clive James describes the "structure" of his influential 2007 book, *Cultural Amnesia*, a kind of example-driven inventory of humanity's brilliant and terrifying creativity. As he assembled his vast compendium over four decades, working from individual parts toward a provisional whole, James started to see that the conventional vehicles of historiography were inadequate to the task of conveying his vision (James 2007, xv):

> In the forty years it took me to write this book, I only gradually realized that the finished work, if it were going to be true to the pattern of my experience, would have no pattern. . . . There could only be a linear cluster of nodal points, working the way the mind—or at any rate my mind, such as it is—works as it moves through time: a trail of clarities variously illuminating a dark sea of unrelenting turbulence, like the phosphorescent wake of a phantom ship. Far from a single argument, there would be scores of arguments.

Thus reads the brief manifesto that serves as prologue to an alphabetized series of memorable cameos, starting with poet Anna Akhmatova and concluding with novelist and biographer Stefan Zweig, stopping along the way to visit with such diverse luminaries as Louis Armstrong, Adolf Hitler, Beatrix Potter, and Tacitus. It's a dramatis personae arrayed in a superficially tidy A–Z order, a nominal sequence that by its obvious insignificance encourages us to seek out alternate ways to understand (and to forge) links between and among them.

James's overall dynamic is thus counterschematic, to be sure, but hardly willy-nilly (Not So Willy-nilly). By casting aside formula-driven paradigms so common to the tAgora, he aims not to undo but instead to foster understanding, not to obscure reality but rather to more faithfully mirror the rich chaos that *actually is* the history of Western Homo sapiens (Homo Sapiens' Calendar Year). By refusing to impose a convenient but reductive pattern, he resists conventional principles of order in search of a new level of fidelity, a mode of representation less compromised by the operative rules and ideology of texts (Ideology of the Text).

In effect, and strikingly, James is pursuing some of the same methods and goals as the Pathways Project, although his subject is not the same. He speaks of nodal points, a lack of pattern, and scores of possible arguments. Most centrally, he describes his book as "working the way the mind . . . works"—parallel to the Project's fundamental credo that *OT and IT mime the way we think*. Even within the arena of the book and page (Arena of the Text), James strives to create a network for navigating, close kin to a morphing book (Morphing Book).

Principles of order

In order to create this kind of representation, both *Cultural Amnesia* and the Pathways Project actively discard two major principles of ordering: *hypotaxis* and *parataxis*. Both of these terms have long histories in the study of rhetoric and communication, and both incorporate the Greek root *taxis*, "arrangement" or "order." The difference between them lies in the first elements of the compounds: Greek *hypo* means "below" and *para* indicates "beside." When authors employ a hypotactic style, then, they are resorting to a hierarchical arrangement, a nested logic where categories are divided into tiered subcategories, like a many-leveled index. A paratactic style, on the other hand, places all parts on an equivalent basis, side by side, and refrains from imposing any sort of hierarchy; as Aristotle puts it, the elements of paratactic logic are like beads on a string.

What these two communicative styles share is linearity: both proceed in one-after-another sequence, from start to finish. Within that single-arced trajectory hypotaxis creates relationships of higher and lower status, with certain elements subordinated to others. Parataxis also works linearly, with the difference that its equivalent parts are not organized into a higher-lower grid or pattern, leaving the reader or listener to supply criteria for interrelationship. For that reason it is perhaps no surprise that parataxis has been identified as a major rhetorical algorithm for oral tradition, in which phrases, scenes, and even performances are understood as existing side-by-side with other instances rather than as tightly configured into a predetermined (and textual) hypotaxis.

Easy examples of these two strategies would be the conventional outline (part I divided into parts a, b, and c, which are themselves subdivided and so on) versus parallel scenes in a double-plotted Shakespearean play. The former provides a road map that not only prescribes a unique route but also ranks the importance of landmarks and stipulates their relationship to one another. The latter sets two series of events side-by-side (Reading Backwards) and leaves it up to the reader or audience to discover the implications of the analogical structure.

But, as it turns out, even the more open-ended strategy of parataxis falls short of an adequate description of oAgora and eAgora activity (Agora Correspondences), primarily because of its ultimate dependence on linearity. Neither hypotaxis nor parataxis can operate outside the frame of sequence.

Sequence-in-the-making

To fill the gap, then, let me suggest the term *polytaxis*, a newly minted coinage that literally means "multiple arrangement." Our tAgora-biased language is unavoidably slippery here, but the main thrust of the term is toward a non-predetermined, always-emergent pattern whose strength and sustainability lie in its ability to take not one but many different possible shapes (Variation within Limits). And the distinction indicated by that first element, *poly*, is categorical: neither "above" nor "beside," both of which defer to spatial order, but rather "multiple."

How does polytaxis work? Well, first it requires the active participation of an OT performer or an IT user surfing through a network of potentials, making choices that engender new sets of choices and constructing reality en route. Only after the fact, only after the pathways have been traveled, is it ever possible to talk about linearity—about a discernible track through a certain selection of nodes—and then it's only a memory of an already completed process and not the process itself. A definitive map becomes available only after the journey has come to an end.

The role of the surfer in both media-technologies is absolutely crucial, as is the ever-evolving nature of the experience. Without these two core features, polytaxis can't happen. For the same reason, it can't happen in the tAgora, which of course has no pathways (Impossibility of tPathways).

And there are other implications as well. The indeterminate nature of polytaxis, which requires surfers to take the initiative but does not mandate choice(s), supports and encourages diversity of experience. No one surfer ever has the final "take" on the network, and even the same individual can configure the elements (which themselves can morph) differently during different excursions. Multiple oral poets will narrate a story in multiple ways, and even the same bard will vary the itinerary from one performance to another. Web-surfers profit from having the interactive network open before them, and the decisions they make will not be identical from person to person or from session to session.

Polytaxis means contingency (Contingency). It also means that everyone can participate, subject to applicable cultural and web-specific rules, and that reality will remain plural (Reality Remains in Play).

From diversity of experience it's but a short step to distributed authorship (Distributed Authorship). Create a website, install links in existing websites, innovate code—all of these are "authoring" activities that depend directly on the efforts of others. New sites are inextricably linked to the larger Internet; links to other sites blaze pathways that didn't exist before; revising or adding code opens up realities that the innovator is complicit in engineering. Like the oral poet who works within a larger tradition—essentially within a constellation of pathways that operates like an IT cloud (Cloud and Tradition)—your role is contributory and shared, not final or supervening (the "final word" being no more than a tAgora myth in any case). Authors who practice polytaxis are always coauthors.

Democracy of reception

Polytaxis has a political dimension as well. Within the code of conduct that applies to transactions in the oAgora and eAgora, it licenses a fundamental democracy in exchange that, while liberating in many respects, may also lead to agoraphobia (Agoraphobia). In other words, a "multiple arrangement" will inevitably free up communication at both ends of the sender-receiver circuit. Reality and experience will be shared and democratic, worked out in partnership, flexible within a rule-governed environment. That's the upside of democracy in virtual environments.

At the same time, tAgora citizens pledged ideologically to brick-and-mortar politics, subscribing without question to the twin illusions of object (Illusion of Object) and stasis (Illusion of Stasis), will find polytaxis unsettling in its lack of linearity and predictability. They will sense something missing, and perhaps even indulge in media-smearing that portrays the oAgora and eAgora as somehow inferior rather than simply alternative. Democracy will seem more like anarchy to those without citizenship in multiple agoras (Citizenship in Multiple Agoras).

Wallace Stevens had it right

So here's the challenge, then. Do we settle now and forever on a repeatable, singular sequence (Recur Not Repeat)? Are we content with limiting our choices to the two possibilities of either a hierarchical or a parallel format? Is a single trip through the multiplex network sufficient? Are we so fulfilled by trekking that we have no need of navigating? Even more basically, can we in good conscience reduce OT and IT to tAgora artifacts?

From a polytactic perspective, the response is obvious. To circumscribe knowledge, art, and ideas via tAgora-specific strategies is to reduce living complexity to a collection of manageable but highly artificial facsimiles. Clive James knows this, and he demonstrates it in *Cultural Amnesia*. Wallace Stevens knew it when he created "Thirteen Ways of Looking at a Blackbird,"[91] a kind of white paper on polytaxis or, for that matter, a kind of polytaxis on white paper.

Stevens had it right—there isn't just one way; there are at least 13. And James has it right—A-to-Z order is merely nominal; we need to find more meaningful (if less conventional) links.

In Pathways Project language, reality remains in play.

Proverbs

Real proverbs serve as behavioral guides in various societies, providing generic, time-tested perspectives on the apparent chaos of everyday life. In this node we'll offer a group of homemade, entirely nontraditional proverbs to help recall how the oAgora and eAgora share similar dynamics (Disclaimer). Originally formulated for understanding OT, these eight "pearls of wisdom" also speak to transactions in the virtual marketplace of IT.

Several of the proverbs appear without change from their original form.[92] Others have been slightly modified to accommodate Internet technology alongside oral tradition (Agora Correspondences).

1. *OT and IT work like language, only more so.* Both media are special cases of language, with additional, denser coding to support the enhanced functionality of each medium. OT uses structural patterning at many levels—phraseology, narrative, story-type, and so forth. IT employs its own set of structures and specialized codes with which programmers and web-designers create systems of pathways for web-surfers to navigate through. Each technology depends for its efficacy on a dedicated register—that is, a rule-governed way of speaking or expressing.

2. *OT and IT are very plural media.* Just as oral traditions dwarf literary works in number and diversity, so the Internet offers us an unprecedented inventory and variety of sites and experiences. Furthermore, no OT or IT ever holds still; everything is constantly varying within limits, taking on one "new" shape after another. Unlike the fixed, tangible items that serve as currency in the tAgora, OT and IT simply can't be confined to a single, stable, counterplural form without the enforced euthanasia of textualization (Resynchronizing the Event). The central truth of both morphing technologies is that reality remains in play (Reality Remains in Play).

3. *Performance makes it happen, while idiom provides the context.* OT depends on performance for its continuing existence; action and involvement—surfing through a network of possibilities—are the hallmarks of the oAgora, and even lie at the root of oral-derived texts as well. Likewise, actually negotiating the ePathways of the Internet (ePathways) is the necessary precondition to making meaning in that arena. Nothing happens in either medium until the performer/surfer begins the journey, and the evolving itinerary is always potential until that same performer/surfer codetermines it through a tiered sequence of decisions. OT and IT can happen only in the oArena (Arena of Oral Tradition) and eArena (Arena of the Web), respectively.

And just as performance drives reality in OT and IT, so both technologies depend on embedded idiomatic implications for their core communication. OT encodes its surface with "more than meets the eye" in terms of traditional, more-than-literal, add-on meanings. A phrase, a gesture, even the performer's costume may harbor whole reservoirs of associated signification. Likewise, IT offers links, portals, clusters of sites, and other emergent, interactive strategies that lead the surfer beyond the immediate and the literal to a richer constellation of implied possibilities (Systems versus Things). Navigating along established but multiply interconnected pathways (always according to the surfer's own initiative) opens up the implied context. Meaning is engaged idiomatically.

4. *OT and IT work* through *rather than in* spite *of their coding.* Largely because we are accustomed to analyzing communication textually, we instinctively try to understand OT and IT through a tAgora lens. Another way to say the same thing is to observe that we are often victims of the agoraphobia (Agoraphobia) and culture shock (Culture Shock) induced by having to manage unfamiliar ways of thinking and communicating. But if we shift our default perspective and confront the oAgora and eAgora on their own terms, then the specialized coding that seems so strange or artificial will make much more sense. That coding, as Lawrence Lessig[93] puts it, is *performative.* Far from serving as a barrier or a clumsy, unnecessary interface, it is the fundamental register—the expressive heart and soul—of the two technologies in question. It's what makes each medium work.

5. *OT and IT function best without depending on published books.* How do you capture Proteus? How do you reduce a living, morphing experience to a page or photograph or even video and still keep it alive and faithful to its true nature? Simply said, you can't. Ideological claims aside, fixed texts do not and cannot faithfully represent such plastic, rule-governed processes (Ideology of the Text). The tAgora—no matter how highly developed—can never house and nurture the expressive ecology (Reading Backwards) of either the oAgora or eAgora. For precisely the same

reason, then, freestanding book editions of OT and one-dimensional how-to manuals for the networked, ever-evolving web will always be deeply unsatisfactory representations of their respective realities. OT and IT operate outside fixation (Accuracy); in fact, their core strength actually derives from resisting fixation.

6. *The play's the thing, and not the script.* By its very nature drama lives to be performed, a truth so self-evident that we've invented a term—"closet drama"—to identify dramatic writing meant for the lonely occupation of silent reading. Yet conventional tAgora assumptions only too often focus on the script as the irreducible core of dramatic art, understanding the comfortably tangible "source" as being "reinterpreted" in various ways. This textcentric attitude not only denies drama its root dynamics; it also reverses its logic. After all, playwrights write not to assemble items complete in themselves, but to enable real-time, flesh-and-blood enactments. Just so with OT and IT. Neither the oAgora nor the eAgora depends in any fashion on a tAgora script. Instead, the morphing technologies are primary and central in and of themselves, and can be only very poorly represented via the default medium of page and book. When we attend a play, we go to experience the performance, not to see how the sacred script gets rendered this time around.

7. *Repetition is the symptom, not the disease.* OT and IT are far too often accused of repeating, of doing the same thing over and over again, perhaps *ad nauseam.* Well, if you're trekking through texts according to the one-way route to which texts confine you, then the second or third or fourth occurrence of a word, phrase, scene, or even whole story clearly does constitute repetition. It happens a first (and unprecedented) time, and you remember that first time when it happens again and note the instance-to-instance correspondence. Along a linear platform that owes its primary allegiance to sequence, repetition can and does take place.

But when—as with OT and IT—the medium is fundamentally contingent (Contingency), when it has no predetermined linear platform, when it requires active cocreation on the part of the user/surfer, repetition is the wrong concept. Recurrence (Recur Not Repeat) is the right concept, because each instance amounts to an independent event and a choice made not on the basis of sequence but rather of fluency in the medium. Another instance occurs not because the first one did, but because the performer/surfer is responding idiomatically to the situation that very moment. "Once upon a time" opens many Grimm Brothers fairy tales not because it's being repeated, but because its *recurrence* idiomatically sets the scene for a certain brand of storytelling. That's why clichés are strictly tAgora phenomena: linearity saps the strength of even the most well-turned phrase after too many iterations in the tAgora. And it's also why OT and IT recurrences (which are not repetitions!) remain fresh and clickable; each one is effectively the "first and only," each is made singular by its unique moment, each one carries coded meaning that emerges with unimpeachable idiomatic force.

8. *Without pathways there is no language, without an individual there is no performance.* Disagreements have raged for decades if not centuries over which is the dominant member in the envisioned contest of tradition versus the individual. Does an OT owe its primary allegiance to what gets passed down from prior performers or to the person who molds it into an idiosyncratic form? The ideology of the individual literary genius has long tilted the scales toward the individual and the unique work—so much so that we have trouble imagining verbal art without a single person fully in control of a singular, well-made item. Similarly, we may question whether the worldwide web (unfortunately too frequently understood as the fixed item it's not) or the surfer has priority in the search for knowledge, art, and ideas.

For OT and IT alike, the notion of distributed authorship offers a way past this agoraphobic dilemma (Distributed Authorship). All performers in the oAgora share some sort of specialized oRegister, some way of speaking, some network of oPathways (oPathways) to navigate. Likewise, all surfers in the eAgora share some sort of specialized eRegister, some way of exploring the web, some network of ePathways. In both cases the languages that these two groups of agora citizens employ is malleable, rule-governed, coded, and idiomatic. Both groups are essentially working cooperatively and online (Online with OT). In the end, as our proverb urges, there is no victor in the imagined contest between tradition and the individual. Both sides are absolutely necessary to the chemistry of the enterprise; both partners are functionally complementary.

Why the proverbs don't work for the tAgora

In telegraphic fashion, and by proverb numbers, here are a few reasons why our OT-IT proverbs just don't work for verbal commerce within the tAgora. For all of their many strengths, and despite our attempts to make them morph (Morphing Book), books can't support the kind of network navigation that characterizes and generates OT-IT expressive power. Briefly:

1. Books aren't language; they're scripts for language.
2. Books operate by fixing knowledge, art, and ideas into singular, inert items; they are limited in the possibilities they present and don't live through morphing.
3. Reading a book means following the textual trail rather than navigating through interconnected pathways.
4. Books don't depend on specialized coding as much as OT and IT or derive as much from that expressive strategy.

5. Books function best as published books.
6. Books reduce the living reality of performances into much-diminished, static, and nonliving reflections.
7. Books support and house repetitions; they can't support recurrence.
8. Books have no pathways: tPathways are impossible. tAgora authorship is individual and nondistributed.

Reading Backwards

The text as tyrant

Let's face it: most Western pages are ruthlessly tyrannical. They mandate a left-to-right, top-to-bottom, one-after-another regimen, and there's simply no appeal to their authority. Words and sentences move eastward, as it were, and paragraphs move toward the south until you reach the frontier of the present reading space and turn the page to cross the next frontier. Even eFiles, like the node-texts in the Pathways Project, follow this demanding convention to an extent, taking advantage of the deeply instilled cognitive habit of linear sequence to streamline communication. Scrolling replaces page-turning, but much else remains the same. Linearity rules.

But what about the hyperlinks that crop up in eFiles and populate webpages? And what about all those opportunities for clicking elsewhere (Getting Started) that await us in the top and left menu-bars of Pathways Project ePages? These pathways certainly aren't textual; they belong to the eAgora rather than the tAgora. And therein lies a categorical difference in both their root dynamics and the "reading" activities they enable.

Opting out

Quite clearly, these links operate according to an alternative logic, one that offers the chance to opt out of text (Texts and Intertextuality) and into surfing—into a parallel mode of communicating. If you decide to take the plunge, you'll be escaping the relentless left-to-right, top-to-bottom, one-after-another march of conventional text in favor of entering another arena altogether (Arena of the Web). And the new node will be connected to the node you've left not by directional default, but rather by the nonspatial logic of related ideas.

What does that process entail? What are the consequences? Well, opting out means a radical shift in your experience, because the next paragraph you read, or the next sentence that unfolds before you, won't be the result of linear sequence. Topic sentences, paragraph-to-paragraph transitions, rhetorical outlines, and the other tools of the tAgora trade can be replaced at any time by eAgora strategies of interactivity, relatedness, and recursiveness. In some ways this nontextual kind of reading has proven uncomfortable for those of us who have pored over texts for most of our lives. We've been taught to depend on the tAgora as the "final word" in communication, and the ascendancy of the eAgora has induced what amounts to culture shock (Culture Shock).

But the eAgora has also opened unanticipated new vistas for discovery, expression, and learning. In place of the confined, even claustrophobic space of the page we're now offered the limitless (and continually expanding) horizon of the Internet, if only we're willing—despite the attendant culture shock or, more specifically, the eAgoraphobia—to opt out of our standing subscription to the ideology of the text (Ideology of the Text).

"Linked from" pathways

As a simple illustration, consider just one specific aspect of the enhanced reading process that the Pathways Project website supports. You'll see that this function exposes the deal with the devil that underlies the enormous success of the page and the book (for the most part invisibly, given how securely our tAgora defaults are set). I'm referring to the "Linked from" feature that appears at the bottom of every node in the Project network: the list of all other nodes that link to it. Here you'll find not the *next* node—there really isn't any such thing, since every one of the more than one hundred can be accessed at any time from anywhere in the network—but rather the nodes that contain a hyperlink leading to the one you're presently reading.

For example, here's a screenshot of what turns up in the well-populated "Linked from" section of the oAgora node:

Linked from: Geting Started, Online With OT, Museum of Verbal Art, Homo Sapiens' Calendar Year, Excavating An Epic, Misnavigation, Footnotes Versus Branches, Stand-alone Book, Systems Versus Things, Proverbs, Audience Critique, Why Not Textualize, Agoraphobia, How To Build A Book, Ideology Of The Text, Agora As Verbal Marketplace, The Three Agoras, Open Source OT

The oAgora: "Linked from" connections.

How does this feature work in real-time reading? Well, when you reach the end of the scrollable text (having resisted all invitations to navigate elsewhere, or having simply hit the back button in your browser to return from elsewhere), you're presented with this list of topics somehow connected to the oAgora within the Project web. Or rather the oAgora is somehow connected to—or from— them. Curious as it may seem to us textcentric readers, in the most basic sense there's no directionality between "here" and "there," only an idea-relationship, so we won't quibble over a primacy that doesn't and can't exist.

All right: no directionality, no inevitable, mandated route toward a single "next." Then it's only fair to ask just how and on what basis these other nodes are linked to the oAgora, isn't it? What's the underlying connection and how does it work? Two answers present themselves.

Answer 1: By juxtaposed ideas   The connection from one node to another can be made not by invoking tAgora convention and linear sequence, but simply by juxtaposing ideas. Since the eAgora lacks a prescribed, unique, take-no-prisoners policy on how you must proceed, textual notions of necessary order and hierarchy are largely inapplicable. There are limits and rules, of course, but there is also enormous, unprecedented freedom. For instance, the Pathways Project site offers you the opportunity—but, emphatically, doesn't ever require you—to explore possible correlations between the oAgora and Online with OT (Online with OT), a node that ponders the similarities between the dynamics of oral tradition and the kind of linking that is the lifeblood of the Project. To take another example, Agoraphobia (Agoraphobia) looks at what it means to try to function according to a wrong set of assumptions in each of the three agoras.

Are these two other nodes apposite to the node you're reading? Do they somehow relate to the oAgora? Most certainly. But does either of them provide the single possible "next" installment in a linear, warehoused inventory of idea-items? Most certainly not. What matters is open-ended and multiple connection rather than singular, writ-in-stone sequence—and for that simple reason the notion of "backwards" loses its meaning. Directionality only reduces the potential of a network.

Answer 2: By your own activities   Connection between nodes also depends crucially on the reader's cocreative contribution. Think about your central role in all of this. You're never compelled to navigate back and read the "Linked from" node, to click back and unearth someone else's built-in logic. (You're never actually required to do anything at all, for that matter.) There's no exclusively defined, compulsory route for you to find and follow toward a conclusion reached by others, as if you were pursuing a treasure hunt of some sort. You won't be served up a chapter or a lecture with a prescribed number and order of topics, nor will you be handed a one-way route map with a preconceived, ultimate destination.

Why not? Because the Pathways Project is at its heart not a *prescription* but rather an *opportunity* for discovering and cocreating reality—something we always do to some extent in every medium but customarily pretend to forgo in the textual "march of convention." In this medium it's you who decide whether to explore—and to share in realizing—a potential connection. You shoulder the responsibility for making sense; you surf the Project network, in whatever direction(s) you wish. Once again, the notion of "backwards" is a nonstarter.

A-directionality and power

All aspects of the website are meant to support creativity in reading, understanding, and learning—and to do so by developing an awareness of the power of a-directionality, that is, the power of nonlinear linkages. And all of those aspects and ways of reading (Getting Started)—by node, by agora, by linkmap, and by branches—relinquish the power of sequence in favor of the very different power of a networked web of options. The "Linked from" entries offer yet another way to construe the relationships that the Pathways Project was built both to explore and to represent. They highlight ideas related to the node you happen to be reading (in some fashion yet to be determined, and then chiefly by you), and they're meant to accomplish at least two objectives.

First, and more obviously, they make you aware of possible connections, immediately enlarging your field of vision on the OT-IT correlation. This kind of open but rule-governed connectivity and potential for variation (Variation within Limits) lies at the core of both communications technologies, both oral tradition and Internet technology, both the oAgora and the eAgora.

Second, the "Linked from" entries straightforwardly call into question perhaps the most central tenet in our communicative ideology of text: they deny the notion that X necessarily leads to Y rather than the other way around, Y leading to X. They insist that X and Y are in some fashion linked and related, but they leave it to you to decide why, how, and with what implications. Nor is this decision-making an aberrant, one-time activity: you'll be called upon to make similar judgments over and over again as you read. Quite a different situation from the predetermined tAgora march of convention.

As does the rest of the Project, the "Linked from" entries dissolve the mirage of object (Illusion of Object) and stasis (Illusion of Stasis) in favor of a living, evolving web of opportunities. You can—indeed you must—discard the codependent pretense of thinking and creating via things. The "Linked from" entries expose objects as endemically limited arenas for thinking and creating and urge us to face the challenge of managing communication without that fiction in place. Embracing a-directionality means committing to your own set of pathways through the network, with scores or even hundreds of decisions for you to make as you surf. And of course, whatever sequence of pathways you choose is merely one option among very, very many. You or someone else can just as easily chart another course later today, tomorrow, next week, or next year. Even your present series of choices is always open rather than closed, always emergent (happening right now, in real time) rather than pre-set. In every important way, any itinerary you follow is continuously evolving (Response) and very much of your own making.

An open network for inquiry

That's why the eAgora in general, and the Pathways Project more specifically, has little or no directionality, little or no "backwards." And that's why the lack of the foregone conclusion that we have come to expect from texts isn't a flaw or a handicap, why the "missing" one-way route map isn't a telltale symptom of a disorganized or second-rate medium. Like its sister technology of oral tradition, a-directional IT is both a uniquely powerful and uniquely innovative platform for construing knowledge, art, and ideas.

It is, after all, the way we think.

Real-time versus Asynchronous

Are you caught up in the moment of surfing through an oral performance (Arena of Oral Tradition) or the web (Arena of the Web), working your way through an evolving, cooperative, real-time process? Are you involved in an emergent partnership that can't be dissolved and rejoined but requires your ongoing attention and participation? Or, alternatively, are you using an asynchronous medium, holding the communicative process at arm's length, stopping the proceedings as you see fit and resuming when the time and place are right? Do you have the luxury to pause and restart without destroying the experience?

Whatever you're presently doing, imagine not just one but both scenarios. And then ask yourself a challenging question: which type of experience is inherently truer, richer, more faithful? Which one qualifies as the more fundamental reality (Reality Remains in Play)?

When your time is your own

We all profit from the multiple advantages of asynchronous communication, whether we're consciously aware of them or not. Think of the many mainstream vehicles that fall into this broad category: brick-and-mortar books, static eFiles,[94] email sent and received, and anything else that serves as a freestanding repository. Such cognitive prostheses help us to dodge the demands of emergence and the dire threat of contingency (Contingency) by offering apparent objectivity, permanence, and stasis. They allow us to defer exclusive, uninterrupted involvement and manage the ever-increasing demands on our time and energy by imposing a sequence—our own designated sequence—on the tasks and responsibilities we face. And all of these advantages are secure, we suppose, devoid of worry or qualification, since the information so dependably contained in these rock-solid media will unfailingly be there waiting for us whenever we're ready to engage it. We, not others, decide when to participate; we, not others, remain in charge of the communication.

So deeply ingrained is this habit that we can easily forget that asynchronous communication is a remarkably recent invention. To be specific, we can trace its origins quite precisely to the founding of the tAgora, about November 22 of our species-year (Homo Sapiens' Calendar Year), the very "day" when Homo sapiens began to encode trading practices via clay counters, the eventual precursors of the tablet (Spectrum of Texts). Not long after that, on December 10 by our calendrical mapping, actual writing and literacy became available. From counters and tablets to papyrus, sheepskin, book pages, and static eFiles, the tAgora has sponsored as well as depended on the peculiar power of disembodied tWords (tWords). Artifacts are created for later, offline consumption; only after an intermission of indeterminate length is the communicative circuit completed, repetitively if the serial occasions arise (Recur Not Repeat). Of course, that chronological and geographical hiatus between creation and use also marks a new kind of technology-supported convenience. With asynchronous media you don't have to suspend your current activities (whatever they are) for an immediate, can't-wait exchange. You can access whatever knowledge, art, or ideas are encoded in the text after the fact of its making and as partially or completely as you wish, whenever the time and circumstances are right for you.

Real time in the oAgora

For an oral traditional performer and his or her audience, however, communication is real-time, not asynchronous. For the exchange to happen, both sides must be present and engaged at the same time and in the same place. If the genealogy spoken by a patriarch isn't conveyed to anyone, its contents aren't shared; it dies. If an elderly woman intones a healing charm with no patient involved, that verbal remedy loses its reason for being; it doesn't cure anyone. If a story is told and retold without an audience, then the two-way dynamic of composition and reception fails; the story doesn't qualify as OT communication. Yes, you can capture any of these empty, futile attempts at performance by introducing an asynchronous medium such as audio, video, or even dictation into text and then playing back your quarry. We may even credit such offline products (Freezing Wikipedia) with successful preservation of the event, even though they amount to an ideological intervention, a kind of imperialistic colonizing of the nontextual under the banner of the textual (Ideology of the Text). But make no mistake: in the oAgora the only viable mode of communication is real-time.

Real time in the eAgora

This is also true for the navigator of ePathways (ePathways), who like the navigator of oPathways (oPathways) is inevitably a partner in the actual shared moment of cocreation. Interacting with a vast array of linked potentials, surfers click and travel in real time. Every trip consists of an ongoing negotiation from start to finish, every itinerary is a work in progress because it requires ongoing participation. Real-time explorations aren't complete until the browser is closed—and in an important sense they're never the last word, because each performance is simply one instance of what's possible. Within the Pathways Project website, for example, you have four methods (Getting Started) of construing reality. You can click on Full Table of Nodes and proceed from node to node in alphabetical order (a linear logic that has no status in this marketplace). You can concentrate on the three principal media environments: the oAgora, the tAgora, and the eAgora. And you can navigate via prenegotiated linkmaps (Linkmaps) or branches. Or you can do none or all of the above. So which strategy is best, most productive, or merely the most preferable? Well, that's the essential point: your journey is what you yourself make of it—moving through an open system of linked alternatives. Just one requirement: you can never escape the contingency at the heart of the process. You can never become unenmeshed, because by doing so you'll exit the web of ePathways and textualize experience. Simply put, there is no reality until you the surfer construct it.

Conventional wisdom is only conventional

Habits of mind notwithstanding, we owe it to ourselves to step beyond our agora-based biases and recognize the diversity of ways in which we communicate. For one thing, asynchronous media represent nothing more—and nothing less—than the accommodation we've settled on since the invention of the tAgora, an accommodation that's been exposed by the invention of the eAgora and the rediscovery of the oAgora. For another, asynchronous technologies have until recently enjoyed an unacknowledged monopoly in "serious" communication, the kind of exchange via which indisputable facts (Just the Facts) must be duly ascertained, recorded, and faithfully transmitted. We've convinced ourselves that such crucial and responsible agora-business can be accomplished only in the tAgora (Responsible Agora-business). Of course, this is fundamentally an ideological claim, tenable only if you've swallowed and fully digested the illusions of object (Illusion of Object) and stasis (Illusion of Stasis), the twin pillars supporting the textual marketplace. If you don't accept these illusions as reality—and the Pathways Project exists in part to refute them—then you'll notice that the tAgora emperor is missing more than a few of his garments.

This is not to say that asynchronous communication doesn't present us with enormous advantages, or that, historically speaking, it hasn't moved mountains in supporting our cultural work. It most certainly does and most certainly has.

But those advantages aren't as trouble-free or uncompromised as we like to pretend.

The price of no pathways

When we deal exclusively with asynchronous media, we by definition forgo real-time involvement, along with all of its own advantages and disadvantages. We restrict our creation, transmission, and reception of knowledge, art, and ideas to one technology, one medium, one way of knowing. We aren't active partners anymore, except at the far end of the communicative process. We put down the book until tonight, by which time we trust it hasn't morphed. We pause the audio or video in order to shovel snow, buy groceries, or share a few unencumbered hours with our family; no matter, we can pick up the film precisely where we left off. As tAgora denizens we know how to smooth over the jump-cuts in life and media use—and we can't influence the pathwayless text of the recorded performance, anyway (Impossibility of tPathways). Asynchronous media allow and foster a staccato experience that we've agreed to interpret as continuous, but let's not mislead ourselves: from the perspective of oAgora and eAgora participation, it's not the same as sharing real-time experience.

Toward diversity: A fieldwork fairy tale

Imagine an ethnographic team from another place and another time entering our twenty-first–century world on a mission to investigate how we communicate. What should they do? Depending on their particular aims and biases, these fieldworkers may decide to concentrate on oral traditions—for example, on the song lines of Australian aboriginal peoples, which serve as maps across their physical landscape as well as mythological digests, providing a kind of oAgora-style GPS facility and identity charter all in one. Or they may opt to focus on the myriad varieties of asynchronous media that proliferate throughout many societies, serving as tangible containers of information that can be read as offline artifacts according to their users' timetables. Or the visiting ethnographers may choose to spend much of their energy delving into the strange and powerful appeal of the Internet, establishing how that ever-evolving and network-dependent technology gained such traction so quickly. Perhaps they'll observe that, in terms of interactivity and navigation through systems, the web appears to imitate the technology of oral tradition. Or, surveying all three agoras, they might even conclude that OT and IT mime the very way we think.

But however this team goes about its work, let's hope that they recognize and understand two fundamental features of communication in contemporary cultures. First, may they come to realize that we are citizens not of any single verbal marketplace but rather of multiple agoras. Second, may they conclude that real-time and asynchronous media, as diverse as they clearly are, both provide absolutely viable ways of making sense of the world. By accepting all three agoras and both kinds of media experience, our imagined ethnographers may just conclude that true, defensible democracy in media means tolerating and appreciating diversity in frame of reference.

Reality Remains in Play

Three brands of experience

"Call me Ishmael," advises the narrator-character through whose voice we hear Herman Melville's *Moby Dick*, a recognized masterpiece in the tAgora. Every edition of the novel ever published starts with exactly those three tWords (tWords) and no others, and every edition of that work (except for shortened, expurgated versions like the one I suffered through in high school) continues according to a uniquely plotted itinerary. We meet Queequeg the harpooner, Starbuck the first mate, Pip the eventually crazed cabin boy, and so many other memorable figures. And they act and interact in specific, definite ways not just on the first reading but on every reading. No alternate beginnings, middles, or ends; no variance in dialogue; no triumph for Ahab. If you've read the book once, you'll recognize its trajectory point by point and scene by scene on the second pass, even more closely on the third pass, and so forth. *Moby Dick* is a singly authored, static, textual object; it will always be verbatim the same.

Now consider how a South Slavic epic singer conducts his verbal business in the oAgora. For present purposes, let's imagine he's performing *The Captivity of Alagić Alaja*, a story-type that follows the familiar story line of Homer's *Odyssey*, not to mention hundreds of stories from other cultures across the face of Europe and Asia. At every level, it exhibits and depends on variation within limits (Variation within Limits). He—and everyone who performs, has performed, or will perform this story—may or may not begin with a generic prologue (called a *pripjev*, or "presong") before entering on the description of a miserable captive crying out from prison. That description may be bare-bones or highly detailed, and may involve a single prisoner or more than one. Negotiations for his or their release—undertaken because the noise is preventing his captor's infant child from nursing and/or sleeping—may involve either the captor or his wife or both, and may be managed through an intermediary scribe or messenger or not. If you've heard the story once, you'll recognize the general flow, but its particular shape in any given performance is highly contingent (Contingency). Since it's emergent and depends on decisions to be made in real time, you can't

204 · Reality Remains in Play

even know whether the hero in prison will find his wife faithful (like the Penelope figure in the *Odyssey* story) or unfaithful (like the Clytemnestra figure in the Agamemnon story) when he arrives home after years of (mis)adventures. The South Slavic singer's story is a performance borne of distributed authorship (Distributed Authorship); "it" can't ever be verbatim the same.

The eAgora offers a parallel, textless experience (and here as always we distinguish between the interactive exchange that is the soul of the Internet as against static eFiles that amount to pixel-texts circulating electronically as tAgora objects[95]). Engage your browser—and remember that even this startup page can morph or be replaced—and where do you go? Bookmarks might be a start, or a Google search, but from that point onward the journey depends wholly on the links you choose to click on, the ePathways (ePathways) you opt to follow or ignore. The itinerary builds in real time, not asynchronously, and cannot be foreordained, and it builds that way for everyone who surfs, has surfed, or will surf cognate ePathways (Real-time versus Asynchronous). Even when you have a specific purpose in mind, even when you aim to reproduce yesterday's surfing expedition, you will always make different decisions about how to handle the alternatives built into the system (Systems versus Things). At every level, your experience exhibits and depends on variation within limits. No, you won't do "just anything"; the eAgora, like the oAgora, is rule-governed and doesn't support merely willy-nilly behavior (Not So Willy-nilly). You can't travel where there aren't any pathways. And yes, you may have a generic idea of what you're pursuing, but that idea is always subject to morphing. The web-surfer's expedition is a performance borne of distributed authorship; "it" can't ever be verbatim.

Lurking below the (textual) surface

Consider for a moment an uncomfortable proposition about the communication of knowledge, art, and ideas. What if reality itself weren't the cut-and-dried, presumably knowable experience we have long taken such pride in imaging via tAgora technology? What if reality morphed, depending on our perspective and those of our fellow travelers, stubbornly resisting the singularity and completion we agree to assign it? What if we peered out from the protected environment of our textual bastion and put aside our most cherished illusions of object (Illusion of Object) and stasis (Illusion of Stasis)? What if we discovered an unsettling truth—namely, that what we know and even how we can know it aren't certain or predictable? What if we concluded that reality isn't a discoverable set of finite things or laws or precepts at all, but (behind Oz's façade) a relative, intangible, emergent web of connections always and everywhere under construction?

Would we be disappointed or threatened? Would we feel a kind of culture shock (Culture Shock) or, more specifically, agoraphobia (Agoraphobia)? Well, if we're ever to escape the default confines of the tAgora and become citizens of all three agoras (Citizenship in Multiple Agoras), we're going to have to come to grips with that unfamiliar brand of reality. Oh, we can merrily go on pretending that texts solve the universe—that they're the prime vehicle for creating, transmitting, and receiving, that they supersede the vagaries of the oAgora and that newfangled, unstable eAgora. Undeniably, that very reductionism has helped us to define our world and ourselves with unprecedented accuracy and precision (Accuracy), or so goes the cultural myth (Ideology of the Text) at any rate. But the oAgora and eAgora reveal that outside the textual marketplace reality operates much differently, as we think and communicate not by tracking through sequences of things but rather by navigating through networks of options. The explicitness and containment with which we reflexively credit the page turns out to be a mirage.

In the oAgora and eAgora reality just isn't fixed, static, or fully ascertainable as a discrete experience. In OT and IT, reality remains very much in play.

Constants, Sir Isaac, and some uninvited guests

Or should we interpret that apparent flux as an illusion, as static on the channel that we can dispense with once we penetrate beyond external, superficial phenomena to more fundamental realities? Some stories from physics can offer a useful perspective.

For instance, what is Avogadro's constant[96]—the number of molecules in one mole of any substance? Look it up: about 6.022×10 raised to the 23rd power. No matter which substance, by the way; a comforting standard in a turgid world. And how long does it take to go from Chicago to New York at a rate of 65 miles per hour? Easy: distance divided by rate yields elapsed time, so a trip of 711.47 miles will require 10.95 hours, plus rest stops. Straightforward enough.

How dependable are such measurements? Well, we take them as invariable and invulnerable, as immune to change of any sort, as the inevitable issue of universally applicable laws that regulate the seeming hurly-burly of existence. As such, these constants rise above background noise and the messy, unpredictable aspects of daily life, providing a foundation for rationalizing apparent differences, for bringing order to apparent chaos.

And, happily, such constants and measurements work perfectly as long as we don't look beyond the universe as defined by Isaac Newton. Indeed, within that frame of reference his basic laws, the platform for so much of classical mechanics, still function with what presents itself as absolute precision. Bridges are built, roads are routed, trips are planned, and products are designed. No apparent slippage; everything intact, on time, and accounted for.

Beyond the (physical) surface

For a long time after Newton's epochal pronouncements in his 1687 *Principia*, there was no reason to question the unqualified coincidence between his views and our observations. But then two uninvited guests crashed the scientific party. Albert Einstein demonstrated that reality wasn't objective, that Newton's laws functioned acceptably only as an everyday-world approximation. At velocities approaching the speed of light, time and space become relative rather than absolute. On the grand scale of the cosmos, gravity and planetary motion show unexpected deviations that can be explained only by considering the role of the observer relative to what is being observed. Although these deviations are hard or impossible to discern in our daily experience of trains and boats and planes, they're unequivocally there, buried beneath Newtonian approximations. On the scale of the cosmos, macroscopically, they're urgently there and they demand explanation. With the advent of relativity theory, one dimension of Newtonian certainty went a-glimmering.

At the other end of the scale, specifically at the atomic level of matter, a movement called Quantum Mechanics[97] exposed a parallel problem with the reigning Newtonian model. As physicists peered more and more closely at the elemental building blocks of matter, they noticed not the regularity of motion predicted by classical mechanics but a veritable maelstrom of activities characterized by their unpredictability. In fact, as Werner Heisenberg discovered, it proved impossible to simultaneously measure the position and velocity of atomic particles, an insight that led to his famous Uncertainty Principle.[98] Once again, this time in the microworld, the laws we had accepted and written into our operating procedures and our conception of reality were shown not to apply.

So what's the upshot of such scientific thinking, which seeks to explore and explain how absolute values and a static vision of reality don't really work? To oversimplify, Newtonian mechanics solves the everyday-scale world, but not the cosmos and not the atomic universe. Newtonian certainty—a version of the myth of fixity and linear outcomes—enjoys unquestioned acceptance in our daily lives, and there is no need to contest its highly functional approximations. There is in fact every reason to continue accepting and implementing the laws of classical mechanics in practically all of what we do.

But let's not kid ourselves. Beyond Sir Isaac's sinecure lie real, undeniable phenomena that put the lie to his approximations, that won't submit to workable compromises. Specifically, they require us to recognize the role of the observer, who is a doer, a participant—and emphatically not an innocent, inert bystander—in the act of experiencing. They require us to recognize that, although relativistic and quantum mechanical dynamics may lie hidden above or beneath our everyday-scale world, they are far more fundamental than the golden rule of *force = mass × acceleration*. They require that we acknowledge a simple but counterintuitive truth: that, quotidian appearances aside, physical reality remains in play.

Texts are like Newton's laws

In a functional sense, texts resemble Newton's laws. As long as we don't question the approximation, as long as we stay within the circumscribed arena they designate and define (Arena of the Text), all is well. The constants apply and the laws work.

But beware the nontextual, where the constants don't apply and the laws don't work. We will never be able to reduce the inherent flexibility of web-powered communication, whether in the oAgora or eAgora, to monolithic, contained reality. In these other venues reality derives, if counterintuitively, from its very immeasurability, its uncertainty, its rule-governed morphing. Outside the world of texts and textual ideology, experience is decidedly different: it thrives on polytaxis (Polytaxis) and involves us by remaining in play.

Back to our three brands of experience

Success in the verbal marketplace is sui generis. Each agora supports its own reality on its own terms. And given the central theorem (Agora Correspondences) of the Pathways Project, what we expect would be two homologous realities—OT and IT—as distinguished from the disparate reality of textual technology. Let's revisit out initial examples, then, and see whether that theorem proves out.

Moby Dick, which some claim is the closest anyone has come to writing the Great American Novel, continues to entrance generations with its Promethean saga of overreaching, its glimpse into the lost world of nineteenth-century whaling, and its terrifying dive into the black depths of the human psyche. It is of course a singly authored work, the sixth of Melville's nine novels, and draws its identity from a stable, invariable text that has prompted a remarkably wide range of interpretations since its publication in 1851. Precisely because it does not vary, because it takes its place in the intertextual history of other American novels and related literary monuments (Texts and Intertextuality), it commands authority as an object, a fixed signpost in the literary culture of the period. Different people and different eras have varied in their understanding of *Moby Dick*, which was remarkably unsuccessful during Melville's lifetime. But not because the story morphed. The book remains exactly the same sequence of words, paragraphs, and pages it was when initially published in 1851. *In the tAgora, reality is circumscribed and static.*

Not so the ever-shifting Return Song of the South Slavic *guslar*, which draws its power from its ability to morph within limits over multiple performances and multiple "authors." Here it's precisely the rule-governed variability of the experience that confers cultural authority, precisely the uncertainty of the journey that is its strongest feature. To confine oral performers to a verbatim text is to render their activity textual, and in the process to sabotage the interactive dynamic between those performers and their audiences. Expressive strength in this arena (Arena of Oral Tradition) stems from emergent, right-now composition and reception, rather than from reducing a system of communication to an object that belongs to another agora. Intertextuality isn't possible in the OT marketplace because there are no texts. Each version is an original in the time, place, and circumstance that it occurs, and the performance recurs rather than repeats (Recur Not Repeat). You can't hold Proteus captive without destroying his natural identity. *In the oAgora, reality remains in play.*

Now picture yourself surfing the web, navigating through the Pathways Project for instance. If we instantly remove all your options—imitating the master plan to freeze and textualize Wikipedia in order to "increase its worth" (Freezing Wikipedia)—you've just as quickly exited the eAgora in favor of a textual venue. Now what you're exploring becomes your not-so-brave old world—tidy, protected, closed-off, and static, not to mention tAgora-cozy. Instead of co-creating experience, you're confined to interpreting an invariable play script, a single route, a pathwayless environment (Impossibility of tPathways). Many interpretations are possible, to be sure, but they all rest on one single, solitary object. Then, if we reverse the procedure and instantly restore those removed links, everything changes (Arena of the Web), and changes radically. Now you're directly responsible for participating in communication that can't be prescribed. Now you must make your own way through a network of nodes in an order and at a depth only you can choose. Now you'll have to deal with sites and domains that actually prosper by being unfixed, by being forever under construction. Now it's up to you to construe knowledge, art, and ideas not by trekking along a one-dimensional road map but by navigating through a multidimensional, interactive grid of potentials. *In the eAgora, reality remains in play.*

Recur Not Repeat

Repetition is a tAgora phenomenon

What do we mean by "repeating?" We mean to do something again, and to redo that something as exactly as possible. The smaller the variation (if any), the better; if there's too much change, the second instance can't qualify as a repetition of the first. With repetition we strive toward a linear sequence of identical acts, all in a row and each taking its meaning from the foregoing instance(s). Think of n, n+1, n+2, n+3, and so forth.

In looking at how repetition works in its home marketplace of communication, the tAgora, let's consider a few instances, ranging from simple to more complex. After that, we'll examine its opposite—*recurrence*, an oAgora and eAgora phenomenon, providing some illustrations of its dynamic function.

1. *Repeating for emphasis.* Perhaps the simplest case and use of repetition is the attempt to emphasize a point we're trying to make, to underline its importance rhetorically. We all remember too many overcrafted political speeches, for example, in which candidates tried to move their audiences by citing and re-citing a particular point or issue, trying to drum their favored position into our heads with a particular catchphrase or soundbite. Many of us have written memos or essays or personal letters whose mission was to persuade their reader(s) by repeating a policy or idea or belief, again often using the same catchphrase so that the cumulative force of linear repetition is maximized. This is classic repetition, where each iteration takes its meaning from the preceding iteration(s). And because this practice depends on leading an audience or reader through a planned sequence of fixed things—rather than navigating and activating option-driven networks—it is also a classic tAgora strategy.

2. *Repetitive practice makes perfect performance.* Classical music performances are in one sense always misleading. We go to the concert hall to hear a Beethoven symphony, for example, and are thrilled by the virtuoso, tightly integrated playing of the strings, woodwinds, brass, and percussion. But what we experience then and there is *only* the performance, the very tip of the iceberg. What's lost to us as an audience for that event is the weeks or even months of repetitive rehearsal—of exploring and practicing small passages within the larger score over and over again, of partial iterations during "sectionals," when the conductor concentrates on synchronizing and drawing out the violins, violas, cellos, and basses, for example. Repetition is the hidden soul of this long, arduous preparation for the momentary experience of performance. And, of course, everything is tethered to a fixed score (with the conductor's interpretation, to be sure) that all players pore over and attempt to master through multiple enactments, private and group-based. Any departure from the linear sequence of "replayings" that constitute rehearsal can only be counterproductive. Behind a successful, real-time, audience-involved performance lies the tAgora process of rendering—and rerendering—text.

3. *Refrains rationalize by repeating.* Or take the example of a simple refrain in poetry, perhaps the earliest refrain in the English language, located at strategic sites in the Anglo-Saxon poem *Deor*. This lament treats the sad fate of the poem's namesake, who has lost his position as court poet to another oral singer, or *scop*, known as Heorrenda. Deor chooses to tell the story of his demise and present misery by indirection. He cites several instances

of tragedy and lost hope from the body of Germanic traditional lore and then closes each elegiac cameo with this refrain:

Ðæs ofereode, þisses swa mæg.
That passed, so may this.

As different as the several ministories are—involving captivity, death, rape, drowning, and other cruel events—each is anchored by this same repeating refrain. Very importantly for our purposes, each instance takes its force from those that precede it. The inherently repetitive refrain serves in effect as an echo that rationalizes the diversity of the episodes. Repetition signals and creates unity within that diversity.

Recurrence is an oAgora and eAgora phenomenon

In the oAgora and eAgora, recurrence is the governing rule and repetition can't exist. What do we mean by "recurrence"? We mean an action or event that occurs as a reflex of the situation at hand and then recurs naturally whenever that situation arises again, if ever. Such recurrences aren't linear in their logic; they don't depend on each other and they don't speak directly, or at least primarily, to one another. Instead they depend on an idiomatic response to a recognized scenario. To put it another way, recurrence takes place in the arenas of oral tradition (Arena of Oral Tradition) and the web (Arena of the Web), while repetition is a creature of the textual arena (Arena of the Text).

Once again, let's look at a few examples to help explain this categorical distinction between the oAgora and eAgora on the one hand, and the tAgora on the other.

1. *Language itself is a fundamentally recurrent medium.* To take the simplest case first, consider how everyday language works (Proverbs). Embedded in social context, you constantly draw on your navigational abilities—not your rote memory—to work your way through a day's experience in social life. If you use the "same" phrase twice during that day, it's not because you recall the first conversation and seek to parrot what you said before. Unless you specifically set out to quote yourself (a textual strategy), you're not striving to copy or iterate or rehash. Phrases turn up because the situation calls for them to emerge—via recurrence, not repetition.

   The idiomatic nature of recurrence is perhaps most obvious when the reflex in question makes little or no literal sense. College students, including my own children, widely practice a telephone-answering ritual that illustrates this phenomenon. When the phone rings, the first words out of the mouth of the person who answers are very often "Not much," in response to an initial "So what's up?" or the equivalent on the other end. Although the answerer might actually be straining to complete a term paper, heatedly discussing international politics with a roommate, or running a marathon, the canonical reply would still be "Not much." Nonsensical? Not at all, because within the focused idiom of the telephone call that mysterious reply has the force of something like "OK, I'm here; what do you want?" And the superficially illogical phrase will emerge not because it builds on the last telephone call, or the one before that, but because it's what the social contract of language (Culture As Network) calls for in this particular situation. In short, "Not much" recurs; it doesn't repeat.

2. *Recurrence in jazz: Improvising along a linkmap.* Simply put, if jazz players repeat it just isn't jazz. Unlike Western classical music, for instance, jazz isn't score-bound. Instead, it requires that instrumentalists improvise along a core melody, navigating the linkmap (Linkmaps) of the tune in question and practicing variation within limits (Variation within Limits). In this scenario no two performances can ever be identical—even if the personnel and the song are precisely the same—and no single performance, however much admired, will ever be the original or final version of the song. Jazz performances amount to recurrence, not repetition.

   Consider Pat Metheny's "When We Were Free," a five-minute, thirty-nine–second version of which is available on the album *Quartet.* If you decide to play this recording (a frozen performance) a dozen times, the last eleven will amount to repetitions of the first experience. No variation whatsoever: the recording memorializes one possible navigation of the basic melody undertaken at a specific time and place and will never change. Although that performance itself involved rule-governed improvisation, it's now an artifact, static and incapable of morphing.

   Not so the more than twelve-minute version of the same song that I heard live at Columbia, Missouri's *Blue Note* venue in 2004. Perhaps spurred on by the enthusiasm of the audience, Metheny soared far beyond what he attempted in the *Quartet* recording, probing many more dimensions of the basic linkmap (Stories Are Linkmaps) and providing an even more imaginative extrapolation of his fundamental musical ideas. But was this twelve-minute performance actually the "same" song in spite of the differences in length, depth, and so forth? Yes, certainly; within jazz conventions "When We Were Free" happened again. It recurred. But unlike the last eleven times I listened to the recording, that performance had nothing to do with repetition.

3. *OT performances recur.* During our fieldwork in Serbia we encountered an epic singer, Živomir Stojanović, who proudly displayed a crudely hand-edited booklet as the source of the oral poem he was about to perform. In other words, he identified a published textual artifact that he was not

only able to read but had himself also modified, presumably according to personal preference, as the source of what we were about to record. This unexpected scenario seemed to call our understanding of composition-in-performance—variation within limits, in particular—into serious question. From the perspective of the Pathways Project, if a *guslar* can read and edit texts, isn't he depending more on tAgora than on oAgora dynamics? Isn't his performance more repetition than recurrence?

But closer examination soon revealed our initial impression to be off the mark. As victims of deeply ingrained textual ideology (Ideology of the Text), we automatically assumed that this performance—along with every other performance of this song, for that matter—would simply amount to a verbatim iteration of that same hand-edited, published text. As citizens of a textual marketplace, we unthinkingly gave first priority to the artifact without considering whether an ironclad, inviolable connection between the text and the performance(s) really existed.

When we backed up an ideological step and checked our recording of the recorded performance against a photocopy of the *guslar*'s "personal edition," we noticed that he didn't follow his supposed source much at all. The first few lines were similar, but after that point he diverged, added, subtracted, and substituted, fashioning something quite different from the textual template. To put it more precisely, the singer wasn't trekking through a text; he was navigating the web of his poetic tradition. And in that fundamental respect his performance was most certainly an example of recurrence rather than repetition.

Remix

A contemporary and an ancient art

As the Wikipedia entry[99] advises, remixing occurs in literature, art, music, and other media. More broadly, cultures are constantly interleaving old and new, domestic and foreign resources—combining religious beliefs and symbols, adapting governments and laws and customs as they encounter "new" cultural environments. The resulting remixes can be frozen into tAgora documents, and the process that produced them is thereby halted and fixed, at least for a while. In this fashion a remix becomes a thing in itself—a freestanding item, but with obvious debts to its constituents.

The possibility of remixing has come into clear focus with the advent of the eAgora, where digital weaving, unweaving, and reweaving is commonplace and expectable. Whereas the tAgora yields and deals in ordered series of invariable linear surfaces, the electronic marketplace offers the tools to reshape reality

(Reality Remains in Play) and the qualified citizenry to use and appreciate the new-media content that results.

What may not be so obvious to us moderns is that remixing is the ruling dynamic of the oAgora as well. Every oral performance is an oPathway-driven surfing of the traditional network (oPathways), responding to different times, places, audiences, new cultural contacts, and other factors. Distributed authorship is the mode of creation (Distributed Authorship), as in the eAgora, and variation within limits is the name of the compositional game, again as in the eAgora (Variation within Limits).

As in other aspects, then, we see the basic Pathways Project homology emerge in the correlative phenomena of eRemixing and oRemixing.

A contemporary remix

A brilliant example of this art form is the *McLuhan Remix* by Jamie O'Neil/Kurt Weibers, who distributes his authorship—which blurs with distributed editorship—between two personas as well as among the content producers from whose work he has drawn. The nearly fifteen-minute video is posted, with his explicit permission, on the Pathways Project website.[100]

Responsible Agora-business

Cyber-detours

Here's the scenario, doubtless only too familiar to all of us. A colleague, friend, family member, or student—or even, perish the thought, one of us—gets "cyber-detoured." In the midst of serious, sustained investigation of Internet resources, navigating through networks and cocreating an experience, he or she (or we) illogically veer(s) offtrack, abandoning the pertinent and productive in favor of the irrelevant and time-wasting. Likely interruptions can include incoming email, updated weather reports, the latest news from RSS feeds, an episode of online gaming, a Facebook encounter, an irresistible Tweet, and myriad other distractions.

Depending on the severity and duration of the detour, it can register as anything from a momentary, attention-deflecting nuisance to a flagrant abuse of the medium. As a second-order reaction to such media-malfeasance, some of us might well find ourselves not merely condemning the outrageous behavior in question but ascribing it to a fatal weakness in the technology itself. What good is a medium that compromises its own mission by offering such built-in distractions? How defensible is agora-business that can so quickly and easily lead to its own demise?

The short answer

The short answer to such questions: tools are tools, nothing more and nothing less. Even the most exquisitely balanced, ergonomically sound hammer can, if wielded without sufficient dexterity, accomplish little more than bruising your thumb. Just so, any technology can be used well or badly. Any medium, and any language, can be engaged fluently or clumsily. In other words, responsibility for conducting and sustaining effective agora-business rests not with the tool, but with its user.

A few longer answers

To level the playing field, let's have a look at how agora-business can go awry in our two other marketplaces: the word-worlds of oral tradition and text. After that, we'll cycle back to the cybersphere with a more realistic (because comparative and contextual) perspective on use and misuse.

Flawed fluency in the oAgora

Not all oral performers are created equal, any more than all speakers of English— or the aspiring poets among them—stand shoulder to shoulder with William Shakespeare or John Keats. Experience with South Slavic oral epic tradition, for instance, teaches that bards range from magisterial to workaday to unsuccessful, depending on their talent and on their fluency in the dedicated creative idiom of the oAgora. And yes, because they are embedded in the flux of everyday reality, individual performances, even those by the very same *guslar*, also show considerable variability. At a third level, singers can find themselves distracted or diverted even within a single performance, veering off (Misnavigation) from an expectable constellation of pathways, losing the thread of the particular story. Such things do occur.

At times like these we recognize that the ideal of continuous, "perfect" navigation amounts to a text-fed fantasy (Texts and Intertextuality); as long as reality remains in play (Reality Remains in Play), nothing happens until it happens. Since the process of oAgora navigation is by nature emergent, contingent (Contingency), and under negotiation, it's also inherently unpredictable and subject to detours. Two anecdotes will illustrate this point.

1. *Preventing performance.* The first involves a portrait of dramatically unsuccessful oAgora activity and its ramifications as sketched by the Slovenian ethnographer Matija Murko,[101] who reported an unusual brand of audience critique that he observed in Bosnia in the early 1920s (Audience Critique). An unnamed *guslar* performed so badly, it seems, that his listeners took a radical step: they covertly greased the single string of his *gusle*, or accompanying instrument, when he stopped for a rest break. As they intended,

this unsubtle intervention left the well-meaning but unappreciated epic singer quite stymied, unable to pursue his particularly unproductive brand of oAgora-business.

2. *Inability to navigate.* The second incident took place during fieldwork conducted in Serbia in the late 1970s by Joel and Barbara Halpern and myself. One afternoon we arrived at the Ilić household, located in our home village of Orašac, intending to record a performance of Christian Orthodox epic from Pavle Ilić, the paterfamilias of his extended family group. But before the old fellow could begin, his impulsive son Dragan snatched the *gusle* from his hands and tried his best to regale us with a favorite story. After a few lines, however, his story-vessel ran aground. Forced to abandon the rash attempt, he shamefacedly relinquished the instrument to his far more fluent father Pavle, who knew how to navigate.

In both of these cases it was clearly the user and not the medium that led to dysfunction. Neither the nameless *guslar* nor Dragan Ilić proved up to the task of accessing and working within their oral epic traditions. Neither was sufficiently fluent in its specialized word-technology (oWords) to communicate effectively. In broad terms, they didn't know how to travel the oPathways of their epic tradition (oPathways). So let's not fault those blameless and longstanding oAgora networks for the failures of prospective oNavigators who simply couldn't manage the exploration.

Flawed fluency in the tAgora

Nor are all readers created equal. In addition to the free-for-all of interpretive license—visible not just in literature, but in law, business, medicine, and every human textual arena—we need to take full account of the kaleidoscope of prior experience and attitudes, and not incidentally of outright misuse of the written medium.

Yes, texts can be and often are misused. Think across marketplaces: if a college student or an analyst in a large corporation can get distracted from intensive, responsible web investigation by the lure of social networking or message-checking, then why can't things go similarly "off topic" in the tAgora? Of course they can and do, as a few anecdotes from university life will show.

1. *A term project goes astray.* Ariadne, a sophomore at a large urban university, is assigned a paper on the sociopolitical backgrounds of the Spanish-American War, and she heads to the campus library to research the topic. Both brick-and-mortar and electronic resources come into play, the latter chiefly as a repository of fixed, noninteractive texts that require reading via the customary rules governing linearity and predetermined sequence. But suppose the journal that Ariadne consults also contains articles on musical trends or popular culture in turn-of-the-century Spain, and fur-

ther that those extraneous contents (extraneous to her core topic, that is) simply prove too attractive for her to resist. Suppose, to reduce things to the most elementary and human level, that our intrepid student's attention falters, and she skips over valuable information essential for her research paper. Is this shortcoming the fault of the resource? Do we attribute the detour to the medium or to the agent trying to operate within that medium? Do we blame the text or the text user?

2. *Manuscripts have their own rules.* Our second example emerges from a real-life episode in academic research. Some years ago I, like all prior investigators, was at a loss to explain the phrase *on sunde* in an Old English poem[102] that links the Christian apocalypse to the widespread destruction by the pagan Germanic storm-giant as he passes over settlements and farms. Literally, *on sunde* seems to mean either "in the water/ sea" or "in swimming." The problem is that neither explanation fits the context, in which the poet is describing how body and soul, flesh and spirit are preserved together. On consulting a photographic facsimile of the original tenth-century manuscript, however, I discovered that the first word *on* ended one line and the second word *sunde* began the next, leaving open the possibility that, since under the scribal rules of the period word-division often went unmarked, this could well be one rather than two words. If that were the case, and taking into account variant spellings common throughout the preserved manuscripts, the Old English expression could in fact be a single word: *onsunde*, also spelled *ansunde* and meaning "safely." This reading makes sense on both levels of the poem—preserving body and soul together and safely. It's a small point, but it illustrates how scholars' misunderstanding of the manuscript medium had led to a persistent error in the printed medium, and thus to bad tAgora-business.

In both of these cases, as with the two oAgora stories recounted above, the technology necessary to the task is present, available, and (in the "right hands") effective. We can't criticize the medium (Accuracy) when it's not to blame, any more than we can fault that state-of-the-art hammer for a blackened thumbnail. In each instance we need to trace the problem beyond the medium itself to the person who fails in some way to harness its power and possibilities, whether through lack of fluency, lack of attention, or a combination of the two.

Just what is fluency in the eAgora, anyway?

With these few thoughts on oAgora-business and tAgora-business in mind, we can perhaps understand cyber-detours in more depth. If oral traditions and texts can be used nonfluently or inattentively, then the incursion of distracting opportunities [oops, there goes my email alert again!] into focused pathway navigation may not seem so outrageous. More to the point, such an incursion may not be misinterpreted as a flaw restricted to and typical of eAgora activities alone.

To put it more plainly, only within the tAgora do such natural and inevitable "diversions" escape our notice, and there's a ready explanation for this peculiarity. Textual ideology has submerged them below the threshold of our active awareness, under the (finally untenable) assumption that textuality freezes knowledge, art, and ideas in a form that keeps them inviolate and immune from change (Ideology of the Text). eTechnology is still very much in the process of being understood and isn't yet our default medium, so perhaps it's only expectable that such momentary departures tend to receive undue emphasis. In a sense the situation isn't so different from aberrant case studies that appear to threaten generally held truths or conclusions.

We look at the wonders of web navigation, which promotes immediate and highly economical access to worlds we could scarcely imagine a decade ago, and even the occasional excursion into Facebook-checking or Tweeting seems wrong or wasteful. Never mind that poring over our sacred texts is rudely derailed by telephone calls, coffee breaks, fire drills, note-taking, or a thousand other activities. Never mind that we programmatically dismiss such interruptions by letting them recede into the background noise of existence, always there but hardly ever foregrounded. Unfortunately, in doing so we let textuality cover its tracks, and we continue to participate in the illusion that it offers the sole dependable standard for nonfrivolous, appropriately engaged agora-business. Culturally set defaults are hard to reset.

Ironically, but from the perspective of the OT-IT homology (Agora Correspondences) quite explicably, this same "text first" ideology has hindered our understanding and appreciation of oAgora communication as well. If a story or genealogy or history seems to vary within limits, as is characteristic of and necessary within the oral marketplace (Variation within Limits), we champions of the book and page cry foul. Never mind the brittle, disembodied, nonconnected, and non-updatable nature of the immutable text; we're quite willing to submerge those glaring deficiencies in our worship of the twinned gods of objectivity (Illusion of Object) and stasis (Illusion of Stasis).

In other words, our understanding of both OT and IT suffers from an ideological short circuit that highlights the unavoidable and expectable static of using media in the living human world. And highlighting the static necessarily means diminishing communication. At the same time, adding insult to injury, this predisposition toward the imagined dynamics of the tAgora measures the nontextual according to (a fantasy of) the textual. That's unfair on quite a number of levels.

Conducting and sustaining responsible agora-business calls for fairer practices across multiple marketplaces, for playing by the applicable rules of each venue rather than imposing a blanket policy for communication. Yet another reason to seek citizenship not in one but in multiple agoras (Citizenship in Multiple Agoras).

Extra-script

Extra- (outside) rather than *post-* (after) a node that's not conventionally *scriptus* (written) at all? But bear with me: in an effort to escape ideological bias and reframe so-called diversions as part of the natural flow of experience rather than a fatal technological flaw, I have a set of propositions for you to consider:

> What if eDiversions are simply alternate sets of pathways for optional exploration and thus part of the overall eAgora network? What if operation within any agora means confronting and selecting among all of its possibilities and potentials? While we're at it, who's to say that Twitter doesn't flesh out the real experiential context of daily life rather than simply divert attention from more "serious" and "directed" communication? Maybe John Lennon was right: maybe "life is what happens to you while you're busy making other plans."

Resynchronizing the Event

Wordsworth had it right

About 200 years ago William Wordsworth put it this way in a poem he entitled "The Tables Turned":

> Sweet is the lore which nature brings;
> Our meddling intellect
> Mis-shapes the beauteous forms of things:—
> We murder to dissect.

A serious charge: "we murder to dissect." Exactly whom or what was he accusing? The answer? In Pathways Project terms, this appears to be a tAgora crime.

From the beginning of the poem on, the principal object of the poet's criticism is in fact none other than the book, which he unconditionally disparages as a source for wisdom. Wordsworth's complaint against books was part of his program for composing poetry, which he felt should depend more on the simple experience of walking through nature—the source of "spontaneous wisdom"—than on the learned, page-turning craft of his immediate poetic predecessors. Quite an indictment of textual ideology (Ideology of the Text).

Em-booking oral tradition

Our advocacy of eEditions (eEditions) as vehicles for studying and representing oral tradition springs from similar concerns and a parallel history. For all of its myriad benefits, the book has done to oral tradition exactly what in Wordsworth's opinion it did to poetry: murdered a living creature by vivisection. The once-vibrant event or experience becomes a corpse, and although an autopsy may bring after-the-fact knowledge of its prior functions, the deed is irreversibly done.

So what's the price exacted by the culturally approved em-booking process? Nothing less than the very viability of the subject under study. A steep price, to be sure, but one that tAgora ideology has conveniently hidden from view. Without examining the implications, we import the "other" into our usual default medium and consider the job well done.

The printed page   Experience has taught us how such euthanasia proceeds in the case of oAgora events. During the early days of "collection" (notice the insulating, object-centered jargon), fieldworkers struggled to extract a dictionary-certified, printable text from the messy reality of multimedia performance. The goal, of course, was to exhibit their elusive quarry within the approved museum space of the printed page (Museum of Verbal Art). When the results fell below the threshold of an acceptable text, editors felt no compunction about "correcting" what their informants actually said and "restoring" what they "meant" to say. Thus the Grimm Brothers and their highly expurgated tales, for example.

The exclusive goal of this culturally sponsored text hunt was to reduce the performance to a document, which collectors and editors assumed had to be the heart of the matter. Many of us still make that assumption (Accuracy), occasionally with a polite but perfunctory nod toward the perhaps 50–70 percent of the performance that's discarded in the process (the intonations, pauses, vocal music, instrumentation, dance patterns, audience reactions, and so many other facets of performances that conventionally get suppressed in the course of conversion to texts).

Audio and video   The advent of audio and video recording raised our awareness, to be sure, making it possible to reach beyond textual remains and glimpse other dimensions of oAgora activity. Still, however, the final published yield of most field recordings is usually only the celebrated but mute transcription. Even when audio or video itself is made available, it's rarely listened to or watched along with the text (or translation). Cultural and historical context is likewise segregated—relegated to an appendix, a companion, or the equivalent—if provided at all.

In short, our default method for representing oral traditions has been to convert events into items. We reduce systems to things (Systems versus Things). We dissect a multifaceted, emergent whole that demands our attention right now, at its own pace and on its own terms, and we settle for a pale reflection of some small part of that immediacy, comfortably static and distanced. We generate an asynchronous artifact that we can control by holding it at arm's length (Realtime versus Asynchronous). In Wordsworth's sense, we effectively murder the living reality of the performance.

Rescuing performances

eEditions, on the other hand, hold out the promise of resynchronizing the event, of reconstituting the experience, of putting the parts back together to create at least a reasonable facsimile of the original whole.

Consider the eEdition of *The Wedding of Mustajbey's Son Bećirbey*[103] as performed by Halil Bajgorić. With the text and translation reconnected to the audio record, and with the commentary, dictionary of idioms, and other materials electronically linked to the onward-moving performance script, users become more than mere readers of texts. To an extent they become part of the audience for that long-ago performance, only now (necessarily) removed from the day (in June of 1935) and place (Dabrica, in the Former Yugoslavia) of its original occurrence.

An eExperience for an eAudience

What's so different? Well, through the agency of the eEdition the performance is once again continuous and multifaceted. Sure, you can stop it by pausing the audio or simply closing the webpage altogether, just as you can close a book and go make a cup of coffee or check your email. But as long as the eEdition is open and all of its systems are active, the potential exists for the "reader" to attend the performance in real time and, to the degree that linked resources restore at least some of the cultural, poetic, and historical context, in real space as well. Halil Bajgorić performs again (Leapfrogging the Text): the story evolves, the vocal and instrumental melodies sound, some of the cultural and linguistic background expected of a fluent audience becomes available. The event happens, again, and you become a member of its audience.

Is this eExperience "the same as" the original that happened in 1935 Bosnia? Of course not, but it's a facsimile of immersion we can manage here and now. It's far more faithful to the original than fussing over the book-bound corpse and trying vainly to imagine what it must have been like while alive.

At the very least, the eEdition avoids the unpardonable sin of murder by dissection.

Singing on the Page

Peaceful coexistence and interaction

The oAgora and tAgora are not sealed off, wholly segregated marketplaces. Nor are oral traditions and texts always and everywhere isolated from one another, impervious to influence from the other technology. Recall as a first principle that three of the four types of oral tradition either may or must involve texts in some way: *voiced texts* are composed in writing, albeit solely for oral performance; *voices from the past* involved both technologies in some now undeterminable fashion; and *written oral tradition* simply cannot be either composed or received without a textual vehicle. The old-fashioned idea that oral tradition and texts form an exclusive binary, or Great Divide, was in its time a useful way to create thinking space for "something else besides literature." But contemporary fieldwork and historical research have taught us that these two technologies not only coexist peacefully but interact in fascinating ways. Moreover, they do so not only within the same community but within the very same individual.

Individual performers who do the once-unimaginable—compose within OT code but in the textual medium—can be described as "singing on the page." Let's examine three cases of this phenomenon, proceeding from the most recent toward the earliest, in an effort to understand just what's transpiring and how the oAgora supports such activities. Starting with an example from a twentieth-century South Slavic epic singer and his transcriber, we'll then look at the nineteenth-century physician/fieldworker Elias Lönnrot, who collected and partially composed the Finnish *Kalevala*. Our third example will consist of the celebrated Anglo-Saxon poem entitled *Caedmon's Hymn*, which scribes seem to have recomposed "orally" even as they copied and recopied it.

Case study 1: Singer versus transcriber

When Albert Lord suggested that I begin my work at the Parry Collection by listening to an audio recording of Halil Bajgorić's performance of *The Wedding of Mustajbey's Son Bećirbey*[104] and making an original-language transcription, I was both intrigued and bewildered. Here, after poring over many textualized performances, I was to gain access to the "real thing," a South Slavic oral epic just as it was performed, without any editorial filter, warts and all. Just one nettlesome problem: a transcription already existed, and by none other than Nikola Vujnović (A Foot in Each World), whose abilities—as a native speaker of South Slavic, a cultural insider with a deep knowledge of the epic way of speaking, and not least a practicing *guslar* himself—far surpassed my own. What need could there possibly be for an outsider to undertake a task that an enormously better prepared insider had already completed?

The answer to that question emerged front and center within the first ten lines of listening and transcribing, as I quickly realized that what I was hearing didn't exactly match what I was reading in Vujnović's elegantly handwritten notebook. Some of the discrepancies were small, and some were larger. I was initially at a loss to explain them, and listened over and over again, trying to discover how I (certainly not Vujnović) had gone astray in my apprehension of Bajgorić's performance (Leapfrogging the Text).

Eventually, however, I started to realize that these discrepancies weren't simply errors; they were performance variants or alternatives. Where Vujnović failed to include *performatives*—extra sounds that a singer inserts to smooth his vocal continuity—the explanation was simple enough. Functional as they were, they passed unnoticed in the oAgora. What was necessary for live performance had no role in silent reading, and the transcriber was acquainted enough with tAgora procedure to know that. So he left them out.

Other discrepancies loomed larger. Where Vujnović wrote *Samo* ("Only") for the singer's *Tamo* ("There") at line 263, or *A opazi* ("But he caught sight of") for the singer's *'Vako pazi* ("So he spied") at line 157, he was recomposing the song within his own personal style or idiolect even as he wrote it down in the notebook. Because he was depending on his compositional fluency, these changes were "wrong" only in a tAgora sense. Within the oAgora they were simply slightly different oWords (oWords), leading to very similar or identical oPathways (oPathways). In fact, they perfectly illustrated the cardinal OT principle of variation within limits (Variation within Limits).

So in none of these cases was Vujnović actually making mistakes. His failure to accurately transcribe precisely what Halil Bajgorić was singing was not a sign of his inattentiveness or inability to hear and render what he heard verbatim (Accuracy). Instead, the discrepancies were a sign of his singer's ability to navigate the networks of his oral epic tradition even as he wrote out a text. Vujnović, a *guslar* in the oAgora as well as a transcriber for the tAgora, was singing on the page.

Case study 2: The 3 percent solution

Elias Lönnrot[105] (1802–84) was trained as a physician, but from his twenties onward he developed an increasing devotion to the language and folk traditions of the Finnish people. In concert with the general nineteenth-century European fascination with finding a people's roots in national epic, Lönnrot traveled through the Finnish countryside, which then encompassed large sections of what is now Russian Karelia, searching for a lost national epic. Not just any epic, of course: what he sought was a cultural treasure comparable in scope and importance to foundational works like the ancient Greek *Iliad* and *Odyssey*, the medieval German *Nibelungenlied*, and many others. His collections of oral poetry—written down from still-living tradition by him and to a lesser extent his collaborators A. J. Sjögren and D. E. D. Europaeus—numbered about two million lines of verse and are preserved in the Folklore Archives of the Finnish Literature Society.

What Lönnrot must have envisioned and what he encountered were substantially different. In place of a long, sprawling epic narrative he was able to find and write down only much smaller stories and story parts. He interpreted these short poems as pieces of a formerly unified master story, calling it the *Kalevala*. From 1835 onward Lönnrot published several editions of his *Kalevala*, editorially assembled from the apparent fragments in his collection. And his reconstructed poem was to prove seminal for the national self-image, driving not only political developments but also myriad Finnish projects in art, literature, film, and music (especially the classical oeuvre of Jean Sibelius) and has been translated into more than fifty languages. It would be difficult to find a more influential modern oral tradition.

But this unique and enormously productive resource would never have existed if Lönnrot hadn't learned to sing on the page. And that singing took various forms: arranging and adapting the material he had collected, sometimes dramatically, not to mention personally creating new, additional verses in the form and style of the indigenous oral poetry. As the Wikipedia article[106] summarizes, the published epic consists of approximately "one third of word-for-word recordings by the collectors, 50 percent of material that Lönnrot adjusted slightly, 14 percent of verses he wrote himself based on poem variants, and 3 percent of verses purely of his own invention."

If we set aside the text-versus-OT binary that fieldwork has shown to be a false dichotomy, we can see that Lönnrot's "interference" was still a type of oAgora activity—of *written oral tradition*, to be specific. He had internalized the rules for composing within the *Kalevala* tradition, and used his competence to modify and even to cocreate within the oral marketplace. Whether an extended narrative ever existed in the Karelian lands or not, what the physician turned epic singer accomplished was to make the oral tradition a continuing and vital force in Finnish culture.

Case study 3: The miracle that morphed

The story of the probably legendary Anglo-Saxon oral poet named Caedmon is extraordinary. According to Bede's famous account,[107] this lowly cowherd regularly experienced a crippling case of performance anxiety at the worst possible moment. In the monastery where he worked, it was the evening custom to pass the harp (probably a six-stringed lyre like the one found at the Sutton Hoo ship burial)[108] around the table after sharing mead and beer. When it reached you, it was your turn to sing—to answer the oAgora call to compose and perform Anglo-Saxon oral poetry.

But not poor Caedmon, who, confronted with what was for him a threatening prospect, fled unceremoniously to the stable, where he spent the night with his bovine charges. However, all was not lost, for during that night an angel appeared to the desolate Caedmon and imbued him with the ability to compose oral poetry. First was a hymn glorifying God's creation, and from that point on he began the practice of turning biblical narratives into orally performed poems, using the familiar, time-honored vernacular medium of oral tradition to spread the word of the gospels and other works. It was a miracle of the first order.

Latter-day reactions to Bede's story have varied widely. Some earlier scholars took it at face value, and tried to decide whether this or that surviving Anglo-Saxon poem was the creation of Caedmon. Never mind that we have only a very few conclusive attestations of authorship, and that even these may well be legendary tag-names for the distributed authorship of the oAgora (Distributed Authorship); textual ideology knows no bounds. More recently, other scholars have interpreted the Caedmon episode as a kind of folk allegory, conjured to explain the transferal of Christian stories to the local, familiar idiom of the Anglo-Saxon poetic tradition.

We may never know with certainty whether someone named Caedmon existed, or, if he did, whether that real-life individual was in any way responsible for some of the oral-derived *voices from the past* that have been attributed to him. Nonetheless, like Homer, the South Slavic Ćor Huso, the Mongolian Choibang, and even the Anglo-Saxon minstrel/oral historian Widsith ("Wide-traveler"), Caedmon remains at the very least a significant way to put a name on an ever-shifting, never-fixed, multiauthored oral tradition. Legendary figures have their own power.

So perhaps it's only fitting that the nine-line hymn that Caedmon is supposed to have composed on his emergence from the stable is so famous. Nor that it's by far the most widely documented of any surviving verse from this era before the Battle of Hastings. Here is my translation of the West Saxon version of *Caedmon's Hymn* into modern English, with small rearrangements and adjustments:

> Now we must praise the Guardian of the heaven-kingdom,
> The power of the Measurer, and his mind-thought,
> The work of the Glory-father, because He established the beginning
> Of every wonder, the eternal Lord.
> He first shaped heaven as a roof
> For earth's children, the holy Creator;
> Then the Guardian of humankind afterward made

Middle-earth, the eternal Lord,
For earth's inhabitants, the almighty King.

Many of the verses or half-lines, separated by extra space at midline in most editions, are variations on oWords that recur elsewhere in the Anglo-Saxon oral tradition of poetry. Given his skill with this specialized language, Caedmon is best understood as an oral poet highly adept at navigating the pathways of this medieval English web of multiform language. He was fluent in the *lingua franca* of the oAgora, and knew how to deploy its poetic idiom, an open-source code that he shared with the poets who composed *Beowulf* and other Old English poetry. Indeed, he was so fluent that he caused oral poetry to do something new, to assume a social function that it had not supported in the past. Whether we explain his remarkable innovativeness and verbal dexterity as the gift of a visiting angel or as reflecting changes in a poetic tradition that took on new duties as the Christian conversion proceeded, we can confidently credit Caedmon with knowing how to manage successful transactions in his oral marketplace.

But that's not the end of this miraculous tale. Recent research has established that the five extant versions of *Caedmon's Hymn* included with the Anglo-Saxon (rather than the Latin) texts of Bede's *History of the English Church and People* behave quite curiously. They don't fit the usual tAgora mold. These variants collectively exhibit option-driven, rule-governed variation typical not of tAgora replication, but rather of oAgora navigation. Such a phenomenon can be explained only as the work of scribes—copyists physically scrawling ink on vellum manuscripts, we should keep in mind—who were recomposing even as they "copied." Katherine O'Brien O'Keeffe[109] puts it very clearly and straightforwardly: "In such a process, reading and copying have actually become conflated with composing."

Like Nikola Vujnović, who recomposed the oral epic performance by Halil Bajgorić as he transcribed the audio recording, these scribes worked within the flexible, systemic (Systems versus Things) idiom of the oral poetic tradition. They weren't doing what we tAgora denizens assume scribes do—namely, reproduce the item verbatim, with the copy nothing less than an exact replica of the original. No, they were writing under oAgora rules, remaking as they went, navigating the OT web (Online with OT). It may seem counterintuitive to us, but these scribes—whose job it was to produce documents—were singing on the page.

Spectrum of Texts: Five Types

Both over its relatively brief history and at the present time, the tAgora has proven a complex arena for communicative exchange (Arena of the Text). To reflect that complexity, this node briefly examines five major species of text that have lived and thrived within its confines: *Symbols of/on clay, Greek letters on papyrus, Latin and runic letters on sheepskin, Typography on paper,* and *Static eFiles in pixels.*

Symbols of/on clay

Within the tAgora we focus exclusively on what transpired from November 22 onward in Homo sapiens' calendar year, the maximum time frame for textual concerns (Texts and Intertextuality). Recently the much-debated connection between numeracy[110] and the origins of literacy has grown considerably clearer, thanks in great measure to the groundbreaking work of Denise Schmandt-Besserat.[111] In books such as *Before Writing* and *How Writing Came About,* she offers much more than a new view of ancient artifacts and their usability. She constructs a coherent explanation of how a simple counting mechanism evolved into an inscribed tablet surface, a surface that amounts to the precursor of papyrus, sheepskin, page, and LED screen, all of which are essentially later avatars of a radical ancient invention. Here's one view of the story:[112]

> About 10,000 years ago, during the Neolithic period, small clay tokens of different geometrical shapes begin to turn up as a fledgling system for keeping track of quantities of grain, jars of oil, and other exchangeable, tangible goods. Evidence indicates a one-to-one correspondence between a token and what it stood for; three cones, for example, symbolized three small measures of grain, whereas five ovoids indicated five jars of oil. At first there were, in other words, no counters that symbolized abstract numbers as distinct from the actual things they represented.
>
> The next step was to devise a method for storing and organizing ever-changing collections of tokens, and one popular solution proved to be the clay envelope or hollowed-out ball, into which the individual counters were inserted before closure. Of course, this otherwise effective strategy meant a lack of ready access to the contents, and to deal with that problem the makers of such containers began to mark the envelope's exterior by pressing the differently shaped tokens into its soft surface before it was sealed and fire-hardened. The result was an external, easily available ledger of hidden contents that could be conveniently accessed at any time without destroying the enclosure.
>
> Once this crucial step was taken, the enclosed tokens became functionally unnecessary to the communication. So, with the transition to a piece of solid clay and its inscribable surface, the tablet—or prehistoric desktop—was born. Later on yet, accountants began to use a pointed stylus to draw token-images on the surface, thus completing the trajectory from a currency of counters to tablet technology. It was from these hand-drawn shapes that ancient cuneiform writing was to emerge.

As long as ten millennia ago, in other words, a brand-new tAgora used the twin illusions of object (Illusion of Object) and stasis (Illusion of Stasis) to create textual precursors in the form of tokens. These counters, like the material goods they represented, were exchanged by their owners under applicable rules and were valued for their tangible symbolism and resistance to change. And why not? Their authority was effectively unchallengeable within the rules of the game. Today you owned seven small measures of grain, and as long as you had seven cones in your pocket tomorrow your grain holdings remained secure. Gathering and ordering your tokens by entrusting them to a clay envelope further certified your ownership (Owning versus Sharing), especially when the envelope's inventory was continuously available on the exterior. And when the bag stopped being an actual bag and modulated into a solid clay object, then the tablet took over as a ready-made cognitive prosthesis.

From the start, then, the tAgora sought to prevent morphing, to forestall variation within limits (Variation within Limits), and freeze systemic transmission (Systems versus Things). It set up a brick-and-mortar technology whose mission was (eventually) to eliminate all flux in the transmission of knowledge, art, and ideas by projecting various cultural realities—always fundamentally Protean—onto concrete tokens and inscribable tablet surfaces. This textual intervention seemed to dispel uncertainty, to secure otherwise slippery or entropic phenomena, to provide its adherents with a firm footing for negotiating the ever-shifting environments and realities they faced.

In order to accomplish these tasks, the textual marketplace mandated a major change in the way we conducted our verbal business: Homo sapiens had to abandon the practice of surfing through networks of potentials in favor of committing to a pathwayless technology (Impossibility of tPathways). And several other key features had to be implemented, among them fixity, ownership, resistance to morphing, and the freestanding status of the items exchanged. This wasn't merely a slight adjustment, because embracing the new technology meant that reality emphatically could not remain in play (Reality Remains in Play). What morphed and was shared had to be reimagined as fixed and owned. In that respect the tAgora was from the start and still remains an arena utterly unlike the ever-emergent, navigable webs of the oAgora and eAgora.

Greek letters on papyrus

Greek letters didn't begin life on papyrus. Invented sometime around the turn of the eighth century BCE and derived from Phoenician writing, the Greek alphabet first turns up on such diverse surfaces (Bellerophon and His Tablet) as clay shards, tombstones, and pottery, portraying everything from simple names to dedications to graffiti to (usually partial) lines of poetry.

Remarkably and atypically, a wine jug known as the Dipylon oinochoe,[113] dated within perhaps fifty years of the alphabet's invention, includes an entire line (and a bit) of hexameter poetry—the OT vehicle for Homer's *Iliad* and *Odyssey*—along its shoulder. The fact that it is written from right to left is hardly unusual, since ancient Greek writing often proceeded *boustrophedon*, which means turning back and forth like an ox plowing a field. The "bottom line" is that early alphabetic writing lacked firm conventions or standards and was put to many different, often informal uses. Standardization was a long way off in the future.

We know from ancient testimony as well as modern research that Homer's great epics—and apparently other epics as well—circulated orally for centuries before being written down. And even when performances were recorded, there was no opportunity for those early tAgora documents to have any direct effect on subsequent verbal transactions (Accuracy) in the oAgora. Taking a snapshot of one possible navigation of the story-web neither called a halt to further navigations nor elevated any one performance above the generative network that produced it. And, once removed from that network, even the most treasured tangible artifact had no way to reconnect.

Practical aspects of technology matter. A papyrus roll of a single book of Homer's *Iliad* or *Odyssey* stretched to an unwieldy twenty feet or more, and very few people had the literacy skills necessary to work their way through this almost unusable item. There were by some accounts more than one hundred versions of Homer at the great Alexandrian Library,[114] and that's only to be expected: fossilizing one performance on an inscribable surface could have no effect on the nature or proliferation of subsequent performances. Each performance was a single realization of web potential, a single surfing expedition—nothing more and nothing less. There was simply no way for one version to win out.

Pity the poor modern editor, then, who seeks to apply tried-and-true principles of editing to the multiple surviving textual records of Homer. Very inconveniently, the whole manuscripts do not agree line for line, nor with the fragments, and even more inconveniently it has proven impossible to solve such discrepancies by creating a genetic family tree or stemma of surviving witnesses. Why? Because those versions don't constitute a conventional family. Unlike the situation with later authors and their works, we can't uncover a genetically based chronology and pattern of influence that explains their variability.

And why not? Because imposing intertextuality—that is, the tAgora *modus operandi* of text-to-text influence—back onto ancient Greek oral-derived epic amounts to a futile and misleading gesture (Texts and Intertextuality). It cannot bear fruit because the modern ideological assumptions of absolute fixity and item-to-item derivation are inapplicable (Ideology of the Text). Which version offers the "best" reading of a particular line or group of lines? To which version do we ascribe the role of "epitome" or "foundation"? These are useless questions, anachronistic misinterpretations of a nascent tAgora, a pre-Gutenberg marketplace that was still millennia away from developing the publishing technology and mass readership we automatically and unthinkingly assume when we think about textual transmission.

So how should we handle the predictable, indeed inevitable variability among the surviving texts of Homer's epics? Well, first we need to recognize that each extant product is the result of a much larger process. The Center for Hellenic Studies has evolved a method, entitled the Homer Multitext Project,[115] that allows the user full access to the "documented" differences among the many surviving readings. What the CHS project recognizes is a very basic but usually overlooked reality: oral and oral-derived works of verbal art do not reside wholly in any tAgora document that reflects one version of them. Our modern equation of the work and the book simply doesn't apply to most ancient and medieval works, which customarily exist in many forms and versions, not to mention the morphing they undergo even during scribal copying (Singing on the Page). Until the technology of the textual marketplace evolves to the point at which we can confidently speak of exact replicas of a single-authored creation intended for the individual reader, we can't equate the work and the text.

Unlike post-Homeric works that don't derive from oral tradition, the *Iliad* and *Odyssey* are tAgora reflections of oAgora processes. As *voices from the past*, they represent the only evidence we have left of an OT that died out so long ago. But, and here is the crucial point for us, we cannot read these artifacts merely as texts, merely as fixed, single-authored, nonmorphing, freestanding items. To do so is to ignore their home agora, from which time and textual technology have inevitably isolated them.

Given their OT origins, and their identity as records of navigation through the ancient Greek oral epic tradition, our responsibility is to return these manuscript-prisoned poems to their oAgora context, at least as much as we can at this late point in time. And that means recognizing such trademark oAgora features as oWords (oWords), oPathways (oPathways), and variation within limits—and the access to the traditional network of meaning that they idiomatically provide. In a sense, we must use textual evidence to reimagine the Homeric network that supported and made possible these navigational records. We must rescue them from the ideology of the tAgora and return them—again, as best we can—to the oAgora.

Latin and runic letters on sheepskin

According to the early eighth-century historian Bede, the Angles and Saxons arrived in what was eventually to be called England (*Angla lond*) in 449 CE. These Germanic peoples possessed no literacy skills, but they did bring with them a thriving oral tradition of poetry that served numerous social functions. Eventually that traditional ecology was to include forms as various as elegies, charms, maxims, battle poems, hagiographies (saints' lives), biblical paraphrases, and the epic *Beowulf*. As time went on, writing and reading entered the picture in ways we can't now precisely recover, but the oral-derived poetry—best understood as *voices from the past* or as *written oral tradition*— remained chiefly an oAgora phenomenon. OT became an important vehicle for the transmission of Christian ideas precisely because it engaged people in a generally available, well-known verbal marketplace using a generally available, well-known source code.

Anglo-Saxon oral-derived poetry survives to our time chiefly in four major manuscripts dated to the last third of the tenth century CE. The contents of these unique collections are diverse, especially the so-called Exeter Book, which houses forms as heterogeneous as charms, riddles, elegies, and religious lyrics. As digests of oral-derived poetry, they reflect the distributed authorship and distributed editorship still characteristic of oAgora-rooted communication even after commission to writing (Distributed Authorship). In other words, they were composed by surfing through the oPathways of Anglo-Saxon oral tradition. The very diversity of forms we encounter in Old English poetry, and their origin in the dedicated code of the oAgora, makes a telling argument for the strength, breadth of application, and persistence of the technology of navigating through networks.

As was the case with the incipient tAgora in ancient Greece, these manuscripts, precious as they are for us, had nothing like a modern textual function. The insular minuscule writing system employed by early medieval English scribes resulted from Irish missionaries' attempts to press Latin letters into service as a vehicle for recording the Germanic language of Old English. For sounds that did not occur in Latin, such as "th," they borrowed letters from the Runic alphabet, or *futharc*.[116] Rhythmic oral poetry, composed and performed in quanta of lines and half-lines, was transferred to a run-on, nonlineated prose format, with little or nothing of modern punctuation and capitalization. And since literacy was rare and restricted largely to the monasteries for many years, these four manuscripts (and the poems scattered through other minor manuscripts) never had a chance to participate in the kind of mass readership community to which twenty-first-century text users are accustomed.

What survives to us amounts to fixed tAgora records of once-flexible, emergent oAgora itineraries, an after-the-fact account of journeys through the web of Anglo-Saxon poetic tradition. Some of these journeys were undoubtedly taken pen in hand, by poets "singing on the page," much as Elias Lönnrot, Bishop Njegoš, and other text-bound performers of *written oral tradition*. Some may be descendants of transcribed oral performances, and therefore *voices from the past*, and still others re-creations of what scribes heard or perhaps even read. Since we know that orality and literacy can coexist not only within the same culture or community but also within the very same individual (A Foot in Each World), many combinations of OT and TT are possible. (In this connection we shouldn't forget about recent discoveries that scribes and transcribers used oAgora code to recompose even as they wrote.)

But the manuscripts that preserve these poetic itineraries, and which descend to us as the only evidence of the OT network that produced them, present themselves solely as texts. What's more, in all but a few cases the available witnesses are unique rather than multiple, with only a single version of most poems extant. Where there are multiple manuscript copies, as is the case with *Caedmon's Hymn*, it quickly becomes apparent that not only is the poem composed in oWords with oPathways, but it actually continued to morph *even as scribes went about copying and recopying "it" in texts*. More broadly, different poems, unrelated by subject or genre, share oWords and attached pathways. Something seems amiss here.

So let's try a more applicable frame of reference. Let's think about the much larger and more generative *process* that yielded these singular-seeming *products*, a process now ironically masked by its surviving tAgora products (How to Build a Book). Conventional wisdom about texts—which holds that the work of verbal art is contained and fixed in the tangible object—cannot explain the real-world phenomena of OT-based or web-based cocreation. It can't predict that variation within limits, the telltale trace of oAgora commerce, can continue even when, as with Lönnrot and his *Kalevala*, the performance is happening in a text. But Old English poems—and so many other *voices from the past* and *written oral traditions*—put the lie to the always unrealistic and now thoroughly disproved binary of OT-versus-text. The truth is that under certain conditions oPathways can and do supersede our usual assumptions about textual encoding. Performances, even records of performances, aren't entirely explained by their textual format.

Like the Homeric epics, Anglo-Saxon poems satisfy these conditions: oAgora species that today survive only as tAgora artifacts. To understand these displaced species, we must interpret them as reflections or traces of living processes rather than as fixed, singly authored, nonmorphing, freestanding items. Strange as it may seem, and counter to the textual ideology that remains our automatic and unwitting reflex, we must make room in the OT performance arena (Arena of Oral Tradition) for composition and reception in letters.

Typography on paper

With the two last types of tAgora activity, *Typography on paper* and *Static eFiles in pixels*, we arrive in far more familiar territory. In the twenty-first century these are our twin default settings for communication: fixed items configured as physical or virtual pages. For these reasons our treatment of these two varieties of marketplace exchange will be much briefer than our considerations of the first three types. Just one cautionary note: let's remember that defaults are inherently the most difficult settings to notice and evaluate because by definition they lie below the threshold of our awareness. Communication "presents itself" in these two familiar vehicles, and we don't usually think twice about the implications built into the vehicles. It's well to remember that all five TT word-markets have their advantages and disadvantages, that none of them is as static or objective as textual ideology insists, and that each of them deserves our conscious attention. Even within the textual marketplace itself let's proceed in the spirit of citizenship in multiple agoras (Citizenship in Multiple Agoras).

The history of printing[117] is a complex and many-sided tale, which Wikipedia tells as a series of nodes that starts with woodblock printing in East Asia around 200 CE, continues through movable type (some 800 years later), lithography, and offset printing to contemporary methods such as laser, dot matrix, inkjet, and digital press printing. Each of these technologies involves not only a physical invention, but also a specific user base and set of specific purposes. All print media were certainly not created equal, either as technologies or as market-making strategies.

As we continue on to the kind of tAgora that Gutenberg's movable type made possible, recall the practical dimensions and effects of this game-changing technology. Instead of the laborious, time-consuming task associated with duplicating manuscripts, multiple exact copies could be produced relatively quickly and easily. Instead of an object that only one person at a time could read (and which could be shared among a group only by reading aloud), a multiply reproduced text could create a mass readership that stretched over time and place, bringing the work concurrently to scores of readers and groups. Texts could become instruments and not ceremonial objects; they could for all practical purposes contain the works they presented. They could demonstrate the features we have identified as important to full-blown modern tAgora communication: fixity, single authorship, exact replicability, resistance to morphing, freestanding status, proprietary nature, and (for texts a positive value) a complete lack of pathways.

Movable type actually first appeared in China around 1040 CE,[118] originally in the form of clay plates. By the thirteenth and fourteenth centuries, wooden and then metal type had been invented in China and Korea, still more than a century before Gutenberg's printing press,[119] conventionally dated to 1440. There is no clear evidence that the East influenced the West in establishing the new technology, but, whatever the case, Gutenberg's machine arrived at precisely the right moment as literacy became more widespread and the demand for texts was markedly increasing.

Over the next five and one-half centuries the reign of the book effectively became absolute, as print technology evolved from the first struggling efforts of small-press tradespeople to the polished, corporate world of twentieth-century commercial presses and large-scale publishing companies. Hand in hand with new inventions and methods went the audiences they were designed to involve and maintain: libraries that developed from unique depositories of one-of-a-kind materials to mega-institutions that drew from publishers' annual lists and subscribed to established journals and a reading public that increased geometrically not only in number but in diversity and demands. The history of the power of the printed book is in large part also the political, social, and even demographic history of its readership.[120]

Static eFiles in pixels

Just because something exists on the web doesn't mean it belongs to the eAgora. Throughout the Pathways Project we carefully differentiate between static and interactive resources—between fixed and morphable entities—on the Internet. Focusing on media dynamics, we reserve the eExperience for online opportunities that involve built-in options and multiple alternative realities. In other words, true eAgora species support emergence and cocreative surfing by incorporating and leveraging ePathways (ePathways).

Consider the range of destinations on the web. At one extreme we encounter static eFiles, such as unadorned PDF documents that contain no links and are posted "as is" for straightforward tAgora-type consumption by readers. Such readers visit these frozen texts not as platforms for surfing but as immutable objects. Their value lies in their categorical resistance to morphing, or so goes the ideological gospel. Apart from the disparity in physical vehicles, there isn't much difference between opening a PDF for scrolling and opening a book for page-turning. For static texts, paper and pixels serve the same fundamental function.

At the other extreme, and counterposed to static eFiles, are facilities like the Pathways Project, which not only permit but require interactive participation. As explained in Getting Started (Getting Started), both the morphing book (Morphing Book) and the wiki-website (Wiki) promote cocreative participation by users in four ways. First, you can read the roster of nodes "straight through," although the only available "sequence" is alphabetical—a nominal and artificial ordering principle meant to suggest the uselessness of purely linear organization in IT (and OT) marketplaces. Second, you can consult the three principal media environments: the oAgora, tAgora, and eAgora. This approach will highlight direct comparisons and contrasts associated with the OT-IT homology and its implications. Third, you can navigate along one or more prescribed linkmaps (Linkmaps), following a trail that someone else has blazed and found rewarding. And fourth, you can click on any one of the myriad links, called *branches*, in any of the nodes. These branches offer pathways to other nodes within the Pathways Project or, more rarely, to external sites and the opportunities they present.

Between these two poles—static eFiles and highly interactive systems—we will find websites that license and require many different kinds and levels of interactivity. Let me emphasize that I attempt no definition or policy that infallibly distinguishes true eAgora experiences from tAgora text-engagement in electronic media, no rule that dependably sorts web experiences into two tidy, mutually exclusive categories. Why not? Because to do so would be to reify the orality-versus-literacy binary in a new arena (Arena of the Web), to replace natural richness and complexity with a false dichotomy. Such open-and-shut theories emerge from (textual) certainty that media-technologies are separable, non-overlapping strategies, and that is an illusion. Nor do web phenomena necessarily remain unchanged in their structure and dynamics over time. A once-static electronic text could well be retooled as a pathway-driven platform for eAgora surfing, while a wiki-site could be reduced to a screenshot and posted online as a static eFile.

Unproductive discriminations aside, our major concern here is to affirm that static eFiles—notwithstanding their accessibility through browsers—belong to the tAgora. As pathwayless documents they support what readers have been doing ever since they consulted clay tokens and tablets to get the final and authoritative word—the "last word" (tWords)—on whatever challenge arose. As such, they foster trekking, not surfing. To put it another way, those early tokens and tablets didn't offer networks; indeed, they worked so well precisely because they *weren't* networked. Neither are static eFiles.

Stories Are Linkmaps

Oral traditions amount to cultural intranets, complex and ever-ramifying networks of options that the performer effectively clicks into being. When a teller performs a story, he or she surfs through a shared intranet, following a series of oPathways (oPathways) and activating certain nodes in the process.

This model can offer a fresh perspective on two long-standing and stubborn questions in OT studies: (1) What does a story consist of? and (2) What happens when a living, performed story is textualized?

What does a story consist of?

In short, and in the OT/IT terms we espouse throughout the Pathways Project, stories are linkmaps (Linkmaps). Just like the alternate pathway sequences offered within the wiki (Wiki) and the alternate reading sequences suggested in the opening pages of *Oral Tradition and the Internet: Pathways of the Mind* (Morphing Book), stories consist of familiar, rough-hewn itineraries within the larger web of oral tradition.

But while the trails are well blazed, performers don't simply trace the footprints left by prior performers (Distributed Authorship) or by themselves. For one thing, the flexibility of the medium means that there would always be more than one set of footprints, each varying in some way from the others. More fundamentally, and although textual ideology (Ideology of the Text) teaches otherwise, specific footprints aren't permanent in the oAgora: they vanish as soon as the story-event ceases.

Navigating linkmaps To grasp how stories consist of linkmaps, consider what actually happens over time.

When tellers perform and reperform a story, some aspects vary while much remains the same. Because the tale is being re-created by surfing along oPathways, which offer options at every juncture, versions will naturally differ somewhat, even when the same teller is involved and other factors are relatively constant (audience, setting, mood, and so forth). But the variation among different performances will also be limited (Variation within Limits), because the teller is traveling the same general route through the OT network. The starting point, the destination, and most of the in-between journey are relatively stable, with differences arising as the inevitable product of a flexible method of creation.

For example, the famous Grimm Brothers tale of "Hansel and Gretel" will unfailingly involve the two title characters, a witch, and a gingerbread house. That much remains constant and expectable. Likewise, the interactions among the principal characters will be identifiable across the spectrum of performances. The general sequence of oPathways through the story-web—let's call it the *story-route*—will retain its fundamental integrity. It must; otherwise, we wouldn't understand the story. And why not? Because we wouldn't be able to surf along with the performer.

At the same time, however, the details of particular performances will inevitably morph. One teller may decide to focus on Hansel's adventurous attitude more than another; Gretel's reactions to the witch may figure more prominently in Tuesday evening's than in Sunday afternoon's rendition; or the gingerbread house may be described in a few words or at considerable length. oPathways allow for—even encourage—these somewhat variant realizations of the always-emergent story (Reality Remains in Play).

The crucial point—for both the teller and the audience—is that the story-route remains the same while small-scale navigation allows for individual creative differences. Fluent in the oAgora medium, we recognize "Hansel and Gretel" at the same time that we can appreciate different tellers' versions.

What happens when a living, performed story is textualized?

To textualize a living story-event is to lose the forest for the trees or, to be more exact, to construe the forest as consisting of only a few dozen particular trees. It amounts to losing the web for the linkmap, to mistaking a single, freestanding, set-in-stone linkmap for the larger story.

Transcription, then edition   Let's think through what happens when we construct a story-text.

1. First comes the transcription, whether in video, audio, or paper format. Remember that while each of these media offers a different reflection of the living event, all transcriptions are fossils. They continue as fixed, non-changeable entities but pay for that status with their media-lives. And at some point—whether before or after the recording—a selection of which performance is to be fixed and memorialized has to take place. Remember: there is no "original," no "epitome," no "finest version."

2. Next, raw transcriptions become formal editions, according to the best judgment of an editor whose responsibility is to make the item understandable to a tAgora audience. In earlier times, the Brothers Grimm saw fit to rewrite the folktales they transcribed from fieldwork, often adjusting the stories' language radically to suit their imagined audience. But even the most scholarly book editions add another level of interpretation and distance, taking us another step away from the living, contextualized event. Audio and video texts may encode more information than the printed page, but they too are interpretations of single performances.

   The tAgora has its own demanding structures, and they do not mesh with OT dynamics (Why Not Textualize?). The more textualized the oral performance, the more limited, artificial, and devoid of life it becomes.

What's lost   By textualizing a story, transcribers and editors detach one realization of the linkmap from the OT web. They take it offline (Online with OT), severing all connection to the network of possibility and implication in which oral traditions are naturally embedded. Consequently, the web of other options and idiomatic meaning is lost, emergent experience is diminished to a flat surface of minimal linear portrayal, and reality no longer remains in play. It's a denaturing process parallel to the eAgoraphobic act of freezing Wikipedia into a linkless, static, forever-fixed document (Freezing Wikipedia).

In short, the price of textualization, of converting the story to a trekable, one-dimensional route suitable to the tAgora, is nothing less than forfeiting its viability in the oAgora. Of course, the story as linkmap still prospers as an OT phenomenon within its natural marketplace and in most cases is not affected at all by the reduction of one of its myriad performances to an item and removal of that no longer viable item to the textual marketplace. There just isn't any feedback loop connecting the dead artifact back to the variable linkmap and the living oral tradition.

Representation of OT performances, as discussed and illustrated throughout the Pathways Project, is more faithfully pursued through eEditions (eEditions). To show how stories are linkmaps, we need to set the textual object aside and exploit the OT-IT homology (Disclaimer).

Systems versus Things

Divergent dynamics

The oAgora and eAgora are linked systems of potentials; conversely, the tAgora amounts to an assembled collection of things.

The first two of these gathering places consist of sets of intangible pathways activated by navigators making their own decisions and choosing among ever-contingent realities. The other is an expansive, generously stocked warehouse of already-finished items accessed by clients seeking an "objective" reality.

The oAgora and eAgora present multiform possibilities, and only in the act of speaking or clicking do potentials produce unique instances. And notice that we said "instances," most decidedly in the plural, not in the singular and epitomized. Given the complexity and interactivity of the linked choices that constitute both oral performances and Internet sessions, a nearly limitless number of actual instances is possible. Indeed, that's the whole point of these two textless technologies—"infinite riches in a little room," to echo Christopher Marlowe.

The tAgora, on the other hand, works like a brick-and-mortar library (Museum of Verbal Art), with an established and well-ordered collection of finite items (Texts and Intertextuality) in place and with new acquisitions always being added to its catalogued holdings. Links versus texts (Agora Correspondences), systems versus things.

Divergent activities

Whether you're surfing through electronic or story-based pathways, you're cocreating the reality as you go (Reality Remains in Play). You the surfer are a full and necessary partner. Nothing happens until you engage the system, summon its open-ended but rule-governed potential, and literally *em-body* its innate power.

Without the hands-on flexibility and generativity of the system that supports oral performance, the oAgora would cease to function. The network would collapse into singularity. All possible stories and versions of stories would fossilize into a unique version of a unique story, a master text repeated verbatim forever. Em-booked and nonmorphing, effectively "writ in stone."

Likewise, without the hands-on flexibility and generativity of the system that supports navigation of the web, the eAgora would cease to function. Its complex route map would collapse into a single one-way street. Hypertext would devolve into a predetermined, invariable sequence with sharply curtailed power to support exploration and representation.

Oral performances and Internet performances would become mere texts, mere dead letters.

Open-ended but also rule-governed

Systems draw their power from an interactive combination of open-endedness and rule-governed behavior. Systems provide users with a frame and a set of techniques within which individuals can create a series of unique instances (Variation within Limits). And because systems are both open-ended and rule-governed, rather than only one or the other, works created within them are both original and intelligible. You aren't slave to a system in the oAgora or eAgora, but neither can you do "just anything." You have to play the game by the rules.

The best analogy is simply language itself, of which OT and IT are highly coded special cases. After all, language operates by balancing the flexibility that fosters creativity with the grammatical, lexical, and idiomatic forms that together provide the vehicle. Subtract that flexibility and language fossilizes, loses its human usefulness altogether. Subtract the grammatical, lexical, and idiomatic forms and anarchy ensues; no one will be able to communicate with anyone else. But meld the two together, combining the ability to morph with systemic rules for allowable variation, and the possibilities for expression become inexhaustible.

Proverbially speaking, OT and IT work like language, only more so (Proverbs).

tAgora: Exchanging Tangible Goods

An agora is a verbal marketplace (Agora As Verbal Marketplace), a site for creation and exchange of knowledge, art, and ideas. The Pathways Project recognizes three agoras, or arenas for human communication (Three Agoras). This node is devoted to the textual arena, the tAgora.

The negotiable currency of exchange in the tAgora is tWords (tWords)—written or printed or onscreen bytes of information that we identify by inserting white space between them and enshrining them in dictionaries. Unlike oWords (oWords), which are spoken, heard, and physically embodied, tWords promote and enable asynchronous communication (Real-time versus Asynchronous), whether they're scratched on the back of an envelope, etched in gold on a wedding invitation, or configured in Unicode-mapped pixels within an email or text message. You participate in the textual marketplace by swapping tangible items that reach beyond exclusive embedding in a single moment or event. These tBytes promise, uniquely, to free you from "right now" involvement and to convey hard, invariable facts (Just the Facts) when and where you or others want to use them—as long as you can get your hands on these textual marvels, of course.

Disembodied transmission

So how does that miracle of disembodied transmission happen? Well, the textually mediated environment (Disclaimer) essentially removes the defining constraints of space and time. Entrust your ideas to a text (Texts and Intertextuality) and they go offline, so to speak. Exchange can happen without the online connections that drive activities in the oAgora (Online with OT) and eAgora, and it can take place anywhere and anytime that the artifact is physically available. The sender inscribes, and the receiver asynchronously reads what's inscribed—one letter after another; one tWord after another; one paragraph, page, and text after another. Put in Pathways Project terms, the cognitive and technological prosthesis of tWords supports the illusion of object (Illusion of Object).

Not insignificantly, that same prosthesis reinforces the cultural fiction of objective reality (Reality Remains in Play), a deeply embedded fantasy that has empowered so many of Homo sapiens' achievements since the relatively recent invention of writing (Homo Sapiens' Calendar Year). Instead of the all-consuming, ever-emergent oAgora event that vanishes as soon as the event is over, or the eAgora website that has morphed significantly since your aggregator last checked it, the tAgora fosters communication via what we take as permanent, immutable artifacts. And because those artifacts aren't subject to built-in contingencies shared by the other two agoras (Contingencies), texts can deliver the message the inscriber intends—exactly, verbatim, with no slippage.

What's more, it will be precisely the same message every time, delivered according to the reader/user's terms and timetable. You can choose to delay the experience until you're ready to start—since you're confident the text can't morph (Morphing Book)—and you can stop and restart just as frequently as you wish. Pick it up where you left off, put it down as often as you like; no need to worry because you're in control. There are no networks to navigate, no pathways to choose among, because texts don't have pathways (Impossibility of tPathways). Texts, which readers necessarily hold both literally and figuratively at arm's length, serve their users as still points largely undisturbed by the hurly-burly of everyday life that swirls around them. Or so goes the ideological folktale (Ideology of the Text).

An ancient witness on the tAgora

No less an authority on knowledge, art, and ideas than the ancient Greek philosopher Plato was keenly aware of the advantages and disadvantages of disembodied textual words as long ago as the late fifth or early fourth century BCE. Here Plato recounts what his mentor Socrates had to say about writing as Socrates addressed his follower Phaedrus in the dialogue of the same name[121] (*Phaedrus* 275D–E):

> Writing, Phaedrus, has a certain strangeness about it, very much like painting, whose creatures, we can say, stand there like living things; but if one poses a question to them, they maintain perfect silence. And it is the same with written words. You might suppose they would speak with understanding, but if you question them at all, wishing to inquire about what they are saying, they always indicate only the very same thing. And whenever any word is written even once, it will be tossed about everywhere, both among those who understand and among those for whom it is not at all a concern. Moreover, such a word does not know to whom it must speak or not speak. And when it is taken wrongly or unjustly abused, it always requires the help of its "father"; for it is not able to defend or help itself.

For all of the many advantages of tWords, we might paraphrase, there also exist serious and inescapable liabilities. tWords may seem to represent pure, uncompromised reality (Reality Remains in Play), but their inertness and detachment from real-time, emergent communication leave them vulnerable to wholesale reconstrual and outright misinterpretation. And they most certainly cannot operate interactively; without their "father," the one who wrote them into the text, they are helpless to respond. Most fundamentally, then, the price of asynchronous, inflexible, noninteractive representation is the impossibility of living exchange (Museum of Verbal Art).

Offline and into the tAgora is where oWords (and eWords) go to die.

Agora-mirrors

Before proceeding any further, let's highlight a built-in structural correspondence among the three nodes on principal media types: the oAgora, tAgora, and eAgora. From this point on—and across all three involved nodes—the internal section headings and organization will follow a mirroring logic. In other words, immediately below this paragraph you will find sections entitled "Genus and species" and "Word-markets," followed by another with the subheading of either "Public, not proprietary" or "Proprietary, not public," depending on the agora in question. In fourth position you will encounter a brief discussion of "The evolutionary fallacy," and so on. The purpose of this mirrored organizational strategy is to help emphasize the comparisons and contrasts that lie at the heart of the Pathways Project. For a complete list of the inter-agora parallels, which also charts the structure of each of the three principal nodes, visit Agora Correspondences (Agora Correspondences).

Genus and species

Of course, all texts are hardly identical. In fairness, we should recognize that the tAgora is—like the two other verbal marketplaces—an inherently complex and heterogeneous arena (Arena of the Text) in its own right. Indeed, it would be a crippling mistake to collapse that complexity into overgeneral, simplistic remarks about all texts belonging to a single, absolutely uniform category. That would amount to the same blunder as deciding that all oral traditions are essentially identical (an error that has been made only too frequently and which handicapped our understanding for a long while), or that all ePhenomena answer one narrow definition. Agoras can't be understood as archives or mausoleums; each of them bristles with supported activities that show real diversity in their relatedness.

So how do we customarily think of texts? Primarily, by default, as sequences of letters, spaces, words, paragraphs, pages, chapters, and so on. These are some

Gutenberg Press.
Courtesy of artnet.com
and Wikimedia.

of the major reading codes used for post-Gutenberg, book-based transactions within the tAgora. They all take part in the tWord program, and collectively they constitute a repertoire of familiar, standard signals that we learn to use, both as consumers and as creators of texts. But the printed page isn't by any means the sole species within the genus "Text."

Early manuscripts didn't use most of these modern tWord codes, which developed hand-in-hand with the platform of multiple identical copies made possible by the printing press and its computer-driven descendants. The unique manuscript of the medieval English epic poem *Beowulf*, for example, presents the Anglo-Saxon epic entirely without poetic lineation and almost wholly without the punctuation or capitalization we require today, leaving to prospective editors the challenging job of imposing our now-conventional reading cues back onto texts that never used them. That's an irony we conventionally submerge in the name of (unexamined) standardization.

At the other end of the historical spectrum, with conventional books in the middle, stand static eFiles of pixel-pages,[122] as well as audio and video files. These

Beowulf manuscript. Permission from Kevin Kiernan of The British Library Board for the third edition of *Electronic Beowulf* (2011).

items (and they manifestly are items rather than experiences) also qualify as species within the genus "Text." Why? Because they operate by foreclosing on variation and by transmitting identical, stable messages—at least until computer-enabled mashups and remixing begin (Remix). All of these texts are typically used and exchanged as fixed, complete products, whether as downloaded manuals, purchased music, films licensed for distribution, or whatever. Although they can certainly be carved up in innumerable ways after the fact, the reality remains that they represent integral wholes ordered by a designated and unique linear sequence. We customarily buy or rent eBooks, eSongs, and eFilms not to cocreate them, but to "read" them as texts. Although they're digital-only, such static eFiles belong most essentially to the tAgora.

Word-markets

Consider a few of the myriad word-markets in which text-exchangers have characteristically plied their trade, the last two very much in use today:

- scratching symbols and numbers on clay tablets,
- inscribing Greek signs onto papyrus,
- adapting Latin and runic letters to spell early English on sheepskin,
- printing and distributing easily replicable and identical brick-and-mortar books, or
- sharing static eFiles within a virtual community.

Each of these tAgora transactions will be examined below, with special attention to the rules that govern its particular dynamics. Meanwhile, here are a few of the questions we should keep in mind as we consider what's been swept under the rug of unchallenged conventions. What are the rules and conditions underlying exchange? Who owns the product and who gets to use it? How do texts gain the unchallenged authority they unquestionably enjoy? How do texts transfer knowledge, art, and ideas? Most generally, how is the tAgora categorically different from those other twin-sibling marketplaces, the oAgora and eAgora?

Proprietary, not public

The tAgora is fundamentally proprietary. It restricts access to exchange by requiring potential users to qualify as owners, not sharers (Owning versus Sharing), of its contents. Generally speaking, then, it's the antithesis of an open-source marketplace like the oAgora or eAgora. Of course, we must always remember that any agora can and does impose certain restrictions on those who practice exchange within it. The eAgora imposes its passwords, firewalls, and member-based privileges, and the oAgora makes some transactions more public than others. But as a rule the tAgora is by far the most doctrinaire of the three marketplaces in requiring ownership as a blanket provision for conducting legalized verbal business.

Not surprisingly, the word *proprietary*[123] stems ultimately from Latin *proprietas* ("owner"). It appears initially in English about 1450, with the narrow sense of "possessing worldly goods in excess of a cleric's needs." The year 1589 marks the first attestation of the more generic modern meaning, "held in private ownership." From the beginning, then, and throughout its history, this word amounts to code for sequestering by an individual (Getting Published or Getting Sequestered) as distinguished from providing broader access for a community (In the Public Domain). It speaks to the acquisition of tangible goods, to owning rather than sharing.

Ownership is absolutely central to proper and continuing tAgora function (consider the positive spin engendered by the contemporary advertising euphemism "pre-owned") and can take a wide variety of forms. Access depends upon legal possession, whether by a single person, a group, or an institution. A unique author creates a unique text, sells it for money and/or rights to a publisher, who then establishes the rules for exchange with those who wish to read it. And this proprietary, monetized, and legally controlled chain of transmission derives inevitably from the categorical difference between OTs and texts.

OTs, on the one hand, circulate virtually among the eligible members of a community. They are enacted and reenacted by various performers over different times and places in an arena that prizes emergence and morphing, and which depends crucially on a navigable, multidimensional network rather than a collection of static, one-dimensional things (Arena of Oral Tradition). Authorship in the oAgora, as in the eAgora, is thus distributed, not unique (Distributed Authorship).

Texts, on the other hand, circulate as fixed entities, complete in themselves, and are transferred only in strict accordance with the legal regulations of the tAgora marketplace. Books are not emergent, they do not morph (except within the Pathways Project), and they have no pathways. Most fundamentally, they do not involve networks of potentials. Again we return to our default concept of ownership, of *proprietas*, a characteristic of the tAgora but not the other marketplaces. It's difficult or impossible to own the truly virtual and interactive, as contemporary skirmishes over digital content illustrate only too painfully and effectively.

The evolutionary fallacy

With the variant dynamics of the oral, textual, and Internet arenas in mind, it's easy to see why "oral evolves to written" and "written evolves to electronic" are fallacies traceable to the ideology of the text. If we model our understanding of all verbal commerce on a singular creation attributed to a singular author and consumed by a singular audience (one-by-one), then the necessarily plural identity of performer(s), OTs, and audience(s) will appear primitive and underdeveloped. Likewise, we'll fail to understand and credit the plural identity of web architects and surfers with their shared but diverse experiences in the eAgora.

In either case, nonwritten, nontextualized communication will seem to lack something, to fail to measure up according to our ideologically imposed criteria. After all, until only too recently collectors of OTs have unquestioningly subscribed to an implicit rank-ordering by converting the living webs that support oral traditions into freestanding objects suitable for display in the Museum of Verbal Art. Taxidermy trumps the living. And how many times each day do you hear or read about people bemoaning the informality and impermanence of the web? Confronted by the virtual world, whose riches lie in its rule-governed flexibility and ceaseless morphing, they too undergo a kind of medium-specific culture shock and feel compelled to "diss" whatever isn't text (Culture Shock).

But of course it's not just a matter of one situation—one agora—evolving progressively and inevitably toward another. Each arena operates according to its own idiosyncratic economy. The oAgora uses a different currency of exchange than the tAgora—embodied versus entexted words, oWords versus tWords. And the eAgora uses eWords (eWords), similar in many ways to oWords and far removed from tWords. Both the oAgora and eAgora sponsor code—like the patterned speech of the oral arena or the URLs and HTML of the Internet arena—that depends for its power and efficacy on its performative nature. oCode and eCode actually cause something to happen, and to happen recurrently (Recur Not Repeat) and idiomatically. None of the three currencies is inherently better, more valuable, or more advanced than the other two. Each is simply the coin of its particular realm.

This is not to claim that any arena is entirely homogeneous. Nor is it to contend that they never interact (A Foot in Each World), or that hybrid agoras can't form; they do and they can, in fascinating ways. The back-and-forth transmission of blues songs between the oAgora and tAgora is one example; the Somali oral contest poetry that has now migrated to the Internet is another. Just more reasons why it will always prove a fatal mistake to posit a one-way developmental trajectory, to view verbal technology as working its way inexorably from a text-deprived Dark Age, toward a thoroughly evolved and fully textual us, and on the way to a (fascinating though in some quarters feared) virtuality. We need to resist the ideologically driven assumption that limits our imagination, our allegiance, and our citizenship to the textual arena (Citizenship in Multiple Agoras). We need to learn to manage the natural diversity of human communication, to think within the cognitive frames of OT and IT as well as textual technology (TT).

Five TT word-markets

Let's sharpen the focus of these general remarks by visiting five tAgoras to investigate who "shops" there (both writers and readers) and how their economies work, at least in broad terms. For this purpose I've chosen examples (Spectrum of Texts) that range all the way from some of the earliest extant inscribed objects through the most modern textual documents, all the way from symbols and numbers scratched on clay counters dating to 8000 BCE through the static, pixel-imaged eFiles we summon to our computer screens today.

One important word of caution and definition before embarking. Here we distinguish carefully between two media experiences: cocreative navigating through an interactive web with interactive sites that belong to the eAgora, versus tAgora trekking through linear, one-way texts that just happen to be configured in pixels rather than on paper. Just because we encounter something on the Internet doesn't qualify it for inclusion in the eAgora, in other words. What matters is whether the experience involves rule-governed flexibility and morphing (OT and IT) or static items (TT).

The examples are intentionally highly diverse, engaging different chronological periods, geographical areas, compositional styles, modes of reception, and cultural functions. But within that diversity they also have something vital in common: they all depend upon several key tAgora features (Accuracy)—fixity, single authorship, exact replicability, resistance to morphing, freestanding status, proprietary nature, and a lack of pathways. They also share the function of masking contingency, a crucial dynamic in the textual marketplace. The degree to which these features can be implemented using the technology of the time varies, of course, and we must be careful not to impose anachronistic restrictions. Still, within the tAgora the most basic rule is survival of the "fixed-est."

These five cases, which include numeracy as well as later-arriving literacy, collectively span about ten thousand years. But let's not lose our perspective. As ancient as Mesopotamian cuneiform, the oldest script, demonstrably is—dated to at least 3200 BCE—it arises fully 346 days into Homo sapiens' species-year, on or about December 10 in calendrical terms. That's roughly 94 percent of the way through our history. Archaeologists have placed the invention of numeracy, as opposed to literacy, some eighteen species-days earlier, on approximately November 22. This set of arresting facts might well surprise us, blinded as we are by the ideology of text.

Think about the implications. If late November is the earliest possible date for the founding of the tAgora, a date before which there cannot possibly have been a textual marketplace of any kind, then the oAgora must have been the only word-marketplace open for cultural business for more than 90 percent of our existence as a species. When we add the observation that OT remains the most widespread communications technology worldwide on a per capita basis, the status of texts as the default medium in the wired West—for the moment, at least—seems ever more misleading and in even more serious need of reexamination.

Here, then, are the five tAgoras for your consideration:

- Symbols of/on clay
- Greek letters on papyrus
- Latin and runic letters on sheepskin
- Typography on paper
- Static eFiles in pixels

Real authors

Authors—in our highly ideological sense of the term as *individual creators of original, unique, objectifiable, and usually published works*—have proven themselves the movers and shakers of the modern tAgora. Their works exist as freestanding textual objects, made available to consumer-readers in multiple copies via print technology. Ownership and protection are core concerns and are controlled legally. Internal tAgora rules prevent another person, or another publisher, from conveying the "same" work, which is understood as initiated by a single person and licensed by a single publisher, without arranging some sort of permission or fee.

On the other side of exchange, the audience or readership for such texts can be remarkably diverse, since the textual medium relaxes or eliminates all constraints on their reception. Today an elderly woman from the Netherlands may pick up a book that yesterday found its way to a library bookshelf in Cape Town, South Africa, where it will be read by dozens of people of various ages, genders, ethnicities, and life experiences. To the extent that a given book penetrates diverse tAgora communities, it may contribute to remixing culture. But as the nonmorphing, pathwayless objects they are (except in the Pathways Project, and then only to a limited extent), books themselves are authored tAgora objects and don't undergo remixing.

Outside the familiar realm of typography—beforehand, afterward, and alongside—the ideological aim is similar, even if these other textual media affect how that core ideology plays itself out. Clay tablets are certainly fixed, to the degree they can be, but also eminently reusable for other purposes, and the ascription of authorship from the ancient world is of course far less dependable than a twenty-first-century book review—less meaningful in many cases as well. Still, the fact remains that there *were* performers and authors whose performances and works *were* recorded on tangible, exchangeable surfaces. Even if the traditions behind those fixed versions continued to morph, the tablets themselves were meant and deployed as permanent items, as stable points of reference. Ideologically they followed the same overall recipe for the transmission of knowledge, art, and ideas as do printed books: fixity, ownership, and licensed consumption. And all of it was author-ized.

This is also true with manuscripts, whether Greek letters written on papyrus or Latin letters on vellum or sheepskin. Although papyrus did not easily lend itself to repurposing, it was cheap and readily available. Likewise, sheepskin was often scraped clean of earlier writing to accommodate something new in the form of a palimpsest. In their uniqueness, and in the difficulties associated with their (re)production and their limited user bases, these media certainly diverged from the modern book. But the larger point is that the works written into ancient and medieval manuscripts were for the most part attributed to specific authors. Whatever other factor we cite, they were understood as created by real-life individuals. Other than *written oral traditions*, which employ oAgora technology in a written medium and amount to singing on the page (Singing on the Page), these manuscript works belong to the tAgora marketplace. Their nondistributed authorship was as textual as ancient and medieval media could support.

On the other side of the ledger, in the post-typographical world, eFiles have proven only too malleable and reconfigurable. Although they were in almost every case intended by their individual authors for bona fide tAgora trade, their digital makeup has proven dramatically less fixed than analog paper pages. This vulnerability has of course given rise to unanticipated manipulation of all forms of electronic files, and thus to legal wrangling over who can own, change, and retransmit works encoded (and recoded) with the aid of eAgora tools. Authorship of original works is still understood as real and important, however, and even the mashups and remixing that sometimes ensue are also seen as yielding authored items that require authorial attribution. It's as if unforeseen ePathways (ePathways) cropped up in what are meant to be tAgora works.

In the end, authorship—as we customarily mean the term—is not at all an archetypal, universal role or function that arose as a necessary condition of verbal art or communication in general. It was not with us from the beginning of Homo sapiens' calendar year, but arose only in late November (numeracy) or early December (writing) as an enabling cornerstone of the tAgora. And with the advent of the eAgora it is once again fading into the background, or, more precisely, into the distributed authorship that powers the IT network. While there are thus no true authors in the oAgora, and while a fair-minded search finds the eAgora to be similarly authorless, the textual marketplace is by necessity categorically different. It depends for its existence and operability upon the concept and the reality of singular, original, fixed-and-static things.

In a word, the tAgora constructed authors, and authors constructed the tAgora. Without that reciprocal relationship this marketplace's ecology will utterly fail.

Five real authors

In the five examples of tAgora activity examined earlier, we can see authorship emerging through the different types of media from different periods. Consider the dynamics of the various TT arenas. The clay tablets that stem from counting technology encode information that had to be compiled by someone, whether a merchant, government official, record keeper, historian, or whomever, and it was intended for consumption as an objective, static item. The second and third types worked similarly. Given the assignment of duties typical of the textual marketplace in ancient and medieval times, delegation reigned: professional scribes no doubt wielded the stylus and pen, but the result was nonetheless an authored, owned object prized for its permanence. Whether the encoding involved Greek letters on papyrus or Latin and runic letters on sheepskin, the intent—however imperfect the result from a post-Gutenberg perspective—was to deposit the work into an authored textual vehicle. With the era of paper-based typography the picture becomes clearer because more familiar: books and pages trace their origins to real, fully empowered authors, even when they're anonymous. And static eFiles are no different in this regard. In every case authors are the builders of the tAgora, and their edifice-making creates a platform on which they can ply their communicative trade.

tAgora sharing and reuse

In the textual arena sharing and reuse are governed by applicable legal rules, which restrict free exchange of the tangible, fixed, owned items that real authors produce. The oAgora, which allows and promotes open exchange (subject to cultural assignments by gender, age, or some other parameter), actively depends on network-based sharing for the continued function of its marketplace. Without such sharing it cannot survive the test of time; it can't serve its ever-changing constituencies via the unique power of its ever-morphing, public-domain technology. And the eAgora likewise depends fundamentally upon navigation and webs of potentials to deliver its function. Once the virtual world moves beyond static files and owned resources to interactivity and pathway dynamics, it works by engaging networks that must always remain under construction and open to individual, emergent navigating. The tAgora, on the other hand, exists by standing firm as a bulwark against unlicensed sharing and reuse.

Ironically, where contemporary tAgora practices have begun to unravel is actually in the opportunities presented by digital representation. New-media technology has shown itself able to outstrip, or at least to circumvent, longstanding rules about copyright and fair use. Faced with this novel instability, publishers struggle to find ways to maintain their grip, to affirm their owner-ship, but suddenly the old strategies aren't working anymore.

Nor is this a vulnerability exploitable only by IT pros. Digital manipulation tools put unlicensed transfer, remixing, and mashups into the hands of Every-surfer. Issues associated with politics, artistic freedom, and identity have desta-bilized every level of the textual marketplace, which must discover new ways to keep its business functioning. Models for electronic publication of newspapers, books, and music are constantly being proposed and tested, for example, and some dedicated solutions are successful in specific ways. But whether the old system of item-based exchange can survive—at least in anything like its present form—remains very much in question.

Certainly the tAgora is not about to collapse; one of the major points of the Pathways Project is to illustrate that we live in a world of multiple agoras and that we should aspire to multiple citizenship (Citizenship in Multiple Agoras). But neither can tAgora users ignore the radical shifts in the ways that we now create and transmit knowledge, art, and ideas. In an increasingly wired envi-ronment, with open-source initiatives and web-driven empowerment, can non-navigable texts command their traditional authority? Can texts sustain the near monopoly they've enjoyed for centuries? Almost certainly not; sooner or later the tAgora has to come to terms with users more and more adept at exploring pathways, and consequently more impatient with pathwayless media. tAgora rules and operating procedures will need to be amended, and in some cases wholly reformulated.

Verbatim means no variation

Verbatim literally means "word for word," and names a highly prized quality in the tAgora. Of course, we need to specify that we're dealing in tWords here, in the textual currency of this particular marketplace and not in oWords or eWords, since these other kinds of thought-bytes thrive on rule-governed variation (Varia-tion within Limits). And variation is anathema to those who crave verbatim replication, who deal in repetition rather than recurrence. The text promises capture, preservation, nonslippage—it fosters trekking linearly through its well-mapped territory one word, paragraph, page, chapter, and book after another.

Over the five textual types examined earlier we saw different versions of the myth of fixity so central to the core philosophy of the tAgora. Tablets and man-uscripts aspire to the verbatim accuracy that we can envision once the "thing-ness" of static media presents itself, and in their time and place such ancient and medieval vehicles maximized available "word-for-word" potential—tWord for tWord, that is. Until recently, variations among tablets or manuscripts were viewed as errors, as scribes' real-world failure to accomplish their goal of perfect recording and transmission. Now we've learned that scribes, and more modern text-makers as well, can recompose in writing, sometimes by surfing oPathways.

Post-Gutenberg, we have the wherewithal to control tWords with absolute accuracy, and the contracts negotiated in the textual marketplace demand no less. Likewise with the static eFiles that, while assembled and conveyed electronically, are essentially texts that belong most importantly to the tAgora. As our media have supported a closer approach to the ideal of verbatim accuracy and transmission, in other words, our tolerance for unlicensed sharing has diminished. An individual might lend a copy of *Robinson Crusoe* to a friend, but a publisher will still charge $10 even for an ePub copy. With the demise of variation and the rise of verbatim replication, the tAgora has tightened up its policies for exchange.

The contrast to language

Our proverb teaches that "oral tradition works like language, only more so" (Proverbs), and the technology of the eAgora mirrors that of the oAgora. But things are very different in the tAgora. Echoing the proverb, we might observe that "texts don't work like language, they commodify it." How can that be, you ask, when the very tWords you're reading clearly qualify as in-use, dictionary-approved integers for communication?

Most basically, a tWord is not an oWord or an eWord, and a text is not a network for navigation. Texts are spatialized road maps that define a single route, scripts for readers' activities that achieve unprecedented economy by reducing the options built into language to a single choice. Simple conversations make the point. We do not converse or interact by exchanging fixed texts; instead, we depend upon the variation inherent in language to construct and react as we proceed. There can be no predictable (because preexisting) "page 2" of a conversation, which is by nature fluid and rule-governed rather than predetermined. Language itself is always emergent, full of more possibilities than we can imagine, while texts are static and resistant to morphing.

OT takes advantage of the rule-governed pliability of language and adds more source code. On top of the grammar and syntax of everyday speech, performers learn and deploy a specialized mode of expression characterized by idiosyncratic features and idiomatic implications. That's what we mean by the "only more so" of the proverb. And IT does likewise, using a multiform code that causes things to happen as the surfer, navigating through webs of potentials, cocreates the experience. The oAgora and eAgora function by extending the natural properties of language, not by resisting them.

On the other hand, this very resistance is the secret of effective exchange within the tAgora. Writers and readers operate under the assumption that their journey can be charted and replicated exactly, that they can march in tandem from point A to point Z without detours. Of course, texts can be interpreted in different ways, as contemporary literary and philosophical theory has emphasized, and we should not lose sight of that reality. And textual media are responsible not only for unprecedented kinds of storage and (limited) accessibility but also for the ways in which we conceive of knowledge, art, and ideas. We cannot overestimate the power of what remains, for now, our default technology. But texts themselves aren't language.

Repetition versus recurrence

What does it mean to say that something repeats? The scenario is familiar enough: a discrete and itemlike event happens once, then it happens again, and so forth. A best-selling novel, for instance, may be published one year and reprinted the next, so that the title repeats on the bookstore or library shelf. Or consider a poetic refrain that appears at the end of every stanza, so that each iteration echoes those that precede it. Or the chorus to a song, which will dependably repeat after each verse. All of these cases are clearly repetitive because subsequent occurrences derive their meaning primarily from earlier ones within a finite, closed context. The chain of meaning is linear and contained, deriving from direct correspondences from one item to the next.

Recurrence, on the other hand, stems not from linearity and containment but from an idiomatic connection between a sign and its significance. Recurrent phrases don't draw their meaning from the last instance; they resonate against collective cultural fluency. Thus OT phrases speak primarily not to their immediate surroundings but to the larger referents to which they're linked. The situation in the eAgora is homologous. When you click on a link, you're taken to the linked site not because of the last visit but because of the established idiomatic connection between the sign (the URL) and its significance (the destination website). Surfing through the web, like surfing through an oral tradition, is a recurrent rather than repetitive activity.

Only when the route system of pathways gets converted into a textual landscape defined by its lack of options can true repetition actually arise. It's a matter of what activities are supported in each agora. Linearity leads to inflexible sequence, to an ideal of precision that has reigned since early December of our species-year. But linearity also runs the risk of generating the worn-out signifiers we call clichés, which are categorically impossible in OT and IT language. To each marketplace its own: recurrence drives verbal exchange in the oAgora and eAgora, while repetition is a creation of the tAgora.

Imposed copyright

In everyday tAgora life we're quite comfortable with the phenomenon of copyright. It's what we expect as the default condition of creating, sharing, and consuming texts of any sort, no matter the medium (books, films, music) or the particular marketplace store where we shop. This expectation is so strong and operates so far below the radar that many of us initially accepted its awkward, agoraphobic application to digital, electronic media (Agoraphobia)—and thereby hangs a still-developing story.

But perhaps we don't fully grasp how unnatural an imposition copyright is across the other two agoras. It demands the ability to own a tangible thing, rather than share an evolving experience, and owning just isn't a viable category in the oAgora and eAgora. If the dynamics of sharing knowledge, art, and ideas involves navigation through linked options instead of trekking through texts, there isn't any "thing" to "own." Only when instances get epitomized, only when emergent experiences get converted into singular, pathwayless artifacts, can they be possessed and exchanged as copyright-protected objects in the tAgora.

As powerful a force as copyright has become in the text-trading we tend to take as the norm (remixing and mashups notwithstanding), it functions as intended only within the object- and stasis-oriented tAgora.

Survival of the "fixed-est"

To put it another way, the ideologically driven textual ecology will naturally select which verbal artifacts are to be understood as viable. Single members of that ecosystem—whether individuals, groups, or corporations—will claim that they "own" a particular work, and the operative legalities will bear out that claim. If it's recognized as a tangible item, you can indeed own it. And if you own it, you can restrict its use. There exists a brick-and-mortar thing to restrict.

In the textual arena, strength and continuity reside not in ongoingness but in stasis, not in rule-governed flexibility but in invariability. The tAgora is a word-market for asynchronous, disembodied, nonsystematic communication. In this marketplace the survival of the fittest means the survival of the "fixed-est."

There are no pathways in it.

Texts and Intertextuality

What is a text in the Pathways Project?

For the purposes of the Pathways Project, the term "text" refers to a tAgora item, an objective and static thing. It is ownable (Owning versus Sharing) and available asynchronously (Real-time versus Asynchronous) as a whole entity. It is exchanged under applicable rules, very often under stringent copyright laws rather than Creative Commons licenses or open-source agreements. A text does not vary within limits. It supports trekking through lines and pages and volumes, not surfing through networks as in the oAgora and eAgora (after all, even morphing books can morph only to a limited degree). It is conventionally the creation of a single individual, rather than the product of distributed authorship (Distributed Authorship). Most basically, with the exception of the reader's own individual trajectory of discovery and reception, reality does not remain in play within texts.

Still, and in harmony with the Pathways Project policy (Disclaimer) of avoiding oversimplification and respecting diversity within all three agoras, let's be sure to emphasize that "text" also designates a broad spectrum of possibilities (Spectrum of Texts). All the way from symbols of/on clay in the third millennium BCE to static eFiles in pixels, the genus of text consists of many different, culturally defined species. But in one way or another, they all occupy the tAgora, which contrasts markedly (Agora Correspondences) with the fundamentally homologous oAgora and eAgora.

Textless agoras

Thus defined, texts cannot exist in the oAgora or the eAgora. The closest we can come to oAgora texts is an audio or video facsimile of a performance, but in fact these multimedia reflections don't really belong to the oral marketplace. Why not? Well, you can't navigate them because they have no pathways (Impossibility of tPathways). Nor do they sponsor interactivity or variation within limits. Similarly, true texts can't prosper in the electronic marketplace for precisely the same reasons.

With these things in mind, how broadly does the term and idea of *intertextuality* apply across the three agoras?

Etymological background

As one perspective, consider that the word derives[124] from two distinct and well-known roots. *Inter* straightforwardly means "between," stemming from Latin, while the history of "text" is more complex. Its Proto-Indo-European root, **tek*, signifies "make," and has many ancient Greek derivatives. But Latin *textus*, the past participle of *texere* ("to weave"), means literally "a thing woven." In Later Latin it narrows considerably to indicate a "written account, content, characters used in a document," and then in fourteenth-century English comes to mean "wording of anything written." Once woven, texts are difficult or impossible to unweave (thus the miracle of Penelope's unweaving the "text" of Laertes' shroud to hold her suitors at bay for twenty years in Homer's *Odyssey*).

Intertextuality depends on textual ideology

If we ideologically condone the myth that knowledge, art, and ideas can be contained in brick-and-mortar artifacts, then we can hypothesize interrelationships between and among the works so contained. An early novel, construed as a self-contained entity, can easily be understood as exerting influence on a later novel, for example. As we further concretize and locate those works = texts by specifying their individual authors and historical-cultural contexts, we can begin to construct a relationship of intertextuality to explain them. "Between-texts" becomes an operative field for inquiry and interpretation.

Not so in the oAgora or eAgora. If reality remains in play, and in these two agoras that amounts to the central algorithm of communication (Reality Remains in Play), then we're simply not dealing with texts. Only if we're willing to subscribe to the twin illusions of object (Illusion of Object) and stasis (Illusion of Stasis) can we conjure the kinds of fixed items to which the *inter* in *intertextuality* refers. The presence of pathways, which support cocreativity and distributed authorship, is anathema to this "between-texts" approach.

In the end, texts and intertextuality are possible only in the tAgora. In the oAgora and eAgora the operative dynamic is recurrence (Recur Not Repeat) rather than repetition, variation within limits rather than fixity, and built-in contingency rather than freestanding authority (Contingency). If we propose to transact responsible agora-business (Responsible Agora-business), then we must we prepared to become citizens of multiple agoras (Citizenship in Multiple Agoras).

Words, worlds, and multiple fluency

Pathwayless texts constitute one very viable world, familiar and extremely useful, and we must not sell short a marketplace that has made such enormous difference to Homo sapiens from early December of our species-year onward (Homo Sapiens' Calendar Year). But navigation through networks is another world altogether, an oWorld that long preceded writing technology and an eWorld that, although only very recently discovered, is already opening tremendous new vistas for thinking, expressing, transmitting, and learning.

To put it as directly as possible, tWords (tWords) aren't the same as oWords (oWords) or eWords (eWords). Fluency in all three agora-languages—giving each one its due—must be our goal.

Three Agoras

Comparisons and contrast

The following table demonstrates some fundamental similarities between the oAgora and the eAgora—between OT and IT—as well as their mutual differences from the tAgora (Agora Correspondences).

Agora Correspondences and Differences

	oAgora	eAgora	tAgora
realities	virtual, emerging	virtual, emerging	*brick-and-mortar*
units	oWords	eWords	*tWords*
routes	oPathways	ePathways	*No tPathways*
authorship	distributed	distributed	*individual*
audiences	open	open	*selective*

Disparate realities

To start with our current cultural default (for the moment, at least), tAgora technology lives and functions not in a virtual but in a *brick-and-mortar* world. Books and pages provide tangible vehicles for word transactions; ideas are inscribed in actual objects you can hold in your hand (or so goes the accepted fiction) (Ideology of the Text). Textual exchange then depends on swapping these objects, whether by purchasing, borrowing, photocopying, scanning, or some other means. tAgora reality is also *directed*, in that all of its rhetorical cues—ordered sequences of words, sentences, paragraphs, numbered pages, chapters, and so forth—serve as ready guides to decipherment. The organization of book contents is not merely an empty convention or ritual gesture; it amounts to a mandate for using those contents in a single-minded, carefully delimited fashion. The book and page don't support detours because veering offtrack would defeat the linear logic of the medium.

oAgora and eAgora technologies, on the other hand, live and function in *virtual* worlds. Neither OT nor IT has any use for brick-and-mortar reality. Oral performers surf their intangible traditions, drawing from a large, untextualizable constellation of potentials. Likewise, eNavigators surf the intangible web, creating, transmitting, and receiving knowledge, art, and ideas without recourse to physical objects. To put it plainly, the nonvirtual reality of the tAgora is an inhospitable venue for OT and IT. Its environment is all wrong.

Correspondingly, the reality of the oAgora and eAgora is never predetermined but always *emerging*. As performers or clickers work through their networks, they must commit to decisions at every turn. On the OT side, storytellers may need to make several important choices within the first few minutes of their performances: for example, whether to describe the opening scene briefly or in great detail, whether to include an anecdote or not, whether to spin a characterization this way or that. Similarly, net-surfers' itineraries are always in-the-making, forever under construction until they quit their browsers. In both cases nothing is set in stone because neither kind of performance is a book. Both kinds of events keep on developing even as they're happening (Reality Remains in Play), with no closure available (or even possible) until the surfing sessions stop.

With these correspondences and differences in mind, let's consider four fundamental aspects of the three agoras: units, routes, authorship, and audiences.

Units

The first aspect is the deceptively simple matter of the unit or thought-byte employed in each agora. Oral performers and their audiences communicate in a language of *oWords* (oWords), acoustic signs that identify pathways leading to meaning. Naturally, these signs are voiced and heard rather than written and read, but their most salient qualities are their composite structure and highly idiomatic meaning. They just aren't the same as "our words."

In many oral traditions the most basic single "word" is at minimum an entire phrase—not one but a group of our textual words. For example, South Slavic epic singers, or *guslari*, speak of the smallest "word in a song" as a whole ten-syllable line, from two to five or six tWords in length.[125] Such oWords aren't bound by white spaces or enshrined in dictionaries; within OT they take the form of integral, indivisible units of utterance and meaning, no matter how large they get. They amount to atoms within the physics of OT communication, if you like.

Such oral performers identify everything from whole poetic lines to entire performances as single "words," understanding them as the fundamental units that support the OT medium. Though it may seem counterintuitive to cultures that depend heavily on texts, these OT bytes are composite wholes that can't be subdivided without destroying their meaning. To put it another way, oWords are typically made up of not one but many tWords, and dismembering oWords produces only nonsense oSyllables, component parts that can't bear meaning by themselves.

eWords (eWords) are parallel to oWords in a number of ways, perhaps most obviously at the level of web addresses, or URLs, which are also made up of several distinct parts joined together. URLs of course make sense only as wholes and can't be subdivided without destroying their functionality. Thus, http://www.oraltradition.org consists of a protocol (*http://*) plus the worldwide web designator (*www*) plus the domain name (*oraltradition.org*) that itself includes a site label followed by a domain suffix. Each part plays a crucial role, but each one is by itself insufficient to access any ePathway. The composite address, construed as a single, indivisible "word," is what makes the link work.

Again like oWords, eWords are also densely coded and highly idiomatic. Just as the oWord "green fear" in Homer's *Iliad* stands for "supernatural fear" in the specialized language of oral epic tradition, so http://www.43things.com[126] prescribes the route to a social networking site in the specialized language of the web. Notice the special semantics of these megawords: in neither case does the unit or thought-byte transparently describe what it means. Neither of the two constituent elements of "green fear" has any dictionary-supported connection to supernatural agency, and the "43things" URL will dependably leave the un-initiated scratching their heads. But both the oWord and the eWord function very effectively once their idiomatic force comes into play, with the designated composite signs standing by convention for more-than-literal meanings.

tWords (tWords), on the other hand, are units defined by white space on either side and certified by inclusion in dictionaries. As the lowest common denominators of textual communication, they can theoretically be combined in myriad ways to produce meaning. The sky's the limit.

But then the process of textualization, the defining activity of the tAgora, enters the scene. Sequencing and fossilizing tWords in particular paragraphs, across particular pages and chapters, and along the one-of-a-kind linear land-scape of the book severely limits their inherent possibilities (Indigestible Words) even as it creates a unique and directed communication. tWords now serve not only their singular meanings but also the particular combinatory arrangement in which they are fixed—a pathwayless text (Impossibility of tPathways). It's easy to see which of these two masters holds the upper, and determining, hand. Text-making requires the sacrifice of multiple options for the greater (and singular) expressive good.

Mapped tWords are rooted in place. For that reason they can't recur in coded, idiomatic combinations without repeating, and repetition eventually produces only the tired, empty language of clichés (Recur Not Repeat). Not so with re-current oWords and eWords, which stand as living, emergent signs that OT and IT surfers can click on or not, as they choose. In the oAgora and eAgora, navigating pathways is always an unfolding process that happens in the mo-ment, decision by decision. There's always and continuously more than a single way to proceed, more than a single reality to engage.

By contrast, tWords do their tAgora work by productively limiting options, by foreclosing on potentials in favor of a prescribed order and sequence. tWords are items for thing-based exchange, not pathways for virtual navigation.

Routes

Within the oAgora and eAgora, words are surfing signals. oWords provide route markers for *oPathways* (oPathways), and eWords for *ePathways* (ePathways).

In the arena of oral performance (Arena of Oral Tradition), storytellers pro-ceed by clicking on oWords like "Once upon a time" and navigating along oPath-ways through the story-web of a Grimm Brothers fairytale. Because they're surfing through a flexible network of potentials rather than trekking along a sequence-ordered page, their itinerary is anything but fixed. On the contrary, the route they happen to choose remains fluid and ever-evolving, taking shape in present time under the interactive influence of factors like individual cre-ativity, audience reaction, the time and place of the event, and so forth. At its core, the act and art of storytelling is the process of choosing among options, of navigating through narrative hyperlinks. oPathways keep the performer's options generatively open, allowing the story to emerge as it's (re-)made.

ePathways work similarly, as any given day's experience with the Internet attests over and over again. In the arena of the web (Arena of the Web) we open our browser to a designated startup page (which we may, of course, change) by deploying an embedded eWord, the equivalent of invoking an oWord like "Once upon a time." From that point on, every decision we make immediately reconfigures our options, shifts our frame of reference, and presents us with new options. We can of course choose to "read" the web like a book—plodding along precisely the same sequence of ePathways again and again, day in and day out, flattening the multidimensional network into the equivalent of a printed, unnetworked page. But to do so is to limit eAgora commerce to what can be transacted in the tAgora—although without the dedicated book-and-page medium appropriate for tAgora transactions. To get the most out of each communications technology, we need to recognize what each agora can support and use each set of tools to its greatest advantage.[127]

Part of that recognition means coming to grips with the arena of the text (Arena of the Text), and with the fact that "*tPathways*" don't, and can't, exist. Texts prescribe one-way routes according to a singular, well-developed plan. They depend on sequences of tWords, pages with numbers, chapters, and so on. Much can be gained by guiding readers in this way, and it would be categorically wrong to diminish the value of texts, which support the tAgora so well. But the one-way highway, for all of its obvious and demonstrated advantages, is distinctly different from the option-driven technologies native to the oAgora and eAgora.

Authorship

European literature from the ancient world onward has always assumed *individual authorship*. We celebrate the achievements of Homer, Chaucer, Milton, and Shakespeare, happy to be able to affix their names to great works like *The Odyssey*, *The Canterbury Tales*, *Paradise Lost*, and *Hamlet*. But there's more to this unexamined assumption than first meets the eye.

The ideological pressure to identify verbal art as always and everywhere a tAgora phenomenon is extremely strong, so strong that we've often created pseudoauthors where no believable evidence exists. Thus the exalted place of Homer at the fountainhead of Western literature, even though "Homer" seems to be an anthropomorphic legend, a mythic figure who never existed (at least in the form we've imagined him). Thus the prominence of the shadowy figures of Caedmon and Cynewulf in discussions of the earliest English poetry. Never mind that Caedmon the cowherd poet is almost certainly legendary, or that the only evidence for the otherwise unknown Cynewulf is a group of poorly matched runic signatures that could have been inserted by anyone.[128] As tAgora citizens we feel compelled to appoint individual authors for all verbal art, no matter what its true origins.

Not so in the marketplaces we've called the oAgora and eAgora, where *distributed authorship* is the empowering rule (Distributed Authorship). OTs, which at their root consist of performance-instances that naturally vary from one to another over time and different performers, just can't be traced to single authors. Like language itself (as distinct from texts, which are scripts for language), no one person is wholly responsible for their invention or maintenance. And IT creations evolve in cognate ways—open-source software, for example, actively depends upon multiple, distributed authorship for its continuing utility. It simply can't live and develop in any other way.

If we're willing to peer behind our comfortable but unexamined assumptions, we'll soon recognize that even in the tAgora individual authorship is to some extent an ideological conviction rather than a fact (Just the Facts). Even verifiably individual authors respond to prior and contemporary authors, creating texts that owe a significant debt to other people and other texts (Texts and Intertextuality). In the oAgora and eAgora, however, the picture is much clearer and more categorical: OT and IT are by their very nature collective, distributed enterprises. They represent community activity (How to Build a Book), the joint work of many hands.

Audiences

Everything else being equal, OT and IT support far more democratic marketplaces than do texts. The oAgora and eAgora involve and engage relatively *open* audiences, while the tAgora is more *selective*.

The reasons for this contrast are straightforward. The oAgora places performer and audience on a fundamentally democratic footing, setting them up as interactive partners in an evolving process. In many cases anyone can attend an oral performance, and, given enough time and energy, anyone can learn to navigate the tradition and perform (some more fluently than others; talent does matter) (Audience Critique). Of course, certain OT genres restrict their audiences and/or potential performers by gender, age, ethnicity, the time or place of the event, or some other factor. But even in the most exclusive scenarios the very ongoingness of tradition—the reality that OTs continue to live and prosper by being shared within a community over time—assures an audience that is *open* and participatory to a significant degree.

The eAgora operates similarly by promoting the root dynamic of sharing and thus opening its resources to all surfers. As with OT, IT can constrain that basic democracy in a number of ways via proprietary software, password-protected sites, and other strategies that diminish universal access for the sake of privacy or of financial or political gain. Nonetheless, the ability to browse through an unprecedented array of interactive resources—far more extensive than any conventional library holdings—represents a media-democracy more radical than any we have known outside the open-access, "online" experience of the oAgora (Online with OT).

The tAgora, on the other hand, *selects* its audience by configuring its substantial assets in an exclusive, protected environment. At the macro level, books cost money and are controlled by distribution networks. On the micro level, the rhetoric of the page is as restrictive as it is powerful.

Consider the implications. Only if you can afford to join the book conversation, only if the text exchange actually includes you, and only if you've managed to internalize the operative textual conventions can you hope to succeed in the marketplace of the tAgora. Granted, it's a very efficient system in its own right, but it's accessible only if you've met the demanding (and for some individuals or even whole cultures, quite impossible) admissions requirements. In short, the tAgora has a double edge: in applying highly selective criteria for membership, it also disenfranchises a whole host of potential users.

Transacting business in the "wrong" agora

It's proverbial that being in the wrong place at the wrong time, or for the wrong purpose, can lead to serious trouble. Nowhere does this adage prove truer than in the three verbal marketplaces we've been describing, where agoraphobia is only too prevalent (Agoraphobia). OT can't live and prosper in the tAgora, because it can't be flattened onto a page without changing its fundamental nature, without reducing it to a faint shadow of itself and making it something it isn't. Nor does IT do well in the tAgora, because its ePathways simply can't be translated to brick-and-mortar representation. The nimble nontextuality of Wikipedia, or even the ever-increasing uselessness of hard-copy software manuals, provides evidence enough of this non-fit (Freezing Wikipedia).

Or think about one of the most celebrated media-related issues of our time: unauthorized file-sharing of musical and video works of art. Ironically, perhaps, this kind of "illicit" traffic reflects the typical and natural flow within the oAgora and eAgora, where sharing constitutes nothing less than each medium's lifeblood. After all, what's the *modus operandi*, even the core ethics, of OT and IT? To transfer freely, to distribute ownership (Owning versus Sharing), to treat knowledge, ideas, and art as open-source creations whose value stems in part from community access and the culture of remixing (Remix).

That's the way it always has been and always will be in the oAgora. Subject to specific cultural guidelines, OTs pass unencumbered from one person, group, place, and era to another. They work not like possessable texts but like a common language that can't be owned, protected, or denied to prospective users. OT traffic closely resembles IT traffic in that respect.

But when precious copyrighted items, such as top 40 hits or blockbuster films, are suddenly thrust into the open-access environment of the eAgora as manipulable digital entities, something cataclysmic happens. Their history as individually authored, legally protected objects is in effect rewritten; their status utterly changes. For better or worse, the rules of the tAgora are suspended and "the work" is exchanged under a new set of rules. Just like OT, it's now eligible for (or at least vulnerable to) sharing, sampling, and remixing.

It's now a tAgora product living in an eAgora world.[129]

tWords

tWords are the designated means of exchange in the tAgora, the default currency of the textual marketplace. More to the point, given the control exerted by textual ideology over most aspects of our daily lives (Ideology of the Text), tWords are customarily the only currency we hold and spend. Agoraphobia (Agoraphobia) is so powerful that it's hard even to conceive (Culture Shock) of any other communicative unit for our verbal transactions.

How are tWords defined? Chiefly in three ways: typographically, lexically, and linguistically.

Typographically, we identify and delimit text bytes by inserting white spaces between them. It wasn't always so, of course. Writing appeared on Day 346 of Homo sapiens' calendar year, with Gutenberg's press arriving only on Day 363 (Homo Sapiens' Calendar Year). For the 17 species-days in between, handwritten media varied wildly (Spectrum of Texts) in their conventions about spacing, capitalization, lineation, and so forth. No surprise there, since there was no way of creating and enforcing any sort of broadly recognized standard.

Lexically, we define tWords by enshrining them in dictionaries and lexicons, customarily with supporting information about their derivation from other languages, their pronunciation, and their array of meanings. Dictionaries don't hold still, of course, any more than languages do, and new tWords and new meanings are added with every new edition. But the latest official lexicon serves as the source and standard for establishing and maintaining the grand periodic table of elemental words.

Linguistically, we speak of tWords as linked closely to the *morpheme*, which Wikipedia[130] defines as "the smallest linguistic unit that has semantic meaning." In some ways the most fundamental of the three perspectives, this definition needs qualification in order to square up with the typographical and lexical definitions. First, only a free or root morpheme qualifies as a word in itself (the *beat* in *un-beat-en*, for example); the other two parts (*un-* and *-en*) are understood as bound or system morphemes, rather than words in themselves. Second, we need to be aware that multimorphemic units, such as the entire combination *unbeaten*, are not only possible but very common.

Within the textual arena (Arena of the Text), an inherently pathwayless environment (Impossibility of tPathways), tWords contribute crucially to the relentless, one-way march from letter to letter, white space to white space, left to right (in most Western tAgoras, at any rate), paragraph to paragraph, page to page, chapter to chapter, and volume to volume. Trekking through texts, readers silently process a highly economical and just as highly restrictive code, following a predetermined map assembled not by a group (Distributed Authorship) but (usually) by a single individual. Variation within limits (Variation within Limits), the stock-in-trade of oWords (oWords) and eWords (eWords), would be counterproductive for the item-based verbal transactions supported by the tAgora.

tWords work for the same reason that texts work—because they actively resist morphing (Texts and Intertextuality).

Variation within Limits

Suppose our foundation myth celebrating completeness (Illusion of Object) and fixity (Illusion of Stasis) didn't explain the world of communication in all its diversity. Suppose there existed an alternate mythology, heretical to the tAgora faithful but defensible and applicable in its own right. Suppose further that this alternate media-story offered a better explanation (Responsible Agora-business) of the expressive dynamics typical of the oAgora and eAgora. What would such an explanation look like? What features would it support and maintain? What assumptions would it make? Just how would that story go?

OT networks

We can begin to answer these questions by highlighting core characteristics of verbal exchange in the oral marketplace (Arena of Oral Tradition), as explored throughout the Pathways Project. Here are some of them: Oral tradition doesn't repeat, it recurs (Recur Not Repeat). It employs oWords (oWords) rather than tWords (tWords) to communicate its message. It is accurate (Accuracy) not in the familiar (but under-the-radar) terms insisted upon by textual ideology (Ideology of the Text) but rather on its own cocreative, emergent terms. Instead of seeking to foreshorten and limit experience, OT creates a frame of reference in which reality remains in play (Reality Remains in Play). Instead of restricting even the most independent-minded reader to an exitless one-way street, it uses oPathways (oPathways) leading to a web of linked options and to variant but always related versions (Not So Willy-nilly). Most fundamentally of all, OT operates by surfing through networks rather than trekking through texts.

All of these features point toward a rule-governed flexibility that licenses innovation and creativity within a powerful and highly resonant idiom. What's more, that signature power derives—however counterintuitive it may seem—not from monolithlike immutability but from variation within limits.

An analogy from telecommunications

The everyday technology of radio and television transmission and reception offers a simple comparison to the rule-governed media environment of OT and IT. In this technology a carrier wave[131] serves as the regular, recurring vehicle and platform that supports the broadcasting of specific, uniquely configured sound and video. In the case of radio, for example, the center frequency of the carrier wave provides the singular call number for the particular station, whether modulated by amplitude (AM) or by frequency (FM). As you move off that center frequency, reception will suffer, initially with increasing static, and will eventually founder. By continuing to move through the frequency spectrum you may well encounter another station you can listen to, but the original experience will be unavailable in the new frame of reference.

Which of these two dimensions, we might ask, is the more important, the carrier wave or the input signal? Which is primary, the vehicle or what it's conveying? In a sense the best answer to this question is "yes." The carrier, whose function is to establish the basic structure and set the outer limits for the exchange, can transmit an infinite diversity of input signals—films, talk shows, advertisements, news updates, or whatever other material is to be broadcast. But both dimensions—the generative, recurrent pattern and the unique modulations—must be part of the synergistic process if the communication is to succeed. Without the cyclical rhythm of the carrier wave, content can be neither sent nor received. On the other hand, without the input signals "written onto" the wave, even the most advanced megawatt radio or television station can transmit nothing but silence. In other words, both morphing and well-defined limits are essential to the physics of effective telecommunications.

OT code as performance platform

OT code functions like a carrier wave, precisely because it's a platform for performance; but we also need the input signals exchanged between a performer and audience. Just as with radio and television broadcasting, we have symbiotic, interacting aspects. The specialized language, or register, is the vehicle for whatever specific narrative is being (re-)created and received. By the same token, the actual content emerges only when the network is activated by users. Without the shared code (Owning versus Sharing), OT performance is impossible; without OT web-surfers, the code is nonfunctional. To put the matter proverbially (Proverbs), *without pathways there is no language; without a surfer there is no performance.*

As illustration of how OT code works, consider some examples of oWords from two particularly well-studied traditions. Let me emphasize that these are merely a few among myriad possibilities, cited here to give at least a small idea of the resources of a dynamic system of expression and reception (Systems versus Things).

Arming and disarming   In South Slavic oral epic, as in many other oral epic traditions, the hero is armed in a highly conventional fashion before he or she enters battle. Audiences hear—and expect—an elaborate description of armor and weapons, as well as an often equally detailed and equally conventional preparation of the hero's horse. Performance variables such as the attentiveness of the audience or the nature of the occasion will influence the poet's surfing of the traditional oWord, but it's not unusual to hear 100- or 200-line versions that mention everything from boots, spurs, and helmet to sword, spear, bow, and pistols. Likewise, the poet may choose to insert a long list of equine-related activities from grooming through saddling and mounting, or he may be content with a briefer navigation of the arms-horse intranet. Shared code for this recurring pattern constitutes what many have called a "typical scene," with the generic template adapted to the specifics of individual characters, situations, and events. This oWord, best understood as a morphing unit, thrives by varying within limits.

Against this background, in his poem entitled *The Death of Prince Marko*, the South Slavic singer (or *guslar*) Tešan Podrugović portrays the demise of one of this tradition's greatest heroes as the ultimate dis-arming. As Marko recognizes his imminent fate and nears his demise, he finds a quiet, deserted site in which he forsakes all future battles in a highly idiomatic way. Instead of donning armor and weapons, and instead of grooming and readying his faithful horse Sharats, the celebrated hero does precisely the opposite: he kills Sharats and destroys or discards his famous weapons one by one. Outside the epic oCode and the associations built into it, this series of actions is dramatic in its own literal terms. But because Podrugović is working within a familiar pattern known to his oAgora partners, his unique adaptation of the oWord or typical scene is also a powerful instance of variation within limits. Heroes conventionally arm for life-or-death combat; this hero now disarms to die.

Getting back home   Across the Indo-European family of languages, the long-absent hero struggling to find his way home is an extremely common story-type, possibly the most widespread and oldest tale we have. Conventionally, this epic pattern of Return, or *nostos* in ancient Greek, begins with the hero mired in captivity and trying to negotiate an escape, usually through the agency of a powerful female. (It is worth noting that the implied backstory involves his prior participation in a composite army aimed at rescuing a kidnapped fiancée or wife, as part of an army led by a duplicitous or at least undependable leader.) At any rate, within the story-pattern the hero manages to exit his imprisonment and returns, always in impenetrable disguise, to test the loyalty of family and colleagues and to defeat the rivals vying for his mate. In the larger morphology of the story, however, it is his mate who holds all of the cards; she may prove faithful or unfaithful to him, with both options very much in play within well-collected traditions. A secret signal shared between them is the tipping point for the narrative, and keys either a reunion (the positive ending) or a deadly conflict and sequel (the negative ending). Even our *Odyssey*—very much the portrayal of the faithful spouse, of course—contains the seeds of the alternate climax. There are no fewer than nine mentions of the Agamemnon-Clytemnestra-Orestes family triangle as a parable-like contrast to Odysseus-Penelope-Telemachos, and Agamemnon's ghost actually discusses the two story-alternatives in Book 24.

Against this background, or carrier wave, Homer configures his *Odyssey* as a specific realization of a generic pattern, as a rule-governed variation within limits. Audiences fluent in the OT idiom (experienced navigators of the Return web) will recognize the pattern early, and will know in general terms what to expect. Long separated from his homeland and community because of the Trojan War and its aftermath, Odysseus negotiates with Calypso for his release and, with the powerful Athena's help, eventually finds his way back to Ithaca. Like all *nostos* heroes, whether in Greek or other traditions, he infiltrates the company of suitors in disguise and defeats them in athletic contests before dispatching them altogether. Penelope poses the secret riddle of the olive tree bed that only her true husband can solve, and their exchange leads to recognition and resolution. Return epics from other traditions—as widely separated as British, South Slavic, and Balochi—reveal the broader morphology: variations include names of characters and places, faithful and unfaithful mates, culture-specific athletic challenges, different secret signs, inclusion of slaughter or not, and of course opposite outcomes. Most crucially, however, all of these details are contextualized by the Return pattern, which provides a shared vehicle for performance and reception.

IT networks

We can continue to answer our opening questions about alternate mythologies of communication by highlighting core characteristics of exchange in the electronic marketplace (Arena of the Web), as explored throughout the Pathways

Project. Here are some of them: IT doesn't repeat, it recurs. It employs eWords (eWords) rather than tWords to communicate its message. It is accurate not in the familiar (but under-the-radar) terms insisted upon by textual ideology but rather on its own cocreative, emergent terms. Instead of seeking to foreshorten and limit experience, IT creates a frame of reference in which reality remains in play. Instead of restricting even the most independent-minded reader to an exitless one-way street, it uses ePathways (ePathways) leading to a web of linked options and to variant but always related versions. Most fundamentally of all, IT operates by surfing through networks rather than trekking through texts.

All of these features point toward a rule-governed flexibility that licenses innovation and creativity within a powerful and highly resonant idiom. What's more, that signature power derives—however counterintuitive it may seem—not from monolithlike immutability but from variation within limits.

IT code as performance platform

IT code functions like a carrier wave, precisely because it's a platform for performance; but we also need the input signals exchanged between a navigator and the Internet (and ultimately the site-builder). Just as with radio and television broadcasting, we have two symbiotic, interacting aspects. The specialized language, or register, is the vehicle for whatever specific web expedition is being undertaken. By the same token, the actual content emerges only when the network is activated by users. Without the shared code, IT performance is impossible; without IT web-surfers, the code is nonfunctional. To put the matter proverbially, *without pathways there is no language; without a surfer there is no performance.*

As illustration of how IT code works, consider some examples of eWords. Let me emphasize that these are merely a few among myriad possibilities, cited here to give at least a small idea of the resources of a dynamic system of expression and reception.

Clicking through options When you click on a link, it's the morphology of the underlying URL-system—not the linkname—that empowers your journey. Even though the linkname itself is nominal, it depends for its meaning and efficacy on the rule-governed code from which all unique URLs are generated. Once you register your domain name, effectively activating its potential, variation within limits prescribes that you affix a universally idiomatic protocol, such as *http://*, and a contracted-for suffix such as *.org*, *.com*, or *.net*. If you install addresses that follow this template of structure and morphology, they will successfully connect to web destinations. If, on the other hand, the addresses lack the carrier-wave syntax required for all input signals, they will fail. Clearly, the highly generative but limited nature of the link-driven network means that you can't go just anywhere; in fact, "anywhere" has no meaning in the context of multiple but restricted options. To travel an ePathway and reach your destination, you must click on a link to a viable URL.

Of course, this initial step is merely the prologue to an ongoing, ever-evolving, and inherently unpredictable story that takes shape in real time rather than asynchronously (Real-time versus Asynchronous). As such, it can't be flattened into a predetermined, optionless blueprint. It has to be "lived through" as an emergent experience. No sooner than the first click brings you to your initial destination, you're immediately presented with another choice to make: explore that node, whatever it is, then get ready for the next step, whatever it may prove to be. So you select another ePathway from among all routes available, and travel somewhere else, but your cocreation of reality still isn't by any means "complete." Why not? Because you have multiple options at every juncture, choices that appear because of a prior choice you've made, and together they offer almost infinite variety—always within limits, of course. In fact, the whole notion of completeness in eNavigation is fundamentally illusory. Until you close your browser, the ever-expanding diversity of links offers a continuous opportunity for performance, for personal, highly individual surfing within an option-driven system.

Building and friending　Taking a step back, consider the process of building the complex and diverse network that you travel by clicking on eWord routes. Web-designers work within languages defined as much by their options as by their set structure; once again, the carrier wave/input signal analogy proves applicable. Unless designers install appropriately configured code, their sites will founder. To create interactive facilities in the eAgora, web architects must be fluent in the dedicated language of that marketplace. At best, the lack of suitable, coherent code will translate to a static eFile, a species of text (Spectrum of Texts) that will not foster two-way exchange. At worst, nonidiomatic eCode will fossilize into meaningless junk and a broken link.

Social networking involves some highly successful—because nimbly interactive—facilities, none more popular or more highly used than Facebook. eCode is operative at a number of levels in the virtual community enabled by this megasite, which leverages variation within limits in powerful and innovative ways. The continuous building-out of the site deploys idiomatic programming language to create opportunities for friending, writing on walls, tagging photos, issuing invitations, convening real-time group discussions, and much more. The inner workings of the site are invisible to the end user, but they support and license every action undertaken by every participant.

But that's hardly the end of the story. These same participants are building as well, cocreating within a flexible, interactive environment, adding and revising within patterned constraints. While site architects provide the shared platform for all activities on Facebook, millions of surfers contribute the always-developing content, stimulating emergent behavior on the part of their friends in a never-ending personal and collective navigation of multiple, networked eCommunities. Just as in OT, the option-driven nature of the code—most essentially its variation within limits—is the crucial and enabling feature of the joint process. Website designers and individual users alike work within a language that supports rule-governed exchange, that meshes the generic and recurrent with the particular and unique. And again as in OT, one aspect is useless without the other. Even the most elegantly programmed site lies dormant until a surfing partner accesses it and begins to convert its potential into kinetic reality. Code just doesn't work unless there are architects and surfers to modulate and activate it.

The "other" mythology of communication

In short, our standard myth of fixity and completeness—the default and sustaining credo of the tAgora—cannot explain the thought-traffic characteristic of the oAgora and eAgora. To understand the dynamics of OT and IT, we need to explore another mode of creating, expressing, and receiving: variation within limits. Although the textual marketplace has trained us to distrust morphing and to value instead a message and a medium that (seem to) resist change, the oral and electronic marketplaces actively depend on and profit from rule-governed morphing. It is, then, up to us as responsible, cosmopolitan citizens of multiple agoras (Citizenship in Multiple Agoras) to update our cognitive firmware and to understand the inimitable power and efficacy of navigating through networks of oPathways and ePathways.

Why Not Textualize?

Why aren't oral traditions always immediately written down or otherwise recorded just as soon as text-making becomes an available option? Why not take advantage of the newest, most advanced, most secure technology?

Imagine a smoothly functioning oAgora, with its interactive web of links connected and functional. Performers and audiences conavigate along pathways established by earlier performers and audiences, constructing their shared reality as they go. The system of pathways (Systems versus Things) provides both a framework of established connections and the freedom to surf. It offers, in other words, both an idiomatic vehicle for tale-telling, healing, lamenting, or recounting history, and at the same time enough flexibility to adapt to the present, then-and-there particulars of the unique performance situation. Meaning derives from working creatively within a prescribed set of malleable rules—just like language, only more so (Proverbs).

The option of another agora

At some moment in a culture's media-history, the text (Texts and Intertextuality), or more precisely the possibility of making texts (written, printed, audio, or video), appears on the horizon. From our twenty-first–century perspective, imbued as we are with the ideology of the book (Ideology of the Text), this new possibility may look like an irresistible opportunity, a godsend for the deprived. Suddenly OT is ripe for harvesting (or should we say colonizing?), and the supposed potential benefits of em-booking are many.

As far as we text-consumers are concerned, the maddeningly protean tale or charm or dirge or historical narrative can finally be captured, fixed, and preserved once and for all. At last we can convert ceaseless change into the solid and permanent reality of pages or a CD or DVD. Later, and on a timetable entirely our own, we can revisit that same manufactured object as many times as we wish. What's more—and this is crucial—"the work" won't have morphed in the meantime. Our long-elusive quarry's been caged; we're in control. Or such is the self-serving fantasy of those who live and communicate within the tAgora.

Dead letters

Let's step outside that default marketplace of books and pages for a moment, and ask a simple question. What possible purpose could such beautifully fashioned text-objects serve in an oAgora that simply has no use for text-objects? Consider the stark realities of the situation. Because they won't plug into the network of exchange, because they don't consist of pathways, texts have no intrinsic value, no negotiable worth. Their tWords are disembodied and em-booked (tWords). They're dead letters.

Of course, someone can always reperform the transcript of a prior OT event for a performer, who can then include the story or song or proverb in a living repertoire. Such a process reembodies the transcript's silenced, spatialized words and reconnects its contents to the living network. In this way the event-turned-item can reenter the oral performance arena (Arena of Oral Tradition) and become OT once again. This sort of "re-oralizing" event has indeed occurred—for example, in American blues music—but worldwide and historically it's the exception to the rule. When it does occur, notice what's actually happening: someone is retranslating an item (Accuracy) from the language of the tAgora to the language of the oAgora, converting a performance-derived script back to a performance.

Customarily, though, an OT performance once em-booked usually exits the oAgora for good, exerting no influence on subsequent oral performances because it's no longer linked to the living pathways of the tradition. A tAgora reduction of an oAgora event is literally out of the loop.

Texts are for foreigners

Small wonder, then, that oral traditions are almost always recorded and converted into books by an agent or agents from outside the traditional culture and not by members of that culture.[132] oAgora citizens don't yearn to transform their smoothly functioning word-markets to serve an economy in which they don't participate. Although it may be cognitively challenging (Agoraphobia) and even uncomfortable for us to reset our default tAgora notions (Culture Shock), the truth is that from inside the oAgora texts just don't make sense. All they can do is get in the way, hindering the natural dynamics of exchange. OTs cannot be reduced to fixed items via an agenda invented and implemented from outside the oAgora and still retain their integrity. As we see elsewhere, OTs stand a far better chance of survival as networked pathways in the eAgora.

Wiki

What is a wiki?

Derived from the Hawaiian word for "fast, quick," the web term *wiki*[133] names an electronic site for collaborative activities. In its most open form, it is a compendium to which anyone can contribute by adding or editing existing materials, subject to approval (reediting) by the community of contributors. Wikipedia is perhaps the best-known example.

And how about the Pathways Project wiki?

The Pathways Project wiki is evolving along a trajectory toward an open-access facility. In its beginning stages, all of the contents were created by one person, John Miles Foley, but even from the very first entry (or node) onward the network has been open to and surfable by anyone who wished to access it. As the wiki develops, it will welcome input from others in the Contributions section,[134] as well as track the surfing of visitors through its web of nodes (with their permission, of course). Both the new content and the trails that visitors blaze will become part of the resource in order to foster growth through distributed authorship (Distributed Authorship).

This wiki will thus go well beyond *Oral Tradition and the Internet: Pathways of the Mind*, the book-based component of the Pathways Project, in two ways. First, even before the book is published, the electronic component has used the strategies of the eAgora to add depth, dimension, and interactivity to the experience of exploring its core topic: the homology between oral tradition and Internet technology. Second, the wiki will continue to evolve—in ways that naturally cannot be foreseen—after publication of the brick-and-mortar component; in other words, it will retain the advantage of remaining forever under construction.

Further Reading

No book, oral tradition, or website is self-contained. Questions seek answers, answers beget more questions, and ideas evolve in unpredictable ways. As a gesture toward what the Pathways Project provokes, I offer a brief and highly selective list of resources that will assist the reader or surfer in following some of the issues and proposals raised by the book and wiki-website.

Policy

These references are provided according to a carefully designed policy: "Further Reading" is intended not as a conventional academic bibliography, but primarily as an optional extension of the Project to serve the needs of nonspecialists. In other words, there is no attempt to include "all" relevant books, articles, and sites on any subject (an illusion in any case), and I have specifically excluded items that demand an expert's preparation. Within this policy, the Further Reading section emphasizes resources on oral tradition because that is my principal field and, of the three agoras or marketplaces (Three Agoras), the oAgora, in my experience, usually requires the most explanation. The Project's dependence on Wikipedia[1] and other electronic entries is intentional, both because of the ready availability of primary information and the second-level opportunities presented by those entries' links out to other eAgora-based information. We have tried to limit broken links and discontinued sites by including only those sites successfully accessed as of February 25, 2012. As with any aspect of the Pathways Project, this section is open-ended, suggestive, and eligible for ongoing development through the website.

On matters associated with the oAgora, the online journal *Oral Tradition* offers more than five hundred articles on the world's oral traditions, from ancient times to the present; this amounts to more than twenty-five years of contents on an open-access, free-of-charge platform[2] that supports search by keyword, author, and combinations of terms. In addition, a Summative Bibliography[3]— also open-access, free-of-charge, and searchable—collects every book, article, film, audio recording, or other material ever cited in the journal, and an annotated bibliography of the oral-formulaic theory[4] is likewise available on the same terms.

Albert Bates and Mary Louise Lord Collection, University of Missouri. http://oraltradition .org/articles/lord_collection

Ali, Samer M. *Arabic Literary Salons in the Islamic Middle Ages: Poetry, Public Performance, and the Presentation of the Past.* Notre Dame: University of Notre Dame Press, 2010.

Allt, Peter, and Russell K. Alspach. *The Variorum Edition of the Poems of W. B. Yeats.* New York: Macmillan, 1957.

Amodio, Mark. *Writing the Oral Tradition: Oral Poetics and Literate Culture in Medieval England.* Notre Dame: University of Notre Dame Press, 2004.

Bagby, Benjamin. *Beowulf* (DVD), produced by Jon Aaron and Charlie Morrow. New York: Other Media, 2007.

Bauman, Richard, ed. *Explorations in the Ethnography of Speaking*, 2nd ed. Cambridge: Cambridge University Press, 1989.

———. *Verbal Art As Performance.* Prospect Heights, Ill.: Waveland Press, 1977.

———. *Story, Performance, and Event: Contextual Studies of Oral Narrative.* Cambridge: Cambridge University Press, 1986.

Bauman, Richard, and Charles Briggs. *Voices of Modernity: Language Ideologies and the Politics of Inequality.* Cambridge: Cambridge University Press, 2003.

Bertsozale Elkartea, ed. *Basque Oral Traditions.* A special issue of *Oral Tradition* 22, ii (2007). Available online at http://journal.oraltradition.org/issues/22ii

Bjork, Robert E., and John D. Niles, eds. *A Beowulf Handbook.* Lincoln: University of Nebraska Press, 1997.

Boyarin, Jonathan, ed. *The Ethnography of Reading.* Berkeley: University of California Press, 1993.

Bradbury, Nancy Mason. *Writing Aloud: Storytelling in Late Medieval England.* Urbana: University of Illinois Press, 1998.

Brill de Ramírez, Susan Berry. *Contemporary American Indian Literatures and the Oral Tradition.* Tucson: University of Arizona Press, 1999.

Brown, Duncan. *Voicing the Text: South African Oral Poetry and Performance.* Cape Town: Oxford University Press, 1998.

Cavallo, Guglielmo, and Roger Chartier. *A History of Reading in the West*, trans. by Lydia G. Cochrane. Amherst: University of Massachusetts Press, 1999.

Clanchy, M. T. *From Memory to Written Record*, 2nd ed. Oxford: Blackwell, 1993.

Daniels, Peter D., and William Bright, eds. *The World's Writing Systems.* New York: Oxford University Press, 1996.

Davies, Sioned. "Storytelling in Medieval Wales." *Oral Tradition* 7 (1992): 231–57. Available online at http://journal.oraltradition.org/issues/7ii/davies

DuBois, Thomas A. *Finnish Folk Poetry and the "Kalevala."* New York: Garland, 1995.

———. *Lyric, Meaning, and Audience in the Oral Tradition of Northern Europe.* Notre Dame: University of Notre Dame Press, 2006.

Eisenstein, Elizabeth L. *The Printing Press as an Agent of Change.* Cambridge: Cambridge University Press, 1980.

Eleveld, Mark. *The Spoken Word Revolution.* Naperville, Ill.: Sourcebooks MediaFusion, 2005.

Evers, Larry, and Barre Toelken, eds. *Native American Oral Traditions: Collaboration and Interpretation.* Logan: Utah State University Press, 2001. Orig. publ. as a special issue of *Oral Tradition* 13, i (1998). Available online at http://journal.oraltradition.org/issues/13i

Finnegan, Ruth. *Oral Poetry: Its Nature, Significance, and Social Context.* Bloomington: Indiana University Press, 1992.

———. *Communicating: The Multiple Modes of Human Interconnection.* London: Routledge, 2002.

———. *The Oral and Beyond: Doing Things with Words in Africa.* Chicago: University of Chicago Press, 2007.

Finnegan, Ruth, and Margaret Orbell, eds. *South Pacific Oral Traditions.* Bloomington: Indiana University Press, 1995. Orig. publ. as a special issue of *Oral Tradition* 5, ii–iii (1990). Available at http://journal.oraltradition.org/issues/5ii-iii

Foley, John Miles. *Traditional Oral Epic: "The Odyssey," "Beowulf," and the Serbo-Croatian Return Song.* Berkeley: University of California Press, 1990. Rpt. 1993.

———. *Immanent Art: From Structure to Aesthetics in Traditional Oral Epic.* Bloomington: Indiana University Press, 1991.

———. *The Singer of Tales in Performance.* Bloomington: Indiana University Press, 1995.

———, ed. *Teaching Oral Traditions.* New York: Modern Language Association, 1998a.

———. "The Impossibility of Canon." In Foley 1998a, 13–33.

———. *Homer's Traditional Art.* University Park: Pennsylvania State University Press, 1999.

———. *How to Read an Oral Poem.* Urbana: University of Illinois Press, 2002. With eCompanion, http://oraltradition.org/hrop

———, ed. and trans. *"The Wedding of Mustajbey's Son Bećirbey" as Performed by Halil Bajgorić.* Folklore Fellows Communications, 283. Helsinki: Academia Scientiarum Fennica, 2004a. eEdition available online, http://oraltradition.org/zbm

———. "Epic As Genre." In *The Cambridge Companion to Homer.* Cambridge: Cambridge University Press, 2004b, 171–87.

———, ed. *A Companion to Ancient Epic.* Oxford: Blackwell, 2005a.

———. "Analogues: Modern Oral Epics." In Foley 2005a, 196–212.

———. "'Reading Homer' through Oral Tradition." *College Literature* 34.2 (2007): 1–28.

Foster, H. Wakefield. "Jazz Musicians and South Slavic Oral Epic Bards." *Oral Tradition* 19 (2004): 155–76. Available at http://journal.oraltradition.org/issues/19ii/foster

Furniss, Graham. *Orality: The Power of the Spoken Word*. London: Palgrave Macmillan, 2005.

Garner, Lori. "Anglo-Saxon Charms in Performance." *Oral Tradition* 19 (2004): 20–42. Available at http://journal.oraltradition.org/issues/19i/garner

———. *Structuring Spaces: Oral Poetics and Architecture in Early Medieval England*. Notre Dame: University of Notre Dame Press, 2011.

Garzía, Joxerra, Jon Sarasua, and Andoni Egaña. *The Art of Bertsolaritza: Improvised Basque Verse Singing*. Donostia: Bertsozale Elkartea, 2001.

Gay, Joshua, ed. *Free Software, Free Society: Selected Essays of Richard M. Stallman*. Boston: Free Software Foundation, 2002.

Goody, Jack. *The Interface between the Written and the Oral*. Cambridge: Cambridge University Press, 1987.

Haring, Lee, ed. *African Oral Traditions*. A special issue of *Oral Tradition* 9, i (1994). Available at http://journal.oraltradition.org/issues/9i

Harris, Joseph C. "The Icelandic Sagas." In Foley 1998a, 382–90.

Harris, William V. *Ancient Literacy*. Cambridge: Harvard University Press, 1989.

Hearon, Holly. "The Implications of 'Orality' for Studies of the Biblical Text." *Oral Tradition* 19 (2004): 96–107. Available at http://journal.oraltradition.org/issues/19i/hearon

Homer Multitext Project. http://chs.harvard.edu/chs/homer_multitext

Honko, Lauri, ed. *Textualization of Oral Epics*. Berlin: Mouton de Gruyter, 2000.

Honko, Lauri, with Chinappa Gowda, Anneli Honko, and Viveka Rai, eds. and trans. *The Siri Epic as Performed by Gopala Naika*, 2 vols. Helsinki: Academia Scientiarum Fennica, 1998.

Houston, Stephen D., ed. *The First Writing: Script Invention as History and Process*. Cambridge: Cambridge University Press, 2004.

Hymes, Dell. *"In Vain I Tried to Tell You": Essays in Native American Ethnopoetics*. Philadelphia: University of Pennsylvania Press, 1981.

———. *"Now I Know Only So Far": Essays in Ethnopoetics*. Lincoln: University of Nebraska Press, 2003.

Irwin, Bonnie D. "The Frame Tale East and West." In Foley 1998a, 391–99.

Jackson, Bruce. *Get Your Ass in the Water and Swim Like Me: African-American Narrative Poetry from the Oral Tradition*. New York: Routledge, 2004. With CD.

Jaffee, Martin S. "The Hebrew Scriptures." In Foley 1998a, 321–29.

———. *Torah in the Mouth: Writing and Oral Tradition in Palestinian Judaism 200 BCE–400 CE*. Oxford: Oxford University Press, 2001.

James, Clive. *Cultural Amnesia: Necessary Memories from History and the Arts*. New York: Norton, 2007.

Johnson, John William. *The Epic of Son-Jara: A West African Tradition*. Bloomington: Indiana University Press, 1992.

Johnson, John William, Thomas A. Hale, and Stephen Belcher, eds. *Oral Epics from Africa: Vibrant Voices from a Vast Continent*. Bloomington: Indiana University Press, 1997.

Jordan, Tim. *Cyberpower: The Culture and Politics of Cyberspace and the Internet*. London and New York: Routledge, 2001.

Kaschula, Russell H. "Mandela Comes Home: The Poets' Perspective." *Oral Tradition* 10 (1995): 91–110. Available at http://journal.oraltradition.org/issues/10i/kaschula

———. *The Bones of the Ancestors Are Shaking: Xhosa Oral Poetry in Context.* Cape Town: Juta Press, 2000.

Kelber, Werner H. *The Oral and the Written Gospel.* Bloomington: Indiana University Press, 1998.

Kelber, Werner H., and Paula Sanders, eds. *Oral Tradition in Judaism, Christianity, and Islam.* A special issue of *Oral Tradition* 25, i (2010). Available at http://journal .oraltradition.org/issues/25i

Klein, Anne C. "Oral Genres and the Art of Reading in Tibet." *Oral Tradition* 9 (1994): 281–314. Available at http://journal.oraltradition.org/issues/9ii/klein

Kolsti, John. *The Bilingual Singer: A Study in Albanian and Serbo-Croatian Oral Epic Traditions.* New York: Garland, 1990.

Lessig, Lawrence. *Free Culture: The Nature and Future of Creativity.* New York: Penguin, 2005.

———. *code 2.0.* createspace.com, 2009a. Available as free download at http://codev2 .cc/download+remix/

———. *Remix: Making Art and Commerce Thrive in the Hybrid Economy.* New York: Penguin, 2009b.

Lindahl, Carl. "Chaucer." In Foley 1998a, 359–64.

Lord, Albert Bates, trans. *"The Wedding of Smailagić Meho," by Avdo Medjedović.* Serbo-Croatian Heroic Songs, vol. 3. Cambridge: Harvard University Press, 1974.

———. *Epic Singers and Oral Tradition.* Ithaca: Cornell University Press, 1991.

———. *The Singer Resumes the Tale,* ed. by Mary Louise Lord. Ithaca: Cornell University Press, 1995.

———. *The Singer of Tales,* 2nd ed., with introduction by Stephen A. Mitchell and Gregory Nagy. Cambridge: Harvard University Press, 2000. With CD.

Martin, Henri-Jean. *The History and Power of Writing,* trans. by Lydia G. Cochrane. Chicago: University of Chicago Press, 1994.

Martin, Richard P. *The Language of Heroes: Speech and Performance in the Iliad.* Ithaca: Cornell University Press, 1989.

———. "Homer's 'Iliad' and 'Odyssey.'" In Foley 1998a, 339–50.

McCarthy, William B. *The Ballad Matrix: Personality, Milieu, and the Oral Tradition.* Bloomington: Indiana University Press, 1990.

McLuhan, Marshall. *The Gutenberg Galaxy: The Making of Typographic Man.* Toronto: University of Toronto Press, 1962.

McLuhan, Marshall, and Quentin Fiore. *The Medium Is the Massage: An Inventory of Effects.* Berkeley: Gingko Press, 2005.

McLuhan, Marshall, and W. Terrence Gordon. *Understanding Media: The Extensions of Man.* Berkeley: Gingko Press, 2003.

Milman Parry Collection of Oral Literature, Harvard University. http://chs119.chs .harvard.edu/mpc/

Nagy, Gregory. *Poetry As Performance: Homer and Beyond.* Cambridge: Cambridge University Press, 1996.

Nagy, Joseph Falaky. *The Wisdom of the Outlaw: Boyhood Deeds of Finn in Gaelic Narrative Tradition*. Dublin: Four Courts Press, 2011.

Niditch, Susan. *Oral World and Written Word: Ancient Israelite Literature*. Louisville, Ky.: Westminster John Knox Press, 1996.

———. *Folklore and the Hebrew Bible*. Eugene, Ore.: Wipf and Stock, 2004.

Niles, John D. *Homo Narrans: The Poetics and Anthropology of Oral Literature*. Philadelphia: University of Pennsylvania Press, 2010.

O'Keeffe, Katherine O'Brien. *Visible Song: Transitional Literacy in Old English Verse*. Cambridge: Cambridge University Press, 1990.

Okpewho, Isidore. *African Oral Literature: Backgrounds, Character, and Continuity*. Bloomington: Indiana University Press, 1992.

Olsen, Alexandra Hennessey. "Beowulf." In Foley 1998a, 351–58.

Ong, Walter J. *Interfaces of the Word: Studies in the Evolution of Consciousness and Culture*. Ithaca: Cornell University Press, 1977.

———. *Fighting for Life: Context, Sexuality, and Consciousness*. Ithaca: Cornell University Press, 1981.

———. *Orality and Literacy: The Technologizing of the Word*. London: Methuen, 1982.

Opland, Jeff. *Xhosa Oral Poetry: Aspects of a Black South African Tradition*. Cambridge: Cambridge University Press, 2009.

Parry, Milman. *The Making of Homeric Verse: The Collected Papers of Milman Parry*, ed. by Adam Parry. Oxford: Oxford University Press, 1987.

Reichl, Karl. *Turkic Oral Epic Poetry: Tradition, Forms, Poetic Structure*. New York: Garland, 1992.

———. *Singing the Past: Turkic and Medieval Heroic Poetry*. Ithaca: Cornell University Press, 2000.

Renoir, Alain. *A Key to Old Poems: The Oral-Formulaic Approach to the Interpretation of West-Germanic Verse*. University Park: Pennsylvania State University Press, 1988.

Rosenberg, Bruce A. *Can These Bones Live? The Art of the American Folk Preacher*. Urbana: University of Illinois Press, 1988.

Rubin, David C. *Memory and Oral Traditions*. New York: Oxford University Press, 1995.

Saenger, Paul. *Space between Words: The Origins of Silent Reading*. Palo Alto, Calif.: Stanford University Press, 1997.

Schmandt-Besserat, Denise. *How Writing Came About*. Austin: University of Texas Press, 1996.

Shuman, Amy. *Storytelling Rights: The Uses of Oral and Written Texts by Urban Adolescents*. Cambridge: Cambridge University Press, 1986.

Smith, John D. "Worlds Apart: Orality, Literacy, and the Rajasthani Folk-Mahabharata." *Oral Tradition* 5 (1990): 3–19. Available at http://journal.oraltradition.org/issues/5i/smith

———. *The Epic of Pabuji*. Cambridge: Cambridge University Press, 1991.

Smith, Mark Kelly, and Joe Kraynak. *Take the Mic: The Art of Performance Poetry, Slam, and the Spoken Word*. Naperville, Ill.: Sourcebooks MediaFusion, 2009.

Stock, Brian. *The Implications of Literacy*. Princeton: Princeton University Press, 1983.

Tannen, Deborah. *Spoken and Written Language: Exploring Orality and Literacy*. New York: Ablex, 1982.

Tapscott, Don, and Anthony D. Williams. *Wikinomics: How Mass Collaboration Changes Everything*. New York: Penguin, 2010.

Tedlock, Dennis. *The Spoken Word and the Work of Interpretation*. Philadelphia: University of Pennsylvania Press, 1983.

———. *Finding the Center: The Art of the Zuni Storyteller*, 2nd ed. Lincoln: University of Nebraska Press, 1999.

Toelken, Barre. "The 'Pretty Language' of Yellowman: Genre, Mode, and Texture in Navaho Coyote Performances." *Genre* 2 (1969): 211–35.

———. "Life and Death in the Navaho Coyote Tales." In *Recovering the Word: Essays on Native American Literature*, ed. by Brian Swann and Arnold Krupat. Berkeley: University of California Press, 1987, 388–401.

———. "Beauty Behind Me; Beauty Before." *Journal of American Folklore* 117 (2004): 441–45.

Toelken, Barre, and Tacheeni Scott. "Poetic Retranslation and the 'Pretty Languages' of Yellowman." In *Traditional Literatures of the American Indian: Texts and Interpretations*, ed. by Karl Kroeber. Lincoln: University of Nebraska Press, 1981, 65–116.

Vaidhyanathan, Siva. *The Anarchist in the Library*. New York: Basic Books, 2005.

Vitz, Evelyn Birge. "Old French Literature." In Foley 1998a, 373–81.

Woodard, Roger D. *The Cambridge Encyclopedia of the World's Ancient Languages*. Cambridge: Cambridge University Press, 2004.

Zedda, Paulu. "The Southern Sardinian Tradition of the *Mutetu Longu*: A Functional Analysis." *Oral Tradition* 24 (2009): 3–40. Available at http://journal.oraltradition.org/issues/24i/zedda

Zemke, John. "General Hispanic Traditions." In Foley 1998a, 202–15.

Zumthor, Paul. *Oral Poetry: An Introduction*, trans. by Kathryn Murphy-Judy. Minneapolis: University of Minnesota Press, 1990.

Notes

Preface

1. http://www.pathwaysproject.org/pathways/show/Contributions
2. http://www.pathwaysproject.org/pathways/show/Mind_Map
3. http://www.pathwaysproject.org/pathways/show/Mashups

For Book-readers Only

1. http://www.pathwaysproject.org/pathways/show/HomePage

Home Page: Welcome to the Pathways Project

1. http://pathwaysproject.org
2. http://www.pathwaysproject.org/pathways/show/Contributions

Getting Started: How to Surf the Pathways Project

1. http://www.pathwaysproject.org/pathways/show/Contributions
2. http://www.pathwaysproject.org/pathways/show/Contributions

Disclaimer

1. http://wordnetweb.princeton.edu/perl/webwn?s=homology
2. See "Static eFiles in pixels" in Spectrum of Texts.
3. http://en.wikipedia.org/wiki/Flip_book

Book versus Website

1. http://pathwaysproject.org

Response

1. http://www.press.uillinois.edu
2. http://www.pathwaysproject.org/pathways/show/Contributions

3. http://www.pathwaysproject.org/pathways/show/Migration_from_Paper_to_Web

Nodes

1. http://chs119.chs.harvard.edu/mpc/
2. http://www.scribd.com/doc/13450393/The-Internet-Medium-and-Poetry
-Transmission
3. http://journal.oraltradition.org/issues/24i/zedda
4. http://www.etymonline.com/index.php?search=accurate&searchmode=none
5. See "Static eFiles in pixels" in Spectrum of Texts.
6. http://en.wikipedia.org/wiki/Ancient_Agora_of_Athens
7. http://www.merriam-webster.com/dictionary/agoraphobia
8. http://journal.oraltradition.org/issues/22ii
9. See "Static eFiles in pixels" in Spectrum of Texts.
10. http://journal.oraltradition.org/issues/22ii
11. http://journal.oraltradition.org/files/articles/5i/7_murko.pdf
12. See "Static eFiles in pixels" in Spectrum of Texts.
13. http://en.wikipedia.org/wiki/Cloud_computing
14. See "An ancient witness on the tAgora" in tAgora.
15. http://en.wikipedia.org/wiki/Contingency
16. http://www.etymonline.com/index.php?term=contingent
17. http://www.thefreedictionary.com/contingent
18. http://en.wikipedia.org/wiki/Book_of_Kells
19. http://en.wikipedia.org/wiki/Marshall_McLuhan
20. http://www.pathwaysproject.org/pathways/show/Table_of_Nodes
21. http://en.wikipedia.org/wiki/Anonymous_(group)
22. http://dichtung-digital.mewi.unibas.ch/2000/Heibach/23-Aug/
23. See "Static eFiles in pixels" in Spectrum of Texts.
24. http://www.eff.org/deeplinks/2010/04/facebook-timeline
25. http://www.digitalpreservation.gov/news/2010/20100416news_article_twitter
_archive.html
26. http://www.nytimes.com/2010/05/02/business/02digi.html?hpw
27. http://en.wikipedia.org/wiki/Open_standard
28. http://en.wikipedia.org/wiki/Remix
29. http://www.youtube.com/watch?v=dXMGF-p4gGI
30. http://creativecommons.org
31. http://text20.net
32. See "Static eFiles in pixels" in Spectrum of Texts.
33. http://43things.com
34. See "Static eFiles in pixels" in Spectrum of Texts.
35. http://oraltradition.org/hrop
36. http://journal.oraltradition.org
37. http://oraltradition.org/zbm
38. See "Pathways versus Canons" in Museum of Verbal Art.
39. http://en.wikipedia.org/wiki/Pierre-Auguste_Renoir

40. http://journal.oraltradition.org/issues/16ii
41. http://journal.oraltradition.org/issues/16ii/gyaltsho
42. http://journal.oraltradition.org/files/articles/9ii/5_bauman.pdf
43. http://journal.oraltradition.org/files/articles/13ii/8_enhong.pdf
44. See "Static eFiles in pixels" in Spectrum of Texts.
45. http://bits.blogs.nytimes.com/2008/07/19/a-book-with-90000-authors/
46. http://de.wikipedia.org/wiki/Wikipedia:Hauptseite
47. http://bits.blogs.nytimes.com/2008/07/19/a-book-with-90000-authors/
48. http://www.etymonline.com/index.php?search=publish&searchmode=none
49. http://en.wikipedia.org/wiki/Google_Book_Search
50. http://journal.oraltradition.org/
51. http://en.wikipedia.org/wiki/Long_Tail
52. For a more detailed exposition, see Foley 2002, 23–25.
53. See Daniels and Bright 1996.
54. http://youtube.com/watch?v=xFAWR6hzZek
55. http://www2.kenyon.edu/AngloSaxonRiddles/texts.htm
56. See "Static eFiles in pixels" in Spectrum of Texts.
57. See Foley 1990, 24.
58. http://en.wikipedia.org/wiki/Venetus_A
59. http://oraltradition.org/zbm
60. http://chs.harvard.edu/chs/homer_multitext
61. See "Static eFiles in pixels" in Spectrum of Texts.
62. http://www.youtube.com/watch?v=H7_ARAF9inI
63. See "Static eFiles in pixels" in Spectrum of Texts.
64. http://www.opensource.org/docs/definition.php
65. http://en.wikipedia.org/wiki/OpenDocument
66. http://www.zdnet.com/news/massachusetts-to-adopt-open-desktop/144466
67. http://ocw.mit.edu/index.htm
68. http://ocw.mit.edu/about/presidents-message/
69. http://www2.kenyon.edu/AngloSaxonRiddles/texts.htm
70. http://oraltradition.org/zbm
71. http://www.pathwaysproject.org
72. For the essay on which this node is based, "The Impossibility of Canon," see Foley 1998b.
73. See Martin 1989; Foley 2004b and 2005b.
74. On *Beowulf* and oral tradition, see Olsen 1998. For a performance of *Beowulf* in the original Old English, see Bagby 2007.
75. On medieval French, medieval Spanish, Old Norse, and Chaucer, see, respectively, Vitz 1998, Zemke 1998, Harris 1998, and Lindahl 1998.
76. On the folk-*Mahabharata*, see Smith 1990.
77. On the Old Testament, see further Niditch 1996 and Jaffee 1998; on the New Testament, see further Kelber 1998 and Hearon 2004.
78. http://en.wikipedia.org/wiki/Alexandrian_library
79. http://en.wikipedia.org/wiki/Book_of_Kells

80. Recently the Book of Kells installation at Trinity College has been upgraded significantly to include well-lighted sample pages on display along with an exhibit on process,
materials, and other medieval manuscripts. Visit http://www.tcd.ie/Library/bookofkells/.

81. http://www.nytimes.com/1987/06/02/books/ireland-s-book-of-kells-is-facsimiled
.html?pagewanted=all&src=pm

82. http://www.bookofkells.com/the-manuscript.htm

83. http://journal.oraltradition.org/issues/22ii

84. http://oraltradition.org/articles/basque

85. http://www.bertsozale.com/english/index.php

86. http://journal.oraltradition.org/files/articles/10i/8_kaschula.pdf

87. http://creativecommons.org/licenses/

88. http://www.craphound.com/msftdrm.txt

89. See "Pathways versus Canon" in Museum of Verbal Art.

90. http://en.wikipedia.org/wiki/Académie_française

91. http://www.writing.upenn.edu/~afilreis/88/stevens-13ways.html

92. See Foley 2002, 184–85.

93. http://en.wikipedia.org/wiki/Lawrence_Lessig

94. See "Static eFiles in pixels" in Spectrum of Texts.

95. See "Static eFiles in pixels" in Spectrum of Texts.

96. http://en.wikipedia.org/wiki/Avogadro_constant

97. http://en.wikipedia.org/wiki/Quantum_mechanics

98. http://en.wikipedia.org/wiki/Uncertainty_principle

99. http://en.wikipedia.org/wiki/Remix

100. http://www.pathwaysproject.org/remix/remix.html

101. http://journal.oraltradition.org/files/articles/5i/7_murko.pdf

102. http://www8.georgetown.edu/departments/medieval/labyrinth/library/oe/texts/
a3.22.1.html

103. http://oraltradition.org/zbm

104. http://oraltradition.org/zbm

105. http://en.wikipedia.org/wiki/Elias_Lönnrot

106. http://en.wikipedia.org/wiki/Kalevala

107. http://www.heorot.dk/bede-caedmon.html

108. http://en.wikipedia.org/wiki/Sutton_Hoo

109. See O'Keeffe 1990, 41.

110. http://en.wikipedia.org/wiki/Numeracy

111. http://en.wikipedia.org/wiki/Denise_Schmandt-Besserat

112. http://www.slideshare.net/macloo/clay-tokens-and-the-origin-of-writing

113. http://en.wikipedia.org/wiki/Dipylon_inscription

114. http://en.wikipedia.org/wiki/Library_of_Alexandria

115. http://chs.harvard.edu/chs/homer_multitext

116. http://en.wikipedia.org/wiki/Runic_alphabet

117. http://en.wikipedia.org/wiki/History_of_printing

118. http://en.wikipedia.org/wiki/History_of_typography_in_East_Asia

119. http://en.wikipedia.org/wiki/Printing_press

120. For a detailed survey, see Martin 1994, 182–506.

121. http://en.wikipedia.org/wiki/Phaedrus_(dialogue)

122. See "Static eFiles in pixels" in Spectrum of Texts.

123. http://www.etymonline.com/index.php?search=proprietary&searchmode=none

124. http://www.etymonline.com/index.php?search=text&searchmode=none

125. For interviews with oral epic singers on the nature of their "words," see Foley 2002, 11–12. The same concept of "word" has been explicitly cited in oral traditions in ancient Greek (the term *epos*), Old English, Mongolian (called a "mouth-word"), Finnish, Estonian, and Sardinian, although the practice is certainly much more widespread.

126. http://www.43things.com

127. The incongruities that naturally arise from trying to conduct purely textual exchange electronically may explain why readers of eBooks and similar utilities so often complain that they have trouble scrolling through long documents on a computer display (whether Amazon's Kindle and other such devices help resolve such incongruities remains to be seen). The eAgora supports interactive, participatory, emergent exploration extremely well, but it doesn't handle textual exchange nearly as well as do texts.

128. Caedmon is described by the seventh-century historian Bede as owing his ability to create OT poetry to an angel's visit, while the "identity" of Cynewulf is based on nonmatching coded signatures within four Anglo-Saxon poems: *The Fates of the Apostles*, *Juliana*, *Elene*, and *Christ II*.

129. Digital rights management (DRM) protocols, which represent a response to some of these problems, can be successful only to the degree that they address eAgora realities with eAgora (not tAgora) solutions. Witness the inefficacy of copy-protection software, often no more than an invitation to hacking—where such hacking amounts for some to assertion of eAgora "rights." On the other hand, the Creative Commons initiative represents an eAgora solution to an eAgora problem. On the cultural and historical implications of eAgora realities, see especially Lessig 2005, 2009b; and Tapscott and Williams 2010.

130. http://en.wikipedia.org/wiki/Morpheme

131. http://en.wikipedia.org/wiki/Carrier_wave

132. See further Honko 2000.

133. http://en.wikipedia.org/wiki/Wiki

134. http://www.pathwaysproject.org/pathways/show/Contributions

Further Reading

1. http://en.wikipedia.org/wiki/Main_Page

2. http://journal.oraltradition.org/

3. http://bibliography.oraltradition.org/

4. http://oraltradition.org/bibliography/

Index

As I set about compiling this index, I began to glimpse another way of shaping and enabling the Morphing Book (Morphing Book), parallel to the Search function on the wiki-website. The strategy? To index the parenthetical cross-references, the brick-and-mortar equivalents of hyperlinks on the website, along with conventional topics. Via this method the reader of *Oral Tradition and the Internet* can "read backwards" (Reading Backwards), moving from nodes that are *linked-to* back to nodes that are *linked-from*. This strategy just adds one more dimension to the reader's potential participation in and cocreation of the experience of surfing this volume. (Note that the parenthetical cross-references are in regular type, while references to the nodes themselves are in boldface type.)

The University of Illinois Press
is a founding member of the
Association of American University Presses.

———————————————————

Composed in 10.5/13 Minion Pro
by Celia Shapland
at the University of Illinois Press
Manufactured by Sheridan Books, Inc.

University of Illinois Press
1325 South Oak Street
Champaign, IL 61820-6903
www.press.uillinois.edu

John Miles Foley was William H. Byler Chair in the Humanities, Curators' Professor of English and Classical Studies, and the director of the Center for Studies in Oral Tradition at the University of Missouri at Columbia. He was the author of several books, including *How to Read an Oral Poem.*